DEVELOPING
BALANCED SENSITIVITY

DEVELOPING BALANCED SENSITIVITY

Practical Buddhist Exercises for Daily Life

by

Alexander Berzin

Snow Lion Publications
Ithaca, New York

Snow Lion Publications
PO Box 6483
Ithaca, New York 14851 USA
607-273-8519

Printed in Canada on acid-free recycled paper.

ISBN 1-55939-094-8

Library of Congress Cataloging-in-Publication Data

Berzin, Alexander.
    Developing balanced sensitivity : a workbook of practical Buddhist exerises for daily life / Alexander Berzin. -- 1st ed.
        p.   cm.
    Includes bibliographical references.
    ISBN 1-55939-094-8 (alk. paper)
    1. Interpersonnal relations--Religious aspects-- Buddhism. 2. Religious life--Buddhism. 3. Group relations training.
    I. Title.
    BQ5400.B47   1998
    294.3'444--dc21   98-22123
                                                                            CIP

Table of Contents

Preface

Buddha taught that life is difficult. Achieving emotional balance, for example, or maintaining healthy relationships is never easy. We make these challenges even more difficult than is necessary, however, for a variety of reasons. Among them are lacking sensitivity in certain situations and overreacting in others. Although Buddha taught many techniques for overcoming hardships in life, traditional Indian and Tibetan Buddhist texts do not explicitly address the topic of sensitivity. This is because the Sanskrit and Tibetan languages lack equivalent terms for insensitivity and hypersensitivity. This does not mean that people from these cultures do not suffer from these two problems: they merely do not organize the various manifestations of them under two general terms. In adapting Buddha's methods for self-improvement to the modern Western context, however, it is necessary to address these issues as formulated in a Western idiom. This book attempts to meet this challenge.

Some people object to learning from ancient sources. They feel that modern times call for new solutions. Nevertheless, the basic obstacles preventing balanced sensitivity are universal. Some modern factors may contribute to the proliferation of our lack of sensitivity, such as overexposure to violence on television and isolating the elderly in institutions. Others, such as dramatic background music in movies, highlight and glamorize overreacting. These factors, however, merely aggravate the deeper causes that have always been present—self-preoccupation, insecurity, fear, and confusion. Furthermore, throughout history, people living through the horrors of war, famine, or natural disasters have become immune to others' suffering. In many societies, only the strong and healthy survive and are visible. Moreover, people have always overreacted to gain attention, as with toddlers showing off when relatives visit. It is cultural self-centeredness to think that we and our times are unique and that we cannot learn from the past or other societies.

My main Buddhist teacher was Tsenzhab Serkong Rinpochey, the late Master Debate Partner and Assistant Tutor of His Holiness the Dalai Lama. I had the privilege to serve for nine years as his interpreter and secretary. Whenever Serkong Rinpochey gave initiations into practices of the highest class of tantra, he explained that five types of deep awareness naturally endow our mind. He illustrated this point with everyday examples. For instance, we each have mirror-like awareness: our mind takes in all the visual information we see. Normally, however, we do not pay full attention to the details. Receiving an empowerment from a tantric master stimulates such forms of awareness to grow. As a result, we attain the five types of "Buddha-wisdom," such as the ability of a Buddha to be attentive to everything. During the years following Rinpochey's death, I reflected deeply on the significance of this point. Gradually, I realized that it suggested a profound guideline for developing balanced sensitivity.

Serkong Rinpochey displayed great flexibility in his teaching style, always adapting it to his audience. Inspired by his example, I set about developing a set of meditative exercises for recognizing and enhancing the five types of awareness as a method for improving sensitivity skills. To make these exercises more accessible to Western audiences, I borrowed several approaches used in self-development workshops. These techniques include having the participants sit in a circle looking at each other and having them work with a mirror. I began to teach these exercises in 1991 in various Buddhist centers around the world and refined the techniques based on experience and feedback. A transcript of one of these courses was published in German as *Fünf Weisheiten: im Aryatara Institut e. V., München (1993)* (Munich: Aryatara Institut, 1994).

Many people found these deep awareness practices helpful and requested me to write a book on the topic. I originally planned to use as its basis a transcript of one of my courses. When I found the material too short for a book, I began expanding the topic and formulating additional exercises on other aspects of the issue. As my work progressed, it soon became apparent that these exercises could be organized in a logical progression to form a complete program for developing balanced sensitivity.

This book of exercises addresses primarily two audiences. The first consists of members of Buddhist centers of any denomination, either within or outside the Tibetan fold, who have reached a plateau in their practice and are looking for additional material to stimulate their progress. Often people reach a plateau when they are unable to apply their meditation to daily life. To meet this need, this program weaves together facets of diverse traditional practices into new exercises. They are directed not only at their customary focus—people in our imagination—but also at other members of a group and at ourselves. These exercises can thus supplement the standard meditation practices of such centers, especially when the centers lack a resident teacher.

The second audience is anyone seeking techniques for overcoming sensitivity disorders, but not persons so dysfunctional that they require professional help. Although the book provides the Buddhist sources for each exercise, undertaking the training at home or in a sensitivity workshop does not require understanding or even being aware of this background. Because this text is a workbook, however, reading it requires sufficient time to pause for reflection after each point or example. This follows the Buddhist pedagogic technique. A tersely worded presentation stimulates a reader to work out the implications. With sincere effort, he or she soon experiences insight and growth.

For a short, introductory course, the following exercises may be extracted from the complete program: Exercises One, Two, Three, Four, Ten, Eleven and Twenty.

The structure of the book derives from a traditional approach to voidness meditation: the four-point analysis. First, we need to identify the problem. Next, we need to understand the technique to dispel the problem, so that we are convinced of its validity. Based on these first two points, we can then follow that technique. The procedure is to eliminate two extreme positions, covered by the last two points. Here, the two extremes are insensitivity and hypersensitivity.

The first draft of this book was completed in Dharamsala and New Delhi, India, during the spring and summer of 1997. During the autumn of that year, I taught different parts of this program in Buddhist centers in Germany, Holland, Mexico, Poland, Switzerland, and the

Ukraine. Based on the responses, I modified the exercises and prepared the final draft during the winter of 1997/98 in Munich, Germany; Raglan, Wales; and Emst, Holland.

I wish to thank the organizers and participants of these courses, as well as Ven. Steve Carlier, Rajinder Kumar Dogra, Dr. Gary Goodnough, Aldemar Hegewald, Dr. Martin Kalff, Sylvie Kämmerer, and Alan and Irene Turner, for their invaluable suggestions. I especially thank Alnis Grants, Thirza Happé, Herman Horman, Burgel Norris, and Alan and Irene Turner for their kind support while providing the facilities for completing this book, and the students of the Aryatara Institute in Munich for being the patient audience for its final adjustments. Lastly, I deeply thank the Kapor Family Foundation for funding the project and the Nama Rupa Foundation for administering the grant.

Alexander Berzin
Munich, Germany
February 27, 1998

PART 1

Dealing Constructively with Sensitivity Issues

1   Identifying Sensitivity Disorders

What Is Sensitivity?

Certain people seem naturally more sensitive than others. Sometimes this is an admirable quality. Partners are sensitive to each other's moods and do not make demands when the other has had a difficult day. Because of this type of sensitivity, our relations are healthier and our lives are happier. Let us call this ability "balanced sensitivity." In other cases, being sensitive is a disability. Insecure people are sensitive to the point that their feelings are hurt at the slightest remark. This syndrome is known as hypersensitivity. At the other end of the spectrum lies insensitivity. Self-centered persons are insensitive to the effects of their words on others and say whatever comes to their heads.

Sensitivity, then, is a variable that encompasses a wide spectrum. It ranges from insensitivity to hypersensitivity, with balanced sensitivity somewhere between. The degree and quality of our sensitivity, however, are not mathematical constants that remain fixed for a lifetime. Through education and training, we can change them if we wish. To do so, we need to look closely at what sensitivity means. Doing this enables us to differentiate the factors that make it an advantage or a drawback. We can then explore various techniques for developing or enhancing the positive factors and for reducing or eliminating the negative ones.

Sensitivity has both physical and mental forms. Physical sensitivity depends on the body's sensory apparatus or immune system. A surgeon, for instance, has sensitive fingers and a person with allergies is sensitive to dust. In this book, we shall deal exclusively with the form of sensitivity that is a quality of the mind and heart. Such sensitivity may be to the environment, business, politics, wildlife, other persons, or ourselves. Here, we shall explore the last two forms.

Sensitivity is a function of two variables—attentiveness and responsiveness—each of which may be either dysfunctional or balanced. With attentiveness, we note the condition of someone, the consequences of our behavior toward him or her, or both. Responsiveness is our reaction to what we notice. We may respond with an emotion, a thought, words, actions, or some combination of the four.

Two additional factors—empathy and understanding—contribute to balanced sensitivity, but need not be present for us to react constructively. Suppose a relative suffers from terminal cancer. Although imagining his or her pain may be difficult, we can still nurse the person with sensitive care. Further, when we come home in a terrible mood, we may not understand what is bothering us. Nevertheless, we can still have enough sensitivity to go to sleep early. The more empathy and understanding we have, of course, the more able we are to react appropriately.

EXERCISE 1
Identifying Sensitivity Disorders

The eighth-century Indian Buddhist master Shantideva explained that unless we can see a target clearly, we cannot shoot an arrow into its bull's-eye. Similarly, unless we can recognize the specific types of dysfunctional sensitivity from which we suffer, we cannot effectively treat them. Therefore, the first step in our program is to consider various forms of hypersensitivity and insensitivity and then to check whether or not we ever experience them. As both are multifaceted disorders, we shall use schematic outlines to unfold their varieties. Although these lists are not exhaustive, they include the more common sensitivity disorders.

Forms of Hypersensitivity

The first scheme presents five sets of alternative forms of behavior regarding others or ourselves. The alternatives are either a balanced way of acting or a hypersensitive one. Pausing after each pair of alternatives, we need to consider which of the cited examples is more typical of us. If neither example fits our pattern, we may try to find illustrations that are more relevant to our personal life. Recalling specific incidents, we need also to consider which of the alternatives leaves us or others with peace of mind and which makes us or others upset. This helps us to pinpoint our problematic areas and to motivate ourselves to do something about them.

(1) We may pay attention to a situation in either a balanced or an overintense manner. Regarding others, we may ask our sick child, for example, how he or she feels or we might pester him or her with this question every five minutes. Concerning ourselves, we may watch our health or be a hypochondriac.

(2) Paying attention to the consequences of our actions may take either a balanced or an anxious form. Regarding others, we may consider their opinion when deciding something or we might be so frightened of disapproval that it disables us from doing what is best. Concerning ourselves, we may take care to do well at school or we might worry obsessively about failure.

(3) We react to what we notice in two ways—either dispassionately or emotionally. Regarding others, suppose we notice someone trying to pass us on the highway. We may react soberly and shift lanes or we might become heated and mutter obscenities. Concerning ourselves, we may react calmly to misplacing our keys and search systematically, or we might panic.

Paying Attention

To the Situation
(of others or ourselves):
   balanced or overintense

To the Consequences of Our Actions
(on others or ourselves):
   balanced or anxious

Reacting

Dispassionately
(regarding others or ourselves)

Emotionally

   Embracing
   (focused on others or ourselves):
      balanced or disturbed

   Rejecting
   (focused on others or ourselves):
      balanced or disturbed

Figure 1: Balanced and hypersensitive alternatives

Furthermore, an emotional reaction may be balanced or disturbing. In either case, the reaction usually takes one of two forms. Either we react by accepting or embracing the matter or we respond by rejecting or eliminating something. The following examples in the death of a loved one clarify this distinction.

(4) We may accept the matter, focus on the deceased, and either compassionately say prayers or obsessively long for the person. Focusing on ourselves, we may either mourn with dignity or wallow in depression.

(5) Wishing to eliminate something, we may focus on the deceased and either responsibly clear away the person's unfinished business or begrudge him or her for having deserted us. Focusing on ourselves, we may either gain the strength to overcome our dependency or punish ourselves who we feel should have died instead.

Manifestations of Insensitivity

The second scheme presents six common manifestations of insensitivity, each of which may also regard others or ourselves. Continuing our introspection, we need to look for traces of the cited examples or of other illustrations we may find in ourselves. When balanced alternatives to a form of insensitivity exist, we need to consider which alternative is more typical of us.

(1) We may not notice or pay attention to a situation. Regarding others, we may not notice that a relative is upset. Our lack of attention may be due to preoccupation with other matters, or laziness, or not caring. Concerning ourselves, we may not pay attention to the fact that our relationship with our partner is unhealthy. This often occurs when we are insecure or have low self-esteem.

(2) Similarly, we may not pay attention to the consequences of our actions. Regarding others, we may not notice that we have hurt someone's feelings. Concerning ourselves, we may not notice that overwork is causing us stress. In these first two forms of insensitivity, our inattention may go beyond not noticing something. We might also deny its existence.

Even if we notice and acknowledge either a situation or the consequences of our actions, we may still not do anything about it. This may take (3) an appropriate form or (4) an inappropriate one. In the former case, a balanced feeling or no perceived feeling may accompany our inaction. In the latter case, a mixed feeling, an overreaction, or no perceived feeling may be present. A mixed feeling is one that has both balanced and detrimental aspects. Except when a balanced feeling accompanies appropriately refraining from action, the other reactions are all insensitive.

Regarding others, we may notice someone who has fallen in the street and not stop to offer help. Our reaction is appropriate or inappropriate depending, for example, on whether or not someone competent is already caring for the person or calling for help. If others have taken responsibility and we would only be in the way if we stayed, we may feel compassion as we pass by or we might feel nothing. The former reaction is balanced; the latter is not. If no one is helping and we do not stop, we may have mixed feelings: we may feel compassion but be afraid to become involved. Alternatively, we may become upset or we might feel nothing.

Regarding ourselves, we may notice that we feel tired. Yet, we ignore this and do not stop working. Our response may or may not be appropriate depending on whether or not we need to complete an urgent task. Further considerations include whether or not we are physically and emotionally able to continue working, and whether or not we have responsibilities that are more important. If not taking a break is the appropriate choice, we may feel a sense of responsibility in ignoring our tiredness. In such a case, our emotions are balanced. On the other hand, we may be insensitive to our feelings. Suppressing resentment, we may feel nothing.

If not taking a break is a neurotic, inappropriate response, we may have mixed feelings in ignoring our tiredness. On the one hand, we may have kind feelings toward ourselves but, on the other, we may be compulsive about work. Alternatively, ignoring fatigue may be an overreaction: we may be upset about personal problems and want to lose ourselves in work. When we are out of touch with our emotions, we may have no perceived feelings as we unnecessarily refuse to take a break.

(5) Even when we notice something in others or ourselves and act in response, we may not feel certain emotions that are typical for the situation. This may occur in a balanced way, in a mixed way, or with no perceived feelings at all. Concerning others, we may attentively care for a sick person, feel compassion, and use maturity and wisdom to dispel any fears that might interfere with helping. In such a case, our sensitivity to the person is emotionally balanced. On the other hand, we might care for the person, feel compassion, and suppress our fears because of not wanting to appear weak. Here, our sensitivity

to the person mixes compassion with a disturbing attitude of pride. When pride prevents caution or when distraction causes suppressed fear to arise, we may become insensitive to the person's needs despite our compassion. We may also care for the person without any feelings at all, like a nurse attending a patient in a cold, businesslike manner, simply as a job. When this happens, we may become insensitive both to the person and to ourselves.

Concerning ourselves, we may follow a special regime when sick and not feel certain typical emotions in the same three manners. We may be concerned about our health and use emotional maturity to dispel our anxiety because we know that a positive outlook will speed our recovery. With a mixed healthy and neurotic attitude, we may be concerned and suppress our anxiety because we want to appear strong.

Not Noticing

The Situation
(regarding others or ourselves)

The Consequences of Our Actions
(on others or ourselves)

Noticing and Not Acting

When Appropriate
(regarding others or ourselves):
   with balanced feelings
   without perceived feelings

When Inappropriate
(regarding others or ourselves):
   with mixed feelings
   with an overreaction
   without perceived feelings

Noticing and Acting

Without Feeling Certain Emotions
(regarding others or ourselves):
   in a balanced way
   in a mixed way
   without perceived feelings

**With Unbalanced Judgment of
What to Do**
   giving what we want, not what
     others need
   giving what others want, not what
     they need
   doing what we feel like doing, not
     what we need to do

Figure 2: Forms of insensitivity

On the other hand, we might be totally out of balance and not feel anything while nursing ourselves. Not feeling anything, however, either positive or disturbing, is different from being dispassionate and calm. Calmness is a state of balance, not an absence of feelings.

(6) Suppose we notice something in others or ourselves, act in response, and feel something while acting. Still, our decision of what to do may be insensitive because our judgment is unbalanced. Regarding others, we may give them what we want, such as economic security, rather than what they want, such as more understanding and affection. Alternatively, we may give them what they want, for example toys or candy to a screaming toddler, rather than what they actually need, more of our time and attention. Concerning ourselves, we may do what we feel like doing, for instance eating a piece of cake, rather than what we need to do, keeping to our diet.

2 Generating a Feeling of Loving Compassion

Feasibility of Improvement

Having examined ourselves honestly, most of us have probably discovered that we have experienced many of the sensitivity disorders outlined. This should not daunt us. Although the task of developing balanced sensitivity is complex and challenging, it aims for a feasible goal that we can achieve.

Everyone is capable of being sensitive. When we were a baby, for example, we noticed when our stomach was empty or our mother was absent. We felt discomfort or loneliness and reacted by crying. If we were totally insensitive, we could never have done that. We would have simply lain in our crib with indifference, feeling nothing and not reacting.

Everyone is also capable of curbing hypersensitivity. As we grew up, for instance, we developed composure so that now we do not cry at the first pangs of hunger. If we were incapable of patient, calm action, we could not simply go to the refrigerator and take something to eat. This shows that we have a basis from which to improve.

Required Skills

The techniques for developing balanced sensitivity focus on two major aspects. The first is becoming more attentive. The second is reacting more constructively and healthily with feelings, emotions, words, and actions. To become more adept and natural at either aspect, we need to eliminate possible blocks.

Some obstacles equally prevent being attentive and being responsive. For example, we may be preoccupied, unconcerned, lazy, or haunted with fears of inadequacy. These disturbing emotions imprison us in loneliness and alienation. We pay little attention to our external or internal situation and do not react. Other obstacles are more specific, although not exclusive to one or the other aspect of sensitivity. When mental chatter fills our head—whether judgments, worry, or just sheer nonsense—we do not pay attention to anything else. When we fantasize the impossible, such as being unworthy of anyone's love, we do not respond to what we notice, or we overreact.

Developing balanced sensitivity, then, requires cultivating confidence, concern, discipline, concentration, and a sober view of reality. In developing these positive qualities and skills necessary for any form of self-improvement, we overcome the obstacles preventing each. Confidence eliminates feelings of inadequacy and self-doubt. Concern does the same with indifference, discipline with laziness, concentration with mental chatter and dullness, and discrimination of reality with belief in fantasy.

Meditation

Meditation techniques suggest ways to develop the skills required for achieving balanced sensitivity. To meditate means to accustom oneself to some positive quality so that it eventually becomes a natural part of one's character. With repeated practice, we can train ourselves to kick a ball over a post. Similarly, through meditation, we can train ourselves to deal more sensitively with life.

Meditation employs various means to generate a constructive attitude or feeling or to recognize one that is already present as an inborn quality. We may develop love, for example, by thinking of others' happiness or by contacting the natural warmth of our heart. The Gelug tradition of Tibetan Buddhism emphasizes the former method, while the Nyingma school teaches the latter in its *dzogchen* (great completeness) system. Western philosophical systems classify the two approaches as rational and intuitive.

Both rational and intuitive techniques require stilling the mind of extraneous thoughts and dullness. We cannot consider others' problems or tap our innate kindness when worry or fatigue overwhelms our mind. Concentration is essential to reach the desired feeling. Once we have achieved that feeling, we focus it repeatedly on other persons or on ourselves, but without verbalization. Silently saying *I love you* may distance us from our feelings or may reinforce uncertainty about our concern. Directly experiencing love, through nonverbally focusing it on someone, builds it into a stable habit. This is the first step in meditation. The second step is to assimilate the new custom by concentrating fully on the warm heart we have nurtured. We feel it is now an integral part of our personality.

The Gelug tradition calls these two stages "discerning" and "settling," or "analytical" and "formal" meditation. The difference between the stages is like difference between actively seeing our newborn infant as our child and then basking in the feeling of now being a parent. The third step is to alternate the first two: focusing the desired attitude on someone and then letting the feeling of it sink in. This reinforces our new beneficial habit.

Basic Approach

This program for developing balanced sensitivity consists of a series of twenty-two exercises based on the structure of meditation. People from any background, however, may comfortably follow its training. The only requirements are a sincere motivation and both knowledge and understanding of what to do.

Any self-development program that can be practiced on one's own offers potential danger for persons lacking a reasonable level of mental health. This axiom is true regarding this series of exercises. If, upon reading a few chapters of this book, we question our ability to deal emotionally with the material, we should not attempt the training. Professional help may be more appropriate as a start. We do not need to wait, however, until we are perfectly balanced before undertaking this program. When we are sufficiently mature so that strong emotions do not destabilize us, we may try these techniques.

Motivation is essential. Without being dissatisfied with our present situation, we do nothing to improve it. We need to look honestly at the quality of our life. More specifically, we need to examine the quality of our relations with others and with ourselves. If we find these relationships deficient, we need to consider whether we want them to deteriorate further. Do we want future relations also to be unhealthy? Do we wish to disable ourselves from helping others because of our inability to form sensitive bonds? Deep reflection on each of these points is crucial for undertaking this program.

Moved to action, we need to search for the causes of our difficulties. Suppose we discover, through the first exercise, that our interactions often contain one or more forms of insensitivity or hypersensitivity. We need to contemplate how our relationships might improve if we were to reduce and eventually eliminate these imbalances. Once we have understood the causal relation between sensitivity disorders and the quality of our life and we are sufficiently motivated, we are ready to look for remedies.

The first step is to learn about positive qualities that can help and the techniques for developing and heightening them. The next step is to think them over and consider them carefully. If they make no sense or do not seem worthwhile, trying to cultivate them is pointless. Once we are convinced of their rationality and personal value, however, leaving them as intellectual knowledge is not sufficient. We need to integrate these qualities into our life through proper training.

Order of Practice

The cleansing of attitudes or "mind training" literature, known as *lojong* in Tibetan Buddhism, recommends generating positive feelings first for oneself and then slowly extending them to others. Westerners, however, seem to have a special problem with low self-esteem and alienation. Many find it difficult to relate to themselves at all, let alone relate sensitively and kindly. Therefore, for Westerners, developing some experience of balanced sensitivity toward others first and then directing it toward themselves seems a more appropriate order.

Many people in the West also experience serious problems in their personal relationships. Since interactions with others can sometimes be too much to handle, following the lead of modern psychology may be better. Treatment often begins with private therapy before working in a group.

Most exercises in this program contain three phases of practice. Their order reflects the above considerations. The first phase involves looking at photographs of various people or simply thinking of them through a mental image, a feeling, their name, or some combination of the three. Traditional Buddhist meditation favors visualization; nevertheless, if our powers of imagination are not vivid, focusing on a photo is more effective. In choosing a picture, one with a neutral expression affords the most open basis for developing sensitivity skills. For many of the exercises, using a photo merely as a point of reference may be more convenient than focusing directly on the picture throughout the process.

Depending on the exercise, the persons we choose for this first phase of practice vary between someone we love, someone with whom we have a close but emotionally difficult relationship, someone we dislike, and a total stranger. People in the first three categories may be currently in our life or from the past. They may even be deceased. If we have previously had a difficult period with someone with whom we have a healthy relationship now, we may work with a photo or image of the person from that period.

Some people may have had a traumatic experience with a parent or relative who abused them. Applying these exercises initially toward such persons is inadvisable. The emotions that arise may be too powerful. After some progress in the training, however, directing these methods at these especially difficult people may be helpful, under proper supervision. The aim of the exercises is not to deny or to excuse their destructive actions, but to heal the damage inflicted. For peace of mind, we need to relate, without emotional upset, to our memories and feelings. We also need balance in relating to the person now if he or she is still part of our life.

The second phase entails working with others in person. During many of the exercises, we sit in a circle and focus in turn on each member of a group. Frequently, we also break into pairs and focus more intimately on one person at a time. In either case, the practices are more effective when repeated with a variety of people. Optimal is to include someone of each sex, someone older and younger than we are, and someone from a different ethnic or racial background. Practicing both with persons we know and with those less familiar is also helpful. If our group lacks members from some of these categories, we may supplement this phase by focusing on magazine photos of people not represented.

The third phase focuses on ourselves. It involves first looking in a mirror and then reflecting quietly without a mirror. It concludes with looking at a series of photographs of ourselves taken over the span of our life. If we do not have photos from a certain period, we may simply think of ourselves as we were then. Snapshots, however, are always preferable since memory rarely produces a clear or objective picture.

This program may be carried out either alone or, preferably, within the context of a workshop under proper guidance. Once we have learned the techniques as part of a group, we may continue training at home, either by repeating the entire sequence of exercises or by focusing on merely those parts that we find most helpful. As with traditional *sadhana* practice—multi-scene mental dramas visualized for establishing a pure self-image—familiarity first with the complete training enables us afterwards to keep the context in mind when deepening our practice of any of its aspects. Occasional review of the entire program, by reading the Table of Contents, refreshes our awareness of this context. When training alone, we may substitute the partner phase of each exercise with focusing on pictures of diverse people taken from magazines or from our photo album.

Practicing these exercises in their proper sequence, with only one per session, brings optimal results. In many of the exercises, each of the three phases has several parts and each part has many steps. We need to spend at least three minutes on each step and, for some steps, we may wish to focus for up to ten minutes. One phase or one part of an exercise may suffice for a session. This allows proper time to integrate and settle our experience. We may repeat each exercise or one of its phases, parts, or steps as frequently as is useful, both before and after proceeding to the next one in the sequence.

Abbreviating the Training

Most people will wish to read the entire book before committing themselves to any form of training. A workbook, however, is not designed for browsing or casual reading. As the style is purposely terse, a first reading requires sufficient time to pause and reflect after each point.

Some people may wish to do only an abbreviated practice. Others may find it useful to work through the sequence of exercises first in a short form before repeating them in full or joining a group. We may abbreviate the training by practicing only several of the exercises, by limiting the scope of each exercise, or by doing both. An introductory weekend course, for example, might include Exercises Two, Three, Four, Ten, Eleven, and Twenty. The topics would be: identifying sensitivity disorders, generating a feeling of loving compassion, imagining ideal sensitivity, affirming and accessing our natural qualities, applying the five types of deep awareness, validating the appearances we perceive, and adjusting our innate mental factors. If time does not permit, we may omit the last two topics. A one-day seminar would comprise: generating a feeling of loving compassion and applying the five types of deep awareness.

If we wish to limit our scope when practicing as part of a group, we may abbreviate by looking at a picture or thinking of only one person during the first phase of each exercise. During the second phase, we might work simply in a circle or facing only one person and, during the third, focus on ourselves only in a mirror or merely without one if mirror practice is normally skipped in the exercise. Those training alone may further abbreviate the program by omitting the second phase altogether.

Posture

Practicing these exercises does not require an acrobatic position or an exotic setting. Sitting comfortably in a quiet place with shoes off is sufficient. We may sit on a cushion placed either on the floor or on a firm bed, or we may choose a firm chair. In each case, we need to sit upright with our back straight, but not stiff, and our muscles relaxed. Maintaining good posture helps to keep the mind clear and alert. Those using a chair need to keep both feet flat on the floor. Those seated on a cushion need to choose a pillow of appropriate thickness and hardness so that their legs do not fall asleep and their back does not become strained. Those sitting cross-legged should place the cushion beneath their buttocks so that their knees are lower than their behind.

Keeping the shoulders down and level, not raised as if working at a desk, is important. Holding the shoulders up at attention creates or accentuates tension in the neck. If we notice such tension, we may find it helpful to raise our shoulders and then to drop them forcefully to release the tension. We also need to keep our mouth and teeth relaxed, not clenched. Resting the hands in the lap, with palms facing upwards and the right hand on top of the left, leaves the muscles in the arms fully relaxed. Moreover, keeping the tongue touching the upper palate just behind the front teeth reduces saliva production so that we are not distracted by a frequent need to swallow.

During the parts of the exercises practiced while sitting alone and thinking of someone, we may keep our eyes either open or closed, whichever feels more comfortable. In either case, bending our head slightly downward is best. Those leaving their eyes open need to focus loosely on the floor and not pay attention to their field of vision. Keeping the eyes open, however, obviously is essential during those parts of the exercises requiring looking at a picture, at other people in a circle, at an individual partner, or at a mirror. During such practice, we may blink normally, without staring.

Initial Procedures for Each Exercise

Beginning each session with a short breathing practice is helpful for turning our attention from previous activities. To do this, we breathe normally through the nose, not too quickly, not too slowly, not too deeply, not too shallowly, and without holding the breath. The healthiest breathing cycle consists of three phases—exhalation, a quiet period of rest, and then inhalation. Silently we count this cycle as one, the next as two, and continue until eleven. We repeat the sequence a second time.

Next, we establish or reaffirm our motivation for practicing the exercise. This helps to prevent our training from becoming mechanical. We remind ourselves, for example, that we would like to achieve balanced sensitivity so that we can use our potentials for the benefit of everyone, including ourselves.

Lastly, we consciously decide to concentrate during the session. If our attention wanders, we intend to return it to its focus. If we become sleepy, we intend to wake ourselves up. To refresh ourselves before the main practice, we may focus for a minute on the point between the eyebrows. While doing this, we need to keep our head level and look upward. This raises the energy in the body. To calm ourselves if nervous or preoccupied, we need to refine our energy. To accomplish this, we may next focus for a minute on the navel, keeping the head level and looking downward.

When practicing with a partner, people often begin to laugh. This frequently happens because of nervousness or because of unfamiliarity with prolonged eye contact. People may also laugh uncontrollably as an unconscious mechanism to avoid personal contact. This syndrome often hides awkwardness or fear. Counting the breath once more and focusing on the navel before beginning the second phase of each exercise reduces the chances of laughter arising. To quiet the energies if laughter erupts, we may revert to counting the breath and focusing on the navel for as long as is necessary.

As an aid for keeping focus, during most of the exercises the group facilitator may occasionally repeat key phrases and the reminder "no mental comments." He or she may do this one phrase at a time for each state of mind that we try to generate or, at minimum, repeat the entire sequence slowly for the final integration at the end of each phase. When practicing alone, we may repeat the phrases to ourselves, silently or aloud. Having a list before us as a visual aid may also be useful. When in a group, we may also say the phrase of the moment silently to ourselves if we notice that our focus has weakened.

Rational and Intuitive Approaches

Some practices in this program take a rational approach, while others take an intuitive one. The rational approach to developing balanced sensitivity is to generate a positive feeling, such as love, using the same approach as when reaching a conclusion through Buddhist logic. We rely on a line of reasoning and an example. This approach is especially useful for persons with blocked feelings or emotions. Such people find difficulty in feeling something spontaneously. Reason provides them an easier access. When they understand why certain feelings are reasonable, they have fewer fears or objections to trying to experience them.

Some persons with blocked feelings, however, find that relying on a line of reasoning is insufficient for generating a constructive feeling. They know intellectually how they *should* feel, but either they still feel nothing or what they feel seems artificial and shallow. Sometimes, this leads to feeling guilty or inadequate. Such persons need to persevere. For example, swimming with a certain stroke may seem unnatural at first. Yet, with repeated practice, it becomes a perfectly normal action. The same is true with learning to feel something positive toward others or toward ourselves. Repeatedly generating a feeling through a line of reasoning leads to slowly beginning to feel something. This occurs as objections and blocks start to weaken. At first, that feeling may seem contrived. Yet, over time, it becomes so natural that relying on reason is no longer necessary to feel an emotion.

On the other hand, people who are emotional often find relying on reason quite alien. They consider feelings generated by logic to be insincere. For such persons, the intuitive approach may be more appropriate. It entails quieting down and working with feelings that naturally arise. The emphasis is on removing any disturbing elements that block or adulterate intuitive feelings.

No matter which type of person we are, looking down on either style is detrimental to progress. Dismissing the rational approach as too intellectual, or the intuitive one as completely irrational, deprives us of reaping the benefits of both. Training with a combination of the two is, in fact, the most effective method for developing balanced sensitivity.

Those who are rationally inclined find that once they begin to experience the feelings they are trying to generate, intuitively oriented exercises reinforce and enhance those feelings. Such exercises convince them that they have a natural source of positive emotions within themselves. This helps them to progress beyond the stage of experiencing their feelings as contrived.

Intuitively inclined persons find that once they quiet down and access their feelings, exercises that rely on reason add stability to their experience. Moreover, such exercises give them an alternative technique for generating positive feelings when they are in a bad mood or when negative emotions overwhelm them. They also find the rational approach useful when the person toward whom they are trying to feel something positive is acting horribly.

Concluding Procedures

We need to conclude each exercise with the wish that such reflection and practice contribute to our becoming a more balanced and sensitive person, for our own and others' sake. We also wish that everyone might achieve this state. Such concluding wishes are known as the "dedication."

If a deep and meaningful conversation abruptly ends with the telephone ringing, the positive energy is immediately shattered and lost. If, however, the encounter ends with a mutual acknowledgment of how wonderful it was and with the wish that the communication deepen in the future, the result is different. The positive feeling created and the insights gained linger with each person. The same is true regarding the positive energy of the insights and experiences gained through these exercises. They become more stable and bring more benefit when we dedicate them toward achieving our goals.

To reduce distraction from disorder or noise, we train at first only in the controlled atmosphere of a clean, quiet room. Many of these exercises may elicit strong emotions. Therefore, practicing them in the protected space of privacy, alone or among sympathetic friends, reduces tension. Gradually, we broaden our endeavor and practice generating constructive feelings in "live" situations. Using the same techniques as when training alone or as part of a workshop, we try to direct these feelings to the people we see in the supermarket, on the bus, or anywhere we happen to be. Such practice helps us to become more sensitive to people's actual situations and not to overreact based on preconceptions.

Over time, the qualities we try to cultivate through these exercises become a natural part of ourselves. Our personality is no more fixed than our athletic skills. With motivation and proper techniques, we can develop either.

EXERCISE 2
Generating a Feeling of Loving Compassion

Since most of the exercises in the program are multistage, let us begin with an unelaborated practice for generating a feeling of loving compassion, which will accustom us to the procedure. Love is the wish for someone to be happy and to have the causes for happiness. Compassion is the wish for someone to be free from suffering and from the causes for pain. To generate these feelings, we shall use the rational technique of relying on a line of reasoning and an example. Here, the reason is that everyone wants and deserves to be happy and not to suffer. The example is ourselves. Just as we have this wish and right, so does everyone else.

The first phase of the exercise begins with looking at a picture or simply thinking of someone we find exasperating—for example, a loud, overbearing uncle or aunt. We try to think how everyone, despite personal shortcomings or obnoxious habits, wants and deserves to be loved and not rejected, just as we do ourselves. Then, looking at our uncle or aunt, we try to recognize that this person is a human being. Like us, he or she both wants and deserves to be happy.

Regarding our relative in this way, we try to generate and direct toward him or her a feeling of loving compassion based on this understanding. We wish our uncle or aunt to be happy and not to suffer, but do not verbalize this wish in our mind. To help maintain focus, our group facilitator or we ourselves may occasionally repeat the key phrase, "loving compassion." We then sit back, figuratively speaking, and try to focus on our feeling. This enables us to affirm and digest it. Lastly, we alternate looking with loving compassion and focusing on the feeling.

During the second phase of the exercise, we sit in a circle with a group and look at each person in turn. Relying on the previous line of reasoning, we think, "Everyone wants and deserves to be happy and not to suffer, just as I do. This is a human being. Therefore, he or she has the same wishes and rights as I do." In this way, we try to generate a loving, compassionate feeling for the person. Actively regarding each person in this way for a minute, we then try to let our feeling sink in by reaffirming and concentrating on it. We may use the same phrase as before and then alternate looking and digesting before going on to the next person.

After this, we pair off with a partner. Without being intense or intrusive, we gently look in the other person's eyes and repeat the procedure. When letting our feeling of loving compassion sink in, we may either continue looking at the person or avert our sight briefly. The other person may find it rude if we shut our eyes.

The third phase begins with looking at ourselves in a mirror and repeating a slight variation of the previous line of reasoning: "Everyone wants and deserves to be happy and not to suffer, for instance others I know. I am a human being. Therefore, I have the same wishes and rights as everybody else." When a warm compassionate feeling arises, we direct it at our image. After a few moments, we try to let that feeling and experience sink in. Putting down the mirror, we repeat the exercise, trying to aim our positive feelings directly at ourselves. We may keep our eyes closed or loosely focused on the floor.

Some people have had particularly difficult periods in their life. They often feel especially negative toward themselves at those ages. They may also feel that they cannot relate to who they were at those times. Even if we do not have this problem, we conclude by looking at a series of photographs of ourselves from representative periods in our life. We try to generate a feeling of loving compassion toward the person whom we see in each. We do this by thinking, "Everyone wants and deserves to be happy and not to suffer, just as I do now. I was a human being then. Therefore, I had the same wishes and rights then as I do now." Such practice is useful for integrating our life's experiences and developing a balanced, holistic attitude toward ourselves.

3 Imagining Ideal Sensitivity

Developing balanced sensitivity requires a clear idea of the goal we wish to achieve so that we can focus our efforts in that direction. A Buddha is a paramount example of someone fully sensitive in the positive sense and totally free of all negative aspects. The descriptions of a Buddha's qualities, therefore, suggest the features we need to achieve.

Qualities Suggested by the Buddha-bodies

A Buddha is, literally, someone totally awake—someone who has overcome all shortcomings and realized all potentials for being of maximum help to others. The qualities of a Buddha are distributed among the various "Buddha-bodies" such a person has attained. A Buddha-body is a collection of a vast array of components, not necessarily physical.

Each Buddha has a *dharmakaya* or body encompassing everything and a *rupakaya* or body of enlightening forms. The former is the collection of qualities that comprise a fully wise, all-loving mind. The latter is the infinite assortment of physical forms in which a Buddha manifests to help others.

If we wish to be fully sensitive in the positive sense, we need qualities similar to both Buddha-bodies. As if we had a body of fully wise, all-loving awareness, we need deep concern about everything and everyone and attention to all details. Understanding each situation and person enables us to know how to help. We also need complete flexibility to respond appropriately, as suggested by having a body of enlightening forms.

Forms of Sensitive Response

Rupakaya has two aspects: a *sambhogakaya* or body of forms of full use and a *nirmanakaya* or body of emanations. The former is an array of subtle forms making full use of Buddha's teachings on altruism. The latter is an assortment of grosser forms emanated from sambhogakaya. The *tantra* literature—texts of advanced techniques for self-transformation—explains sambhogakaya as the collection of all forms of enlightening speech. Nirmanakaya is the full assortment of visible enlightening forms, no matter the level of subtlety.

Perfect sensitivity similarly requires full use of our body and communicative skills. We need sensitivity in how we speak to others and in how we act. Moreover, sensitive physical responses need to span several levels. On a subtle level, we need to show sympathy with our facial expression and body language. On a grosser level, we need to give, for example, a comforting hug, or to help with the dishes.

A body of forms is not like a collection of suits in a wardrobe. To fit an occasion, a Buddha does not choose a particular coarse or subtle form from a fixed repertoire. Instead, a Buddha spontaneously appears in whatever form helping others requires. Similarly, when we are properly sensitive to others, we do not respond with a fixed routine chosen from among a certain number we have learned. Reacting to others with a set response makes us stiff and unnatural. It causes others to feel we are insincere. We need to be flexible and respond spontaneously with heartfelt words and actions.

Qualities of Mind and Heart

Dharmakaya also has two aspects: a *jnana-dharmakaya* or body of deep awareness and a *svabhavakaya* or body of self-nature. The Tibetan traditions offer several explanations. The Gelug lineage and some Sakya authors assert the former to be the fully wise, all-loving mind of a Buddha, with deep awareness of everything. The latter is the "self-devoid" nature or "self-voidness" of such a mind. The self-voidness of something is its total absence of existing in a fantasized, impossible way.

The Kagyü and Nyingma schools and several Sakya authors explain jnana-dharmakaya as the "other-devoid" nature or "other-voidness" of a fully wise, all-loving mind. Other-voidness is the absence from the subtlest level of the mind of all grosser levels, such as conceptual thoughts or disturbing emotions. Other-voidness also implies the endowment of this level of mind with all enlightening qualities. These include compassion, understanding, and the ability to benefit others through restraining from inappropriate actions and through engaging in fitting deeds. According to this position, svabhavakaya is the inseparability of the various Buddha-bodies. The *Kalachakra* (cycles of time) literature offers another variation. Svabhavakaya is also the joyous nature of fully wise, all-loving awareness.

Each of these facets of dharmakaya suggests factors needed for developing balanced sensitivity. Proper sensitivity depends not only on love and understanding. It also relies on the fact that we, our heart, and our mind do not exist in fantasized ways. No one is the center of the universe, nor is anyone totally cut off from others or from themselves. Moreover, no one is incapable of being sensitive. This is because everyone's mind is fully endowed with all abilities, such as the capacity to love, the competence to understand, and the capability to restrain from what is inappropriate.

Dharmakaya
(Body Encompassing Everything)

Jnana-dharmakaya
(Body of Deep Awareness)
   completely wise
   all-loving
   devoid of conceptual thoughts
     and disturbing emotions

Svabhavakaya
(Body of Self-nature)
   devoid of impossible
     ways of existing
   integrated body, speech,
     mind, and heart
   joyous

Rupakaya
(Body of Enlightening Forms)

Sambhogakaya
(Body of Forms of Full Use)
   subtle forms of physical expression
   verbal communication

Nirmanakaya
(Body of Emanations)
   behavioral expression

Figure 3: The Buddha-bodies

Furthermore, when we are properly sensitive, our mind remains free of disturbing thoughts, upsetting emotions, and unsettling attitudes. Our feelings, speech, and conduct are integrated and consistent. Free of the insecurity out of which we project fears and fantasies, our mind is also naturally joyous.

EXERCISE 3
Imagining Ideal Sensitivity

The following three-part exercise takes a more intuitive approach than the previous one. It is suggested by and a composite of several standard meditation techniques. First is the procedure of openly admitting to our previously committed negative actions and purifying ourselves of their *"karmic* consequences." Such consequences are the repercussions that follow from the laws of behavioral cause and effect. An abbreviated practice comes next to reaffirm our motivation for behaving more constructively.

We then adopt the basic technique of tantric visualization practice. In tantra, we imagine that we already have a Buddha's enlightening qualities. We picture acting with them toward everyone around us. Here, we shall use the qualities suggested by the characteristics of the Buddha-bodies. Like a rehearsal for a performance, such practice familiarizes us with the ways in which we would like to act in the future. This serves as a cause for actualizing these skills more quickly. At the end, we strengthen our resolve by adopting the structure of meditation on the four "immeasurable attitudes": love, compassion, joy, and equanimity.

We begin the first phase of the exercise by choosing a form of insensitivity that we have recognized in ourselves. We try to recall an incident in which someone acted like this toward us. For instance, our partner came home excited from work and proceeded to speak only about his or her day. We had a difficult day ourselves and also wanted attention and comfort. We try to recall the pain we felt at our partner's insensitivity. Perhaps we recall that we had blocked our feelings and just stoically listened. If we live alone, we may have had a similar experience when we telephoned a friend. Next, we try to remember an incident in which we acted in the same insensitive way toward someone. The person must have also felt hurt.

Acknowledging the mistake of our insensitive behavior, we regret our actions. Regret is different from guilt. Regret is merely the wish that we had not done something. We regret, for example, that we ate a meal that disagreed with us. Guilt, on the other hand, arises from a strong identification of what we have done as "bad" and of ourselves as therefore a "bad" person. With guilt, we hold on to these fixed judgments and do not let go. It is like keeping our garbage in the house and never throwing it out. To overcome feelings of guilt, we need to realize that our previous actions are in the past. We regret that they happened, but we cannot do anything to change the fact that they occurred. We need to get on with our life and no valid reason exists for having to repeat these mistakes.

The next step in our exercise is to try to feel disgust with our insensitivity. No longer wishing to tolerate the isolation and anguish this disorder brings, we determine to rid ourselves of it. We strengthen our resolve by reminding ourselves of the pain our insensitivity brings others and the unfairness of this. Also, the more insensitive we are, the more hampered we become in our attempts to help others, for instance our loved ones. For their sake, we must overcome our lack of openness and balance. We resolve to try our best not to repeat our action and we reaffirm the direction in which we would like to go. We would like to develop balanced sensitivity toward everyone.

To begin counteracting our detrimental habits, we direct our efforts initially at the person toward whom we have acted insensitively. We try to imagine acting toward him or her in the ideally balanced fashion suggested by the qualities of the Buddha-bodies.

First, we need to quiet our mind of mental chatter. Two techniques are helpful. The first is a breathing exercise called "letting go." We breathe normally, as described in Chapter Two, with a three-part cycle of exhalation, rest, and inhalation. While exhaling, we try to imagine that our verbal thoughts leave us with our breath. We do not expel the thoughts forcefully, but just gently exhale. Before inhaling, we rest in the quiet space between breaths.

To supplement this technique, we may use a dzogchen method. We try to imagine our verbal thoughts to be like writing on water. When we write on water, the letters arise and disappear simultaneously. There is nothing substantial about them. We may try an example by thinking slowly, one by one, each word of the thought "I am bored." Without visualizing the letters, we try to imagine each word to be like writing on water. Most people find that the energy of the thought diminishes significantly. They often experience that it is difficult for the next word of the thought even to arise.

When we have achieved a modicum of mental silence, we look at a photo or simply think of the person toward whom we have acted insensitively. As when quieting our mind of mental chatter, we use the breath and the image of writing on water to try to still our mind of preconceptions and nonverbal judgments. We then try to release our feeling of self-importance by reminding ourselves that we are not the center of the universe. The other person also exists. We honor the conventional boundaries of propriety. For example, we do not pry intrusively into his or her private affairs. Yet, we try to feel that no solid walls stand between us, preventing heartfelt communication. The nonexistence of walls does not leave us exposed, frightened, and insecure. On the contrary, with no barriers obstructing love and understanding between us, we try to relax our defenses and feel no fear.

Experiencing joy at the possibilities of our encounter, we now focus attentively on the person. Trying to look at him or her with warmth and understanding, we also express our concern with appropriate facial expression and body language. If we were to listen to someone's problems with a blank expression, he or she might feel we did not care. On the other hand, if we were to wear an idiotic grin on our face, the person might feel we were not taking him or her seriously. Moreover, if we sit with arms folded, the person might feel we were distant and judgmental.

Exercising self-control to curb any destructive tendencies, we imagine responding with kind words and thoughtful actions. If we are listening to someone on the telephone, for example, unless we occasionally say at least "uh huh," the person suspects we are not even listening. On the other hand, if we say too much, he or she might feel we just want to hear ourselves speak. Moreover, listening with a sympathetic smile in our eyes and nodding our head are often not enough. We need to take more demonstrative steps with appropriate actions. For instance, we might put our arm around someone's shoulders, if this would be of comfort, or offer to help with the person's tasks.

Lastly, we need to familiarize ourselves with these factors. Our group leader or we may repeat slowly, one by one, the following thirteen key phrases in sequence several times: "no mental chatter," "no judgments," "no self-importance," "no solid walls," "no fears," "joy," "focus," "warmth," "understanding," "facial expression," "self-control," "kind words," and "thoughtful actions." With each phrase, we try to look at the person with the state of mind or feeling.

We conclude by slowly thinking the following three thoughts, one at a time, and by trying to feel their sentiment sincerely. "How wonderful it would be if I could become like this." "I wish I could become like this." "I shall definitely try to become like this." Then, we try to think of a shining example of balanced sensitivity—whether a Buddha, a spiritual leader, or someone from our personal life. Looking at a photo or simply picturing the person in our mind, we request inspiration. We try to imagine that warm yellow light radiates from the person and fills us with the inspiring strength to reach our goal. Imagining that the figure dissolves into our heart, we try to feel ourselves glowing with the light of inspiration.

We may repeat the exercise using a form of hypersensitivity that we have also identified in ourselves. We may try to recall, for example, coming home tired. Paying hardly any attention to the person we live with, we retired to the sofa and turned on the television. If living alone, perhaps we forgot to call our friend or our parent. He or she became completely upset and overreacted by accusing us of not caring. We felt hurt at this false accusation: we were merely too tired to chat. Calming and reassuring the person of our true feelings was extremely unpleasant.

Next, we try to remember an incident in which we similarly overreacted when someone behaved like this toward us. Our hypersensitive behavior must have made him or her also feel awful. We then proceed with the rest of the exercise as before. Here, we imagine avoiding the extremes of speaking cruelly or acting rashly.

Feeling Balanced Sensitivity Toward a Partner and Toward Ourselves

During the second phase of the exercise, we face a partner. We try to look at the person with the same thirteen states of mind, attitudes, feelings, and intentions as when practicing with a photograph or with a thought of someone. We may omit, however, the steps of the practice that preceded and followed this procedure. To help us keep mindful, we may use the key phrases as before.

We begin the third phase by looking in a mirror. Again, we repeat simply the sequence of thirteen attitudes, directing them now at ourselves as follows. Stilling our mind of comments, we try also to release our fixed attitudes and to shed our self-judgments. To dispel our fantasies, we note that we are not the most important person in the world or the only one with problems. Moreover, we try to see that there are no walls preventing us from relating to ourselves. Any self-alienation we feel is based on sheer fiction. Unafraid, we try to feel relief and joy at the possibility of being open and relaxed with ourselves. We then focus with warm understanding and try to exercise self-control so as not to overreact with low self-esteem nor to be self-destructive. At ease and at peace with ourselves, we soften the expression on our face and try to look with at least a smile in our eyes. We resolve to speak to ourselves kindly, not to put ourselves down, and to treat ourselves in a thoughtful manner.

With the thirteen key phrases, we repeat the sequence several times slowly. We then put down the mirror and go through the sequence again, but now just feeling the sentiments with our eyes closed or loosely focused on the floor. Lastly, we repeat the exercise while directing our attention at the series of photographs of ourselves spanning our life. Especially helpful is working with periods we would rather forget or about which we feel self-hatred. For instance, we may focus on a time when we acted foolishly in an unhealthy relationship. In place of the phrases "kind words" and "thoughtful actions," we substitute "kind thoughts of forgiveness."

4   Affirming and Accessing Our Natural Abilities

The Necessity for a Pragmatic Technique

Imagining what it would be like to be as perfectly balanced in our sensitivity as a Buddha gives us some idea of the goal we would like to achieve. Comparing our present level of sensitivity with this ideal also helps motivate us to strive toward this aim. Nevertheless, we need more than the power of imagination to reach this goal. In addition, we need conviction in our ability to achieve it and a down-to-earth basis from which to grow.

The breathing technique of letting go and use of the image of writing on water can bring us a quiet mind, at least temporarily. We may reinforce this state by focusing on the sensation of the breath passing in and out our nostrils as we breathe normally. A calm state of mind serves as a platform for reaching deeper levels of inner peace and for seeing reality more clearly. However, it is difficult to generate and implement such qualities as joy, warmth, and tender understanding by merely conjuring them in our imagination. Relying purely on the rational approach of logic is also not so simple. The teachings on Buddha-nature suggest a more pragmatic means to access a working level of these qualities. Following these methods brings confidence that the goal is practicable.

Buddha-nature

Buddha taught that everyone, despite gender, age, or race, could evolve to the state of maturity he had reached. This is because each individual possesses the natural factors that allow for the achievement of Buddha-bodies. He called these factors "Buddha-nature." They fall into three basic groups. Let us present them in the context of how they pertain to the topic of sensitivity.

(1) The most fundamental features that allow us balance in our sensitivity are the mind's other-void and self-void natures. No one's mind is permanently cluttered with endless thoughts or haunting images. No one's heart is eternally plagued with disturbing emotions or upsetting feelings. Moreover, no one's mind exists as inherently flawed or incapable of balance. These other-void and self-void natures are abiding facts. We need merely to realize them.

(2) The basic qualities that allow for balanced sensitivity naturally endow our mind and heart. These qualities are part of our innate stores of positive potential and deep awareness—our "collections of merit and wisdom." In other words, everyone has a certain amount of warmth and understanding. We need merely to remove the obstacles preventing them from functioning fully and to build them up further.

(3) Our mind and heart can be stimulated to grow. Everyone can be inspired by something or someone to reach new heights. This point accounts for the fact that with favorable circumstances our talents can blossom. We need merely openness and receptivity.

Basis, Pathway, and Resultant Levels

Buddhist analysis differentiates basis, pathway, and resultant levels of certain phenomena. The factors comprising the stores of positive potential and deep awareness are among them. Their basis level is their natural occurrence as features of our heart and mind. Just as everyone's face comes with a nose and a mouth, everyone's heart and mind come with a basic level of warmth and understanding. Various practices can enhance these qualities so that they function through a broad range of pathway levels. These levels act as a pathway for achieving the resultant level: the fully matured functioning of these features as part of the Buddha-bodies.

Since everyone has at least a basis level of qualities such as warmth and understanding, we can all recall an incident in which they were functioning to some degree. Memory of personal experience is usually more vivid than an imagined occurrence. Consequently, recollection of a certain feeling acts as a more effective springboard for generating it again. This is the technique we shall employ in the next step of our training.

Acknowledging Our Store of Positive Potential

Positive potential results from constructive behavior and ripens into happiness and joy. Constructive behavior refers primarily to two activities: helping others with loving compassion and restraining from acting, speaking, or thinking under the influence of disturbing emotions. Such behavior results from loving concern and from self-control. Therefore, if we all possess a store of positive potential as part of our Buddha-nature, we must also have a basis level of joy as its result and of loving concern and self-control as its causes. If we can recognize and access these three qualities, we can develop them further.

Happiness or joy is defined as that feeling which, when experienced, we would like to have continue or repeat. This does not imply necessarily being attached to the feeling. We may be content and happy watching our children at play, but not cling to that experience when it is time for them to go to bed. Nor does this definition imply that a feeling we like must be intense to qualify as happiness. The joy of relaxing after a day of work is not dramatic, but is pleasurable and something we would like to repeat.

No matter how dour or depressed we might usually be, we have all experienced moments that we would like to continue. Surely, everyone has savored the enjoyment of lying in a warm cozy bed in the morning. If we remember the simple pleasures in life, we can use them as a foundation for feeling happy to be with someone. They form the basis for extending joy to the person.

Everyone also has a basic level of concern for others. Biologists call it the instinct for the survival of the species. We see clear evidence of inborn concern for others in small children. Almost all youngsters instinctively like to take care of a doll, or to play house or doctor. Moreover, as an adult, we gain satisfaction and fulfillment when, without pressure or obligation, we can nurture, guide, or protect someone. This happens even if the person is not our child. After all, everyone enjoys being a good host or hostess. When we recall the warm concern we naturally feel when preparing and serving a tasty meal to a guest, we have a basis for extending the same regard to anyone, including ourselves.

All of us can also exercise a certain amount of discipline and self-control. We naturally restrain ourselves, for example, from driving our car dangerously. Recalling this ability, we can apply it to restrain ourselves from acting destructively or inappropriately.

Since we each have a basis level of joy, regard for others, and self-control, we can conclude that we all have at least some innate store of positive potential. This means that everyone has acted constructively in the past, to varying degrees. In other words, no one is totally bad. Affirming this is important, particularly regarding ourselves if we suffer from low self-esteem.

Appreciating Our Store of Deep Awareness and Ability to Be Inspired

We all are born not only with a store of positive potential, but also with a store of deep awareness (*yeshey*). Our mind has the inherent mechanism that allows us to gain knowledge, to discriminate between what is appropriate and what is not, and to know what to do. For example, we can see the dishes in our sink, discriminate between their being clean and dirty, and realize that we need to wash them. Moreover, all of us are also capable of focusing. When we wash the dishes, we remain focused on the task and do not drop them. Acknowledging these abilities gives us the self-confidence to sense, understand, and react sensibly, with focused attention, to others' or our own condition.

Lastly, everyone's heart and mind can be moved by something or someone—whether it be music, the beauty of nature, a just cause, or an outstanding person. Recalling the uplifting feeling we gain from whatever moves us, we can harness that feeling for constructive purposes. We can use it to inspire ourselves to transcend the basis level of our remembered good qualities. This enables us slowly to bring these qualities to their resultant level of perfectly balanced sensitivity, which we can only begin to imagine now.

EXERCISE 4

Affirming and Accessing Our Natural Abilities

To gain a more vivid feeling for some qualities that we merely imagined in the previous exercise, here we try to remember our natural experience of various aspects of balanced sensitivity. We then direct these mental factors at others and at ourselves, while trying to continue to feel them.

During the first phase, we focus on a photo or simply on a thought of someone with whom we have or have had an emotionally trying relationship. First, we try to recall the mellow feeling of joy we felt at lying in bed this morning. Directing it at the person, we are happy to be with him or her and we have ample joy to share. Remembering our ability to focus on washing the dishes, we then try to focus our attention fully. Next, we recall the regard and care we took when preparing a meal for a welcomed guest. When we feel this warmth, we also try to redirect it toward this trying individual.

Remembering the understanding we had when we saw the sink full of dirty dishes, we then try to focus understanding on the person. Bringing to mind the self-control we exercised not to drive dangerously on the highway, we try to feel able to restrain ourselves from acting destructively toward him or her. Lastly, we recall the inspiration we felt when watching the sunset and try to feel uplifted so as to maintain our balanced sensitivity.

We repeat this sequence several times, either listening to our workshop leader slowly reciting the following six key words or cuing ourselves: "joy," "focus," "warmth," "understanding," "self-control," and "inspiration." With each word, we generate and direct the state of mind at the person, focus on the feeling itself, and then alternate looking with the feeling and focusing on it.

At first, we work with merely one state of mind at a time. Gradually, we try to combine and integrate all six. To begin the process, we try to put together joy and focus, by using a sequence of just two key words. We then add warmth and graduate to a three-termed sequence. Increasing one at a time, we steadily expand our state of mind to include all six factors at once.

During the second phase of the exercise, we follow the same procedure while facing a partner. During the third phase, we direct these feelings at ourselves, first looking in a mirror and then without one. When we hear or say "joy," we apply the remembered feeling of comfort at lying in bed to feeling at ease and happy to be with ourselves. As a final step, we direct these feelings at the series of photographs of ourselves spanning our life.

5 Refraining from Destructive Behavior

The Need for Ethics

Responding to others or to ourselves with balanced sensitivity entails refraining from destructive, harmful behavior and engaging in constructive, helpful acts. Restraint from destructive behavior sets the foundation. For example, if we have not established a consistent pattern of curbing ourselves from making cruel, sarcastic remarks, others will not trust us with their personal problems. This will happen even if we notice their moods and show concern. Therefore, we need to apply our natural ability for self-control to keeping ethical ground rules for our interactions.

Definition of Destructive Behavior

Each system of ethics, whether religious or civil, defines destructive behavior differently. Some systems have a set of laws established by heavenly authority or by legislature. Destructive behavior is to disobey the law. Others define destructive actions as those that harm others or harm oneself. Knowing what is harmful is difficult, however. The same action may be detrimental to some and helpful to others. Even when directed at the same person, it may be damaging in one situation and not in another. For instance, shouting harsh words to someone may either hurt his or her feelings or rouse the person from laziness.

Buddhist ethics emphasize the importance of motivation and frame of mind in determining whether an action is destructive. Besides causing harm and suffering, a destructive action must also be motivated by greed, anger, or naivety about its consequences. Further, it arises from having no shame and from not feeling embarrassed by anything we do. By these additional criteria, yelling with anger at someone to get out of bed, without caring that we are making a terrible scene or a fool of ourselves, is destructive whether or not it hurts the person's feelings. At minimum, it is a self-damaging act, which brings us suffering. We may be upset for hours.

Ten Destructive Actions

Many physical, verbal, and mental actions are destructive. Buddhism delineates ten that are the most harmful. This is because they nearly always arise from disturbing emotions, shamelessness, and lack of embarrassment. The ten are (1) taking life, (2) taking what has not been given, (3) indulging in inappropriate sexual behavior, (4) lying, (5) speaking divisively, (6) using harsh language, (7) speaking idle words, (8) thinking covetous thoughts, (9) thinking thoughts of malice, and (10) distorted, antagonistic thinking. Irrespective of one's religious background or belief, restraint from them is pertinent for anyone wishing to develop balanced sensitivity.

These ten categories also include other destructive actions. We do not need to kill to cause physical harm. Beating or treating people roughly is also destructive. Taking what has not been given includes not only stealing, but also keeping a borrowed item longer than needed or not returning it at all. Inappropriate sexual behavior is not only rape or adultery, but also sexual harrassment. When working on sensitivity, we need to think as broadly as possible about our behavior and its consequences.

Motivation for Ethical Training

In a Buddhist context, we motivate ourselves to exercise ethical self-control by thinking about the karmic consequences of the ten destructive actions, which will occur primarily in future lives. For example, we will compulsively repeat the pattern of behavior. Moreover, we will impulsively blunder into relationships in which people act toward us in the same insensitive, cruel manner as we have been acting toward others. Not wanting the unhappiness of frustrating, unfulfilling relationships, characterized by a lack of kindness or consideration, motivates us to avoid its causes in our behavior now.

To motivate ourselves to behave ethically, we need not think about future lives if we do not believe in them. Consideration of this lifetime alone can accomplish the same effect. We may recall incidents in which others have acted in these destructive manners toward us and remember how hurt we felt. We may then recall occasions when we have acted similarly and imagine how others must have felt in response. Noting that our destructive patterns repeat and feeling horrified at the prospect of future unhealthy relationships, we determine to free ourselves from these painful syndromes. To do so, we would be willing to give up our negative ways. Our determination strengthens when our primary concern is to stop hurting others.

EXERCISE 5
Resolving to Refrain from Destructive Behavior

During each phase of this exercise we consider the ten destructive actions one by one. The first phase has two steps. We begin by trying to recall specific incidents in which others have acted in these anguishing ways toward us. For example, we might have been ill and someone with us walked too quickly. We try to remember the distress we felt when we could not keep up. Alternatively, we might have stoically endured the person's lack of consideration and repressed our feelings.

Recalling an incident in which we were similarly insensitive, perhaps when walking with an elderly relative, we look at a photograph or simply think of the person. Then, we consider how he or she must have felt. Acknowledging that our negative behavior was a mistake, we regret how we acted. We determine to rid ourselves of this destructive habit, for the sake of both this person and others we may encounter. We must also eliminate it for our own development. Focusing on our older relative, we give our word that we shall try our best not to repeat our inconsiderate behavior. We do the same even if the person in our example has already passed away.

We repeat the procedure with the rest of the ten destructive actions. For stealing, we may recall, for example, someone using our telephone for an expensive long-distance call without asking our permission.

For inappropriate sexual behavior, we may remember someone making an unwanted sexual advance toward us. For lying, we may think of someone who deceived us about his or her feelings or intentions in our relationship.

For speaking divisively, we may remember a person who told us terrible things about our boyfriend or girlfriend to make us break the relationship. For using harsh language, we may recall someone who yelled at us cruelly or who insensitively said something that hurt us deeply. For speaking idle words, we may recall someone who betrayed our confidence and revealed our intimate secrets to others. We may also think of someone who frequently interrupted our work with meaningless chatter or who never let us finish what we were trying to say.

For thinking covetous thoughts, we may remember someone who became jealous when we spoke about our financial success or about how well our children were doing. When the person became lost in thought about how to accomplish what we had achieved, he or she stopped listening to us. For thinking with malice, we may recall someone who became angry at something we said and then plotted revenge. Lastly, for distorted, antagonistic thinking, we may remember someone to whom we spoke about something positive or ethically neutral. It might have been something that we were pursuing to help others or to improve ourselves, such as the study of medicine or basketball. The person responded by thinking we were stupid for being interested in such things.

We may choose more than one person for each destructive action. We may also recall more than one form of each act. The broader the scope of destructive behavior we consider, the more effective the exercise becomes for overcoming insensitivity to the emotional impact of our actions.

The second step of the first phase of the exercise is to focus on someone close to us. We may look at a photograph or just think about the person. Surveying a broad spectrum of forms that each of the ten destructive actions may take, we check if we have ever acted in these ways toward the person. If we have, we think of the pain we caused, admit our mistake, feel regret, and determine to rid ourselves of the destructive habit. If we have not acted like this toward him or her, we rejoice in that fact. Not wishing ever to hurt the person, we then give our assurance that we shall try our best never to act in each of these ways.

The second phase of the exercise begins with sitting in a circle if we are part of a workshop. Either our group facilitator or we repeat key sentences regarding common examples of each of the ten destructive actions. For instance, "I shall not treat you in a rough physical manner," "I shall not use anything of yours without permission," "I shall not push myself sexually on you or your partner," "I shall not lie to you about my feelings or intentions," "I shall not try to part you from your friends by saying bad things about them," "I shall not verbally abuse you," "I shall not betray your confidence by revealing your private matters to others," "I shall not think jealously about what you have achieved," "I shall not think with malice about how to harm you if you say or do something I do not like," "If you are striving to improve yourself or to help others, I shall not think you are stupid, even if what you have chosen is not my own interest." After each sentence, we look at the persons around the circle and silently promise to try not to act in each of these ways toward each of them. During the second part of this phase, we sit facing a partner. Wishing never to hurt the person, we repeat the procedure.

We begin the third phase by looking in a mirror and checking whether we have acted toward ourselves in any of the ten destructive manners. If we have, we acknowledge the problems and pain this has brought and regret the foolish mistakes we have made. We then promise ourselves that we shall make all efforts to stop repeating our self-destructive behavior.

We pledge, for example, "I shall stop mistreating myself physically by overworking, by eating poorly, or by not getting enough sleep," "I shall stop wasting my money on trivial things," "I shall stop engaging in sexual acts that may endanger my health," "I shall stop deceiving myself about my feelings or motivation," "I shall stop speaking so obnoxiously that my friends become disgusted and leave me," "I shall stop verbally abusing myself," "I shall stop speaking indiscriminately about my private matters, doubts, or worries," "I shall stop thinking about how to outdo myself because of being a perfectionist," "I shall stop thinking in self-destructive, irrational ways that sabotage my relations with others or my position in life," "I shall stop thinking I am stupid for trying to improve myself or to help others." The leader of our workshop may repeat these phrases or, if practicing alone, we may say them silently to ourselves. We may also customize the phrases to suit our personal history.

Next, we repeat the pledges to ourselves after putting aside the mirror. Lastly, we look at the series of previous photos of us and consider whether we have been thinking negatively of ourselves as we were then. If we have, we acknowledge the problems and pain we have caused. Admitting that our way of thinking has been self-destructive and feeling regret, we determine to resolve our emotional issues about those times. We cannot change the past, but we can change our attitude toward it and learn from our mistakes. We pledge to try to stop thinking negatively of ourselves during those periods, by using three key sentences, "I shall stop thinking with dissatisfaction about how I was then, wishing that I had acted differently," "I shall stop thinking with self-hatred about myself then," " I shall stop thinking I was stupid then for what I did to try to improve my lot or to help others."

This exercise asks us to confront aspects of ourselves that many of us would rather forget. Consequently, it may make us feel uncomfortable or ashamed, especially while facing a partner. If this happens, we need to reaffirm our positive qualities that we discovered in the previous exercise. With proper effort, we can use them to overcome our negative ways.

6 Combining Warmth with Understanding

The Necessity for Joint Development of Warmth and Understanding

Achieving enlightenment requires simultaneously building up bountiful stores of positive potential and deep awareness. Both are necessary for attaining any of the Buddha-bodies. The frequent analogy is that the bountiful stores are like the two wings required to fly.

Combining warmth and understanding is also necessary for achieving balanced sensitivity. Suppose we have merely warm loving feelings toward others, but lack understanding of their situation. We may be carried away by emotion and act unwisely. Often, we overreact when we are overemotional. On the other hand, if we merely understand the situation, but lack any warmth, we may react to others insensitively.

Each of us has a basis level of both warmth and understanding. When we develop them jointly, we can be of more balanced, sensitive help to others and to ourselves. Let us examine five points that help to combine the two factors.

Taking Others Seriously

Others are real. The people we encounter are not fictitious characters in a movie or anonymous faces in a news report. We may be well informed about the troubles others are facing. Statistics, however, are of little help unless we take their plight seriously. We need to feel concern on a human level.

For example, suppose we were lying in a hospital bed, waiting for a major operation. Most of us would be frightened and worried that we might not survive. Suppose the nurse came to prepare us for surgery. Though we do not wish anyone's pity, we would certainly appreciate him or her showing some warmth and understanding. Knowing all the technical details to prepare us physically is not sufficient. We are real, our fear is overwhelming, and we want the nurse to take us seriously.

If this is true about us, it is also true about others. Everyone deserves to be taken seriously. Moreover, taking others seriously helps them to take themselves seriously. This strengthens their self-confidence, thus helping them to overcome low self-esteem.

Being Unafraid to React

Our actions do not determine the outcome of every event. Nor is the outcome predetermined. If it were, there would be no point in responding to anyone's needs, in offering our help, or in doing anything at all. Others' successes or failure would already be fated. According to the Buddhist understanding, what happens arises dependently on many factors, following the laws of cause and effect.

The main factors affecting what happens to people are their karmic potentials. We can merely try to offer circumstances for their positive potentials to ripen and try to avoid providing conditions for their negative ones to surface. However, if others lack sufficient causes for happiness from their personal history, our best efforts cannot succeed. Similarly, if others lack the causes for tragedy, our worst mistakes cannot cause them a downfall. Still, we are accountable for our actions and need to act responsibly. In providing or withholding circumstances, we contribute to what occurs. Nevertheless, we are not the sole source even of circumstances.

Therefore, fear of responding to others' or our own needs is inappropriate. Even if we make a mistake, we have at least tried. We do not become dismayed or feel guilty when our help fails. Nor do we arrogantly take all the credit when others succeed through our assistance. We can only try to be helpful, with as much warmth and understanding as possible.

For example, suppose we have a baby daughter, or are visiting someone who has, and suppose we are trying to teach the baby to walk. The toddler inevitably falls down. If she stumbles and begins to cry, are we guilty? Is it our fault? Do we stop trying to teach her to walk?

Obviously, the baby's success in learning to walk depends primarily on her development of strength, balance, and self-confidence. We merely provide the circumstances for these potentials to mature.

Thus, we would not be afraid to respond to the baby's faltering steps as we teach her to walk. We would naturally do this with joy, without shouldering sole responsibility for success or failure. Yet, we would also naturally act responsibly. Holding the baby's hand at first, we would remain nearby to catch or at least to comfort the toddler when she stumbles and falls.

Taking in All Information

Even if we have great concern about a situation, we need to take in complete information before responding. If we do this without making judgments or mental comments, we avoid overreacting or responding to something we have merely invented. For instance, suppose we hear our little boy screaming and, rushing outside, we see his arm badly bruised. Instead of reacting with panic, thinking he has broken his arm, we need to remain calm and first comfort the child. Without jumping to conclusions, we need to ask, and to look carefully to see what is wrong.

Other situations in life require the same approach. For example, when listening on the telephone to a friend talking about his or her problems, we need to listen with a quiet mind and open heart. We need to let our friend finish telling his or her story before offering advice.

Acting Straightforwardly

Sitting back and coldly analyzing how to solve others' problems is not sufficient. Of course, we need to figure out what to do. Nevertheless, once we know, we need to act straightforwardly, sensitive to the urgency others feel. Suppose we see someone struggling with bundles and about to drop them. Commenting on how much he or she bought or asking which store the person shopped at are clearly absurd. We need to understand the situation and respond immediately, with consideration and kindness.

Refraining from Offering Unwanted or Unneeded Help

We may help others with warmth and kindness. Yet, if our hidden motivation is to gain a feeling of self-worth or of being needed, we are exploiting them. Understanding this point allows us the sensitivity to restrain ourselves when the most appropriate help is to let people handle situations by themselves. In this way, we avoid others' resentment or rejection because of our pushiness. It also helps us to avert oversensitive reactions of feeling unappreciated, unneeded, unwanted, or worthless when others decline our help.

For example, suppose we have a two-year-old daughter. Feeding her with a spoon made us feel good when she was younger. We felt needed and useful. At some point, however, we need to stop and let her feed herself. Insisting on treating her like a baby, even with an effusive show of affection, is exploitation. It helps neither our daughter nor us.

EXERCISE 6

Five Decisions for Combining Warmth with Understanding

Decisions are most effective when based on reason. Decisions made on a whim or by force are usually not sincerely felt. Consequently, they do not often last. Adopting a procedure from Buddhist logic for reaching a conclusion may be useful. Many meditations use it for equalizing and exchanging attitudes about self and others. As with the rational approach taken in Exercise Two for generating a loving feeling, we reach a conclusion, or make a decision, by bringing to mind a reason and an example. Having consciously thought through a line of reasoning and having reached our conclusion, we then stop all verbal thought. We simply view the imagined or real person while keeping the decision actively in mind. Remaining focused on the person, we let our decision sink in and concentrate on feeling it.

For our decisions not to be partial in their application, we shall adopt an additional technique from the meditations for equalizing our attitudes. We shall direct each decision toward three successively imagined persons: someone we like very much, a stranger, and someone whom we dislike. Then, as in the previous exercises, we shall extend these decisions to an assortment of actual partners and to ourselves.

We begin the first phase of the exercise by choosing, for example, a close family member. Looking at a photo or simply thinking of the person, we proceed as follows:

(1) We try to recall an incident in which someone else did not take us seriously. For example, our mother continued to push us to take a second helping when we told her we were full. On a more painful level, our partner did not even try to change his or her behavior when we said it was upsetting us. Trying to recall how we felt, we direct our

attention toward the close relative we have chosen for the exercise. We consciously decide, "I shall take you seriously, because you, your words, and your feelings are real, as in my own case when I said I was full or upset."

(2) We then try to remember an occasion when someone was afraid to respond to our needs. For instance, we were upset and our friend was afraid to comfort us. Though we did not expect him or her to solve all our problems, we would have appreciated some type of warm and sensitive response. Directing our attention at our relative, we consciously decide, "I shall not be afraid to respond to you. Although I may contribute to your success or failure, I am not the sole source affecting your situation, as with my friend whose comfort I needed."

(3) Next, we try to bring to mind an incident in which someone did not take in all the information about our situation or feelings and jumped to a false conclusion. For example, our mother asked us to pick up some groceries on our way home. We fully intended to do it, but we had to stay late at work to finish some urgent business. By the time we arrived at the store, it had already closed. Seeing us walk in the door with empty arms, she became furious and started to yell how irresponsible we were. We recall how tedious it was to calm our mother and reassure her that we had tried our best. The circumstances were out of our control. We then focus on the family member in our exercise and consciously decide, "I shall take in all the information about your situation, without jumping to conclusions. I shall do this because I wish to avoid overreacting or responding to something I have merely invented, like when my mother imagined I had forgotten the shopping."

An important variant especially concerns interactions with those closest to us. For example, we might remember criticizing something our partner said or did. Losing sight of all other facets of our history together, our partner immediately concluded that we did not love him or her any longer. He or she became either completely depressed or extremely hostile. Trying to recall the effort it took to reassure our partner of our love, we give our relative a further assurance. "I shall keep sight of the larger context of our relationship so as not to jump to a false conclusion over a tiny incident, like my partner did when I criticized his or her behavior."

(4) Next, we try to recall a time when someone did not act straightforwardly when we needed his or her help. For instance, a family member had offered to drive us to the airport so that we would not need to leave our car there during our vacation. Yet, he or she arrived

so late that we missed our plane. We turn to the relative in our exercise and conclude, "Once I have decided to do something for you, I shall act straightforwardly. I shall do this because you experience your problem as something urgent, as I did when I needed to catch my plane."

(5) Lastly, we try to remember an occasion when someone offered his or her unwanted or unneeded help. For example, we were chopping vegetables and our mother corrected the way we were doing it. What was she trying to prove? We focus on our family member and consciously decide, "I shall refrain from offering my unneeded or unwanted help or advice. I shall do this because I do not wish to exploit you to gain a feeling of self-worth or of being needed, as with my mother who could not resist correcting how I chop vegetables."

If we wish to practice more elaborately, we may expand as in the previous exercise on refraining from destructive behavior. After remembering an incident in which someone acted toward us in each of the five insensitive ways, we recall an occasion when we acted similarly toward someone else. Admitting that it was mistaken and feeling regret, we reaffirm our determination to be free of the syndrome. We then give our pledge to the person involved that we shall try our best not to repeat it.

Next, we make the same five decisions while looking at a picture of a stranger or while looking at a photo or simply thinking of someone we hardly know. If we need to repeat the reasons and examples from the first part of the exercise to feel stronger conviction, we may do so. Otherwise, we may omit this step. Lastly, we follow the same procedure while looking at a photo or simply thinking of someone we dislike.

If the examples from the previous part of the exercise seem inappropriate for the stranger and for the person we dislike, we may use the more general examples from the earlier discussion. We decide, one by one, "I shall take you seriously, like when preparing a hospital patient for an operation." "I shall not be afraid to respond to you, like when teaching a baby to walk." "I shall take in all the information about you and not jump to conclusions, like when examining a child with a bruised arm." "Once I have decided to do something for you, I shall act straightforwardly, like when seeing someone carrying a heavy bundle and about to drop it." "I shall refrain from offering unwanted or unneeded help, as when insisting on feeding the two-year-old with a spoon."

During the second phase of the practice, we face a partner and try to focus on the feelings that arise from directing the five decisions toward the person. If we are practicing in a group, the facilitator may cue us with the following key phrases: "real," "no fear of reacting if you need me," "take in all information," "act straightforwardly," and "refrain from giving unwanted or unneeded help." We may also repeat the phrases silently to ourselves.

We begin the third phase by looking in a mirror and directing toward ourselves the same five feelings of combined warmth and understanding. We may modify the key phrases to: "real," "no fear of reacting to what I see or feel in myself," "take in all information," "act straightforwardly," and "refrain from pushing myself to do something unneeded." We then repeat the procedure, putting down the mirror and reflecting quietly.

As a final step, we look at the series of photographs of ourselves spanning our life. We try to see each picture as revealing a real person and to take each of them seriously. We try to feel no fear in dealing with our feelings about ourselves then. Without insisting on a fixed impression based on selective memory, we try to consider all the facts about that period. If our attitude about ourselves then is unhealthy and is causing us pain or blocked emotions, we resolve to act straightforwardly to change that attitude. Lastly, we try not to push the impossible by dwelling morbidly on our wish that we had acted differently. The past is over. We can do nothing to change what has already happened. All we can do now is accept it with understanding, warmth, and forgiveness, and learn from our mistakes. As a prompt, we use the phrases: "real," "no fear of dealing with how I feel about myself then," "consider all the facts," "act straightforwardly to deal with unresolved feelings," and "do not push the impossible; forgive."

PART II

Uncovering the Talents of
Our Mind and Heart

7 Shifting Focus from Mind and from Ourselves to Mental Activity

The naturally occurring internal resources that allow for balanced sensitivity—joy, focus, warmth, understanding, self-control, and a feeling of inspiration—are all factors of mind and heart. To work effectively with these factors requires a powerful conceptual framework. It must be broad enough to include all relevant aspects of mind and heart and to make comprehensible the approaches used for treating each. The Buddhist presentation of mind provides such a framework.

Integrating Mind and Heart

Most Western systems of metaphysics sharply divide between mind and heart. The former deals with rational thinking, while the latter accounts for emotions and feelings. Buddhism, in contrast, groups these three facets under the rubric of one term and includes with them sense perception, imagination, dreaming, sleep, and unconsciousness. By default, Western languages translate the term as "mind."

Viewing mind and heart as two facets of the same phenomenon brings fewer obstacles in integrating understanding and warmth. Any program for balancing sensitivity needs to take this point seriously. A dualistic view of mind and heart contributes significantly to alienation from logical processes or from emotions and feelings. This is especially true if we regard one of them as trustworthy or good and the other as suspicious or evil.

Mind Is Not Some Physical Entity in Our Head

Mind has no form. It is not a material organ found somewhere in the brain. Nor is it reducible to something physical, like the nervous system or the electrochemical processes that describe neurological functions. Mind is also not merely an abstract metaphysical entity that is the fancy of philosophers. From the Buddhist point of view, the phenomenon translated as "mind" is not an entity at all. Rather, the word "mind" refers to the mental activity—both conscious and unconscious—that occurs based on an individual's brain, nervous system, and the physiological processes of the two.

Further, the term "mind" does not refer to the agent of mental activity. Nor does the word refer to a tool that we use to comprehend a sight, to think a thought, or to feel an emotion. The word "mind" denotes only mental activity itself, such as seeing, thinking, or feeling something. It even includes subtle mental activity while asleep.

When we regard our mind as a "thing" inside us, we often project a fixed identity onto it. We imagine, for example, that our mind is incapable of feeling anything or of responding to others. Identifying with our mind, we may judge ourselves as inadequate or we make excuses. We may insist that others accept us because this is the way that we are. If, instead, we view our mind as mental activity, we are more open to the fact that, with a change of circumstances, our experiences change. As we recognize and enhance the positive factors that already accompany our mental activity, we naturally become more sensitive.

When we take this approach, we see that sensitivity does not depend on the competence or worthiness of ourselves as a person. Nor is it the activity of some fixed entity in our head. Therefore, blaming our mind or ourselves for being insensitive or hypersensitive is pointless. Without self-recrimination, we need simply to adjust the attentiveness and responsiveness that accompany our mental activity during any event.

Mind as the Ever-changing Experience of Things

Mental activity always involves an object. We do not just see. If we see, we see a sight. If we think, we think a thought. Moreover, the objects of our mental activity are always changing. One moment we are seeing the wall and the next we are seeing the sight of a loved one. Even if we stare at the wall, our focus constantly shifts very slightly.

In any particular moment, the seeing and the sight do not exist independently of each other. Therefore, when we see something different, our experience of seeing a sight has also changed.

An experience, then, does not have merely emotional contents. We cannot experience a mood, for example, without perceiving some object at the same time. Thus, we cannot feel depressed without simultaneously seeing the wall or thinking about something either verbally or otherwise. Even if our depression is not about anything conscious and we shut our eyes and do not think any verbal thoughts, still we perceive darkness while being depressed. Intellectually, we can distinguish a mood from the objects perceived while in that mood, but we always experience the two together.

Furthermore, a mood is not a monolithic mental entity. It consists of a cluster of factors, such as feelings, emotions, attention, interest, and so on. As the objects we experience change each moment, each of these mental factors also naturally changes—and not all at the same time or rate. Therefore, a mood never remains static.

Confusion about these points often makes us insensitive to the present moment. Before encountering someone, we might imagine that our state of mind would remain the same as it had been until then. Alternatively, we might expect our experience to repeat previous ones with the person. For example, suppose our interaction with colleagues at work was difficult this morning. We became upset at the slightest things they said. Concluding that we are having a bad day, we might assume that the rest of it will undoubtedly be the same.

This does not have to be the case. When we see our family in the evening, we are having a new experience, with fresh mental activity involving different objects. If we are mindful of this fact, we can let go of what we conceived as our previous mood and become calm, warm, and understanding.

Individuality of Experience

Minds are individual. My experience of seeing a sight is never the same as yours. This is because the sight of someone's face that we see depends on the angle and distance from which we look. What we see from the right side at two feet away is different from what someone thirty feet away simultaneously sees from the left. If we each took a picture at the same moment, the two photos would not be the same. Yet, each would be an accurate semblance of the face.

Comprehending this point convinces us that each person's experience makes sense within its own context. This is true regarding not only what people see or hear, but also how they interpret it. Appreciating this fact helps us to overcome the insensitivity of imagining that only what we see or think is correct. Such insight is the bedrock upon which to build a lasting form of conflict resolution.

Suppose, for example, we buy a complex entertainment system for the house. When our partner comes home, we offer to go through the instruction book together. Our partner takes the suggestion as an insult and furiously accuses us of not trusting him or her. We, on the other hand, simply want the intimacy and joy of sharing the experience. Taking our partner's hypersensitive reaction as a personal rejection, we conclude that he or she does not love us anymore.

To resolve this misunderstanding, both of us need to recall the example of two people looking at the same face from different perspectives. Each sees something different and yet each sees something correct. We need to acknowledge the validity of each other's experience of the conversation and accept the background and reasons for the other's response. Once we dispel the arrogant belief that only our experience of the event is correct, we can regain our composure.

Mind as an Unbroken Continuum

Each person's mind, or mental activity, has unbroken continuity. One experience follows another, forming an orderly continuum obeying the laws of cause and effect. Reflecting on this fact, we realize that our lack of sensitivity in some situations and oversensitive outbursts in others have both immediate and continuing effects. Shock waves from them unsettle our own and others' minds. We are responsible for our attitudes and behavior. Denying that they matter does not prevent them from creating problems.

Buddhism explains that mental activity continues uninterruptedly not only in this lifetime, but without beginning or end. Whether or not we believe in past and future lives, we gain stronger motivation to balance our sensitivity when we consider an undeniable fact. The effects of our behavior carry on not only into old age, but also into future generations. If we do not respond sensitively to our children, for example, we affect their psychological makeup. This, in turn, plays an important role in how they will raise their future families. We need to think carefully about our emotional legacy. If we do not wish to burden future generations with psychological fallout from our behavior, we need to work on our problems now.

General Definition of Mind

Training in Tibetan Buddhist logic involves studying ways of knowing (*lorig*). The literature on this topic defines mind as "mere clarity and awareness." Just as mind is not an entity, however, neither is clarity or awareness. Characterizing each moment of our life's experience, they are facets of mental activity regarding an object.

"Clarity" refers to the mental activity of producing a mental object. Here, it has nothing to do with sharpness of focus. Describing this mental activity from a Western point of view, we would say that in each moment our mind creates a mental object. From a Buddhist point of view, we would simply say that each moment of our experience entails the arising or appearing of such an object. Mental objects include sights, sounds, smells, tastes, tactile or physical sensations, dreams, thoughts, feelings, and emotions.

To avoid misunderstanding, we must differentiate between an object and the sight of that object. What we see is a sight—an image on our retina—not actually the object itself. Our mind gives rise only to the sight, which it does by relying on visual consciousness, the object, and the sensory cells of our eyes. Our mind does not produce the object itself. Sights exist only within the context of being seen by a mind, whereas objects, such as our face, exist whether or not anybody sees them. The pimple on our nose does not disappear when we cover it with cream or do not look in the mirror. The only thing that vanishes is our experience of seeing the sight of it.

"Awareness," the second word of the definition of mind, is the mental activity of engaging with a mental object in some way or another. Experiencing something necessarily entails either seeing, hearing, smelling, tasting, physically feeling, dreaming, thinking, or emotionally feeling it. This is the case whether or not that mental engagement is conscious or with understanding. Moreover, producing a mental object and engaging with it are two facets of the same activity. They occur simultaneously, not consecutively. A thought does not arise before we think it.

The word "mere" in the definition of mind implies that producing an appearance of something and engaging with it are all that is necessary for mental activity. Neither focus nor comprehension is required, although these and other mental factors may be present.

"Mere" also excludes not just the necessity, but the existence of a concrete, findable mind or agent "in here" that is making a sight arise or doing the seeing of it. "Mere," however, does not negate the fact that, conventionally speaking, our mind, not our nose, produces and engages with appearances. Moreover, we, not anybody else, see or think them. The mind and person involved, however, are neither concrete nor findable "things" in our head. If we imagine they are, we soon project onto them a fixed identity as, for example, inherently insensitive or overemotional. Consequently, we do not even try to change our personality; we feel that we and everyone else must learn to live with it.

Further, when we conceive of ourselves as a concrete "boss" inside our head who must always be in control, we may create other problems for ourselves. For instance, when we act insensitively or overreact, we may hurl allegations and insults at this chief. We may think that the boss should have been in control, but was not. Switching sides and identifying with the boss, we may then feel guilty. On the other hand, we may be afraid that if no boss was in control, the only alternative would be that our mental activity is out of control. This understanding is also mistaken. "Mere" does not exclude the fact that mental factors of discrimination and self-control can always accompany our thoughts and our feelings.

Significance of the Definition of Mind for Sensitivity Issues

Understanding the definition of mind is crucial for balancing our sensitivity. It enables us to see that regulating the factors that accompany our mental activity changes our personality and experience of life. Consider what happens when we encounter somebody. The framework of our experience is the simultaneous arising of his or her image and the seeing of it. Certain mental factors always accompany each moment of experience, such as some level of attention and interest. If we wish to improve our sensitivity, we need to adjust them. Other factors are optional. We can see someone either with or without the filter of preconceptions and moral judgments. The choice is ours. Still other factors are totally absent, such as a concrete "me" that is looking out our eyes and around whom we crystallize self-consciousness, insecurity, or paranoia.

When we understand these points concerning our mental activity, we can apply them to handle difficult situations with emotional balance. Consider the misunderstanding with our partner over learning to use the sound equipment. He or she accused us unjustly. We can avoid overreacting if we experience hearing these words as the mere arising and engaging with a sound. Recognizing what we experience as merely the mental activity of the moment, we simply go on with the next moment of experience.

Thinking like this does not mean that we ignore our partner's words, with either a blank expression on our face or an idiotic benevolent grin. We understand their meaning perfectly well. Nevertheless, by not identifying ourselves—the one who hears the sounds—as a concrete entity inside us, we avoid taking the words personally. Moreover, by not inflating the words out of proportion, we do not take what we hear as showing our partner's true feelings toward us. Thus, we do not take offence or become defensive or aggressive. We remain sensitive to what is causing him or her upset and we respond in a calm, patient, and understanding manner. If we can do this when a four-year-old says, "I hate you," after we have denied him or her candy before mealtime, we can do the same with our partner.

EXERCISE 7
Shifting Our Focus from Mind and from Ourselves to Mental Activity

The Kagyü style of *mahamudra* (great seal) meditation suggests the next exercise. We begin by relaxing our body and mind of any physical, mental, or emotional tension we may have. We do this through paying particular attention to our posture, by using the breathing technique of letting go, and by applying the image of worry and tension being like writing on water.

Keeping our eyes opened, we look slowly around the room and listen carefully to whatever noises there might be. We try to notice the mechanism that automatically occurs each moment of seeing and hearing. The baseline is the simultaneous arising of sights or sounds and engaging with them. Aimed at an object, such as the clock or its ticking, our mental activity simultaneously produces and perceives the mental objects that constitute what we directly experience. In other words, producing an appearance of something and perceiving it are two facets of the same activity. Once we have recognized what is happening whenever we see, hear, or think about something, we try to accompany our moment-to-moment mental activity with a clear understanding of the mechanism involved.

Verbalizing our understanding is not necessary. We are perfectly able to understand something without saying anything in our mind. Consider seeing a traffic light turn red, understanding the significance, and applying the brakes. We can easily do this without verbalizing that the light is red and we need to stop.

First, we try to look and listen while understanding that we are simultaneously producing and perceiving appearances of objects. Then, we try to look and listen while feeling that this process is happening. Lastly, we alternate realization and feeling, and then try to combine the two. To do this, we need to understand what feeling means in this context.

The English word "feeling" has many meanings. These include a physical sensation, an emotion, a level of happiness or sadness, a level of sensitivity, and an aesthetic sense. A feeling may also be an imagined experience, an urge to do something, an intuition, an impression, an opinion, or a sense of identity or reality. We may feel hungry, angry, happy, sensitive, or creative. We may try to feel what it is like to fly, or we may feel like eating. We may also feel that something wonderful will happen, that we are at an important point in our life, that something is not right, or that we are talented. Here, we are using the word "feel" to mean "have a sense of reality."

We can appreciate the difference between understanding something and feeling that it is happening through the analogy of flying in an airplane. Often during a flight, we are unaware that we are flying. Nevertheless, we can experience the journey with an understanding that we are traveling through the air at high speed. We may also feel that we are speeding in a plane. Here, we do not mean feeling the physical sensation of flying, but feeling the reality of what is happening. We can similarly feel, as we look and listen, that our mental activity is producing and engaging with the audiovisual impressions that we perceive.

Keeping our mental activity unself-conscious is crucial here. This means not conceiving of a concrete, findable "me" or mind inside our head that is the passive observer or active controller of our mental activity. Viewing our experience from the perspective of the removed observer can reinforce a habit of insensitivity. Alienated from our feelings, we may find difficulty reacting to what we observe. On the other hand, if we view our mental activity as a controller or boss, we may strengthen our tendency to overreact. This occurs due to overintense involvement with what is happening and the anxious struggle to manipulate it, arising out of self-importance.

Therefore, we try to experience each moment with an understanding that our mental activity is occurring without a concrete "me" or a concrete mind. Then, we try to look and listen without feeling self-conscious. Lastly, we try to combine both realization and a feeling of no concrete "me" with looking and listening.

In shifting our focus from mind to unself-conscious mental activity, we must also be careful not to deny the conventional existence of our mind or of ourselves. Otherwise, we may face the danger of no longer taking responsibility for what we think, feel, say, or do. We might act in this way because we feel that there is no one accountable or that our experience is out of control. To prevent this from happening, we now try to look and listen while understanding our reality. Although we do not exist as a concrete boss in our head, we are still accountable for what we experience and how we experience it. After trying to look and listen with this understanding for a few minutes, we try to look and listen while feeling accountable. Then, we try to combine both realization and a feeling of accountability with our mental activity as it continues.

Next, we try to notice and focus on the fact that each moment of our experience has different contents, which continually change, like a flowing stream. These contents consist not only of various sights, sounds, or thoughts, but also of diverse emotions and different levels of interest, attention, and so forth. First, we try to add this understanding to our ongoing mental activity of seeing and hearing. Then, we try to look and listen while feeling the flowing change. Lastly, we try to combine both realization and a feeling of continual change with our moment-to-moment experience.

We then try to observe that what we experience is particular to ourselves alone. It depends on our physical and mental perspectives. If we are practicing in a group, for instance, and someone coughs, each of us experiences hearing the sound differently. Some hear it with annoyance as an interruption to their concentration, while others hear it with concern that someone might be sick. If our leg starts to hurt, we may similarly experience either irritation or gentle regard. First, we try to look and listen while understanding that our experience is particular to us. Then, as we look and listen, we try to feel the individuality of our experience, like feeling the uniqueness of ourselves as a person. In the end, we try to experience simultaneous realization and feeling of distinctness as our mental activity continues.

Next, we think how our mental activity forms a continuum and that what we perceive, think, and feel now will affect our future experiences. If we are insensitive to others or to ourselves, or if we overreact to inconvenience, we will continue to experience unhappiness. If we wish to avoid unpleasant experiences, we need to develop a better understanding of life. First, we try to supplement our seeing, hearing, and thinking with the understanding that we will experience the effects of our mental activity. Then, we try to accompany our looking and listening with a feeling for this, like the feeling of certainty we have that we will be happy when we come home and see our loved ones. Lastly, we try to combine joint realization and feeling of cause and effect with our ongoing mental activity.

The final step is to try to understand and feel all these points together as we look around the room and listen. To start the process, our workshop leader or we may repeat slowly, one by one, the eight key phrases: "producing and perceiving appearances," "no observer," "no controller," "and yet accountable for what I experience," "changing appearances," "changing mental factors," "particular to myself alone," and "I experience the effects of my mental activity." With each phrase, we try to look and listen with joint understanding and a feeling for reality.

We begin to combine the points by alternating two phrases that condense three aspects, "producing and perceiving appearances" and "no self-consciousness." Then, we add a third phrase, "accountable." One by one, we add the condensed key phrases: "flowing change," "particular to me," and finally "I experience the effects."

Repeating these phrases too often may distract our attention. It may also cause our practice to become more intellectual than experiential. Hearing or repeating the phrases should merely remind us of our understanding and feeling, and help us to maintain our focus. The main point is to remain fresh in the experience of each moment's mental activity, with mindfulness, alertness, and increasingly more understanding and feeling for the reality of what is happening.

During the second phase of the exercise, we face a partner. To provide an obviously changing object of focus, each of us needs to move our head or to shift position from time to time and occasionally to change facial expression. We do this while following the previous procedure to try to add increasingly more understanding and feeling for reality to our mental activity of seeing the person.

During the third phase, we follow the same procedure while looking at ourselves in a mirror, occasionally moving our head and changing expression. From time to time, we also look away or close our eyes to add variety to the experience. Throughout the process, we focus not only on what we see, but also on our emotions, feelings, and any seeming lack of them that we might experience. Lastly, we repeat the procedure as we alternate looking at the series of photos of ourselves and closing our eyes.

8 Appreciating the Clear Light Nature of Mental Activity

Mental Activity as Clear Light

Many Buddhist texts describe the nature of mind—in other words, the nature of mental activity—as "clear light." Clear light, however, is merely an analogy. It does not mean that we possess, literally, a light source deep inside, like a lightbulb in the recesses of our brain. Mind is neither a source nor an agent that shines a spotlight on objects, rendering them known. Nor is mind the spotlight itself. Rather, the term "clear light" implies that mental activity, by nature, is as clear as empty space. Like empty space, it allows for any mental object—not only a sight, but also a sound or a thought—to arise and be known, as if that object were something visible being illumined in the dark.

The term "clear," then, refers to an absence. In other words, by nature, mental activity is clear of various "stains," which do not adulterate it. There are two types of stains: fleeting and natural. The former can exist; the latter are imaginary.

Fleeting stains may be present but, since they pass, they are not inherent flaws. Some fleeting stains prevent liberation from suffering and obstruct the ability to help others. Examples are disturbing emotions and attitudes. Others, such as conceptual thoughts, do not create such problems. Some may even help to overcome them. Nevertheless, with the attainment of Buddhahood, mental activity continues without them.

Natural stains refer to concrete, findable features in mental activity that would cause it to exist in impossible ways. Such features include inherent flaws and omnipotence to change reality. When we deeply investigate the nature of mental activity, we can never find such features, despite our possible belief in them. Since natural stains are merely imaginary, mental activity is naturally without them.

Our mind operates on two levels. On the grosser level, our mental activity contains the fleeting stains of disturbing emotions and thoughts. On the subtler level, it is devoid of such stains. Both levels of mind, however, are naturally devoid of inherent flaws. This subtler level, also known as clear light or subtlest mind, underlies each moment of our experience. It provides the continuity of our mental activity.

Four Types of Clear Light Nature

Several aspects of mental activity are unadulterated by either fleeting or natural stains and are therefore as clear as empty space. Each of them accounts for the fact that mental objects can arise and be known. Consequently, mental activity has four types of clear light nature: (1) its defining characteristic—merely producing mental objects and engaging with them, (2) its self-void nature—its lack of existing in fantasized and impossible ways, (3) its subtlest level—that which provides its continuity, and (4) its other-void nature—its subtlest level being devoid of grosser levels of mental activity.

In other words, no matter how confused or preoccupied our mental activity may be, (1) it still produces mental objects and engages with them and (2) it still does not exist in impossible ways. Its subtlest level (3) still provides its unbroken continuity and (4) is undisturbed by the churning of its grosser levels. All these aspects of mind's clear light nature allow it to know its objects despite the stains that might temporarily taint it.

Nothing Can Affect Mind's Fourfold Clear Light Nature

Mental activity does not exist or occur in impossible ways. Self-voidness theories explain that this is a permanent fact that is always the case. Nothing can affect its truth. The other-voidness position agrees and asserts the same regarding mind's other three clear light natures. A level of mental activity (1) with a structure of producing appearances and engaging with them, (2) which provides continuity from one moment to the next, and (3) which is devoid of grosser levels, is also permanent. It is permanent in that its presence and functioning are always the case. This is true no matter what appearance mind produces and engages, and no matter what mental factors accompany that activity. Thus, by nature, mind is unadulterated by stains.

In short, although mental objects and factors are constantly changing, mind's clear light natures remain forever the same. From one point of view, disturbing emotions and thoughts affect our experiences. As these factors change, so do our experiences. From another point of view, the structure of our experiences never alters. The subtlest level of our mind is unaffected by disturbing emotions and thoughts because it is devoid of these grosser levels. Our basic mental activity of producing mental objects and engaging with them is also unaffected, although emotions and thoughts are part of it. This latter fact is significant for our discussion.

Relevance of Clear Light to Issues of Sensitivity

When we successfully develop balanced sensitivity, our mental activity of producing appearances and engaging with them is free of all stains. It becomes like clear light. In the terminology of mahamudra, we reach our "naturally unadulterated state" that was always the case. Our clear light activity has never existed with inherent flaws. It was never true that we could not feel anything or that we were too sensitive to deal with difficult situations. Our fears and self-centered attitudes were just passing phases that were not inherent, permanent parts of our personality. The conceptual framework we used for balancing our emotions was very useful, but we no longer need it. We automatically are fully attentive of others and of ourselves. Moreover, we spontaneously react in a balanced manner without any conscious, deliberate thought.

EXERCISE 8
Appreciating the Clear Light Nature of Mental Activity

We begin the first phase of this exercise by choosing someone with whom we presently have or have previously had a volatile relationship. For example, we may choose a relative or friend whom we miss when we are apart, but who frequently annoys us when we are together. We place a photograph of the person before us, making sure to select an image with a neutral expression, not a smile. As we shall be working with a variety of feelings and thoughts toward the person, we need to focus on an image that is more easily open to different emotional responses.

First, we try to experience the fact that mind's clear light nature of producing and engaging with mental objects is never blocked or stained. Focusing on the sight of the person's face in the photo, we try to remain aware of the mental activity that is happening while seeing the image. That activity is simply the simultaneous creation of the appearance we perceive and the seeing of it. Then, recalling an upsetting incident that we had with the person, we try to generate a feeling of annoyance. We stop and observe whether our disturbing emotion prevents the mental activity that produces the sight of the face and our seeing of it.

We then look away from the photo and think of the person, by using a mental image, a feeling, or simply a name to represent him or her. We may keep our eyes either opened or closed, whichever is more comfortable. Again, we try to recall the incident and feel annoyed. Does our annoyance block the person's name or an image of his or her face from arising in our mind and our thinking of it? In fact, we cannot be consciously annoyed with the person without somehow thinking of him or her.

Next, we recall an upsetting situation that had nothing to do with the person and generate a feeling of annoyance, for instance with our work. We look at the photo in this state of mind and examine whether our emotion prevents our mental activity of producing and seeing the sight. Still feeling annoyed with work, we then try to think of the person. Although this may be difficult if we are extremely upset, nevertheless we can at least think of the person's name. In the end, personal experience leads us to conclude that no matter how disturbed our mind may be, it does not affect our moment-to-moment mental activity of producing appearances and engaging with them. We can still see and we can still think. Therefore, no matter how emotionally distraught we may be, we can still be aware of others' situations. Being upset, we might not pay much attention to their situation, but disturbing emotions do not incapacitate us from being able to see or think of it. We try to digest this realization.

Looking once more at the photograph, we consciously think a verbal thought about the person, such as "This is a human being." We investigate whether the thought prevents our mental activity from producing the sight of the face and our seeing of it. We then do the same while merely thinking of the person nonverbally. How can we think this person is a human being without thinking of the person? Next, we think something that has nothing to do with the person, such as "It is time for lunch." Can we simultaneously think that thought and see the photo? Can we think that thought while also picturing the person's face in our mind? Experience leads us to conclude that verbal thought also does not block our seeing or thinking of someone. We try to focus on this fact.

Again looking at the photo, we think, "I cannot relate to this person." Even if we believe this is true, is there some inherent flaw in our mental activity that prevents us from seeing what we see? We repeat the thought while merely thinking of the person and ask the same question. Through this process, we discover another crucial fact that allows us balanced sensitivity. Natural stains also do not obscure or obstruct our mind's clear light nature of merely producing appearances and perceiving them. No matter what we believe, we can be properly sensitive when we see or think of someone. Again, we try to let this realization sink in by focusing on the feeling and conviction that this is true.

Next, we try to experience that nothing can affect our mind's clear light nature of self-voidness—the fact that it does not exist in impossible ways. One impossible way would be that our mind could alter reality—not just our subjective experience of reality, but objective reality itself. When we believe that our mind has this power, we imagine that whatever we think of someone is true, simply because we think it is so. Such a belief underlies feeling that our opinion of someone is always correct. Thinking this makes us insensitive to the person's reality and often leads to overreaction based on belief in fantasy. In this exercise, let us examine this issue only on its most obvious level. We shall explore it in depth later.

First, we look at the photograph with fear and think, "This person is a monster." Do our feelings or thoughts make the person a monster? No, they do not. Someone may act *like* a monster, or we may merely think that the person acts like a monster. However, no one actually *is* a monster, because actual monsters do not exist. Repeating the procedure while merely thinking of the person, we conclude and try to focus on the fact that our mind cannot change reality. Our mental activity does not exist with this impossible power.

Then, we try to experience the fact that a subtle clear light level of mind underlies each moment of our experience and, being other-void, it is devoid of all stains. To do this, we investigate what provides the continuity of our experience of looking at or thinking of the face in the picture. We try to regard the sight and then the thought of the face with annoyance, longing, and finally with jealousy. Since none of these disturbing emotions last and each can be replaced with the next, the level of mental activity that provides continuity must be a subtler one that underlies all emotions. We try the same experiment with a variety of verbal thoughts about the person and reach the same conclusion. The level that provides continuity must underlie and be more fundamental than verbal thought too.

What remains of our mental activity now is merely seeing and thinking of an image of the face. We slowly alternate the two, closing our eyes when thinking of the person if we have not been doing this before. In both cases, there is an arising of an appearance and an engaging with it. The fundamental mental activity is the same. Thus, the common denominator underlying all our experiences and providing their continuity is the mental activity of merely producing appearances and engaging with them. We try to focus for some minutes on that realization.

Lastly, we try to incorporate these insights into our moment-to-moment experience, by looking at the photo and using the key phrases: "producing and perceiving appearances," "unaffected by emotions or thoughts," "not inherently flawed," "incapable of changing reality," and "always there." First, we work with one realization at a time as we go through the sequence. Then, we try to be aware of increasingly more points simultaneously, by working first with two phrases, then three, four, and finally all five. As with the previous exercise, we do not repeat the phrases more than once every few minutes. Otherwise, they become distracting. We then repeat the procedure while merely thinking of the person.

Next, we sit in a circle with a group and repeat the entire exercise two or three times. Each time, we alternate looking at a different person in the group and merely thinking of him or her for the entire sequence. With someone we know fairly well, we can generate disturbing emotions by trying to remember incidents in which we might have been impatient with the person, felt superior or inferior, and so on. With people we do not know well or whom we do not know at all, we may try to recall an emotional incident from our life also during the first step. When we meet someone new, we can often be upset about something that happened with somebody else.

During the second part of this phase of the exercise, we repeat the procedure while facing a partner, alternately looking at the person and merely thinking of him or her while closing our eyes. When generating various emotions during the first step, we may either do the same as when sitting in a circle or use the nervousness and shyness we might feel now if we do not know the person.

During the third phase, we alternate looking at ourselves in a mirror and merely picturing our image or thinking our name. We follow the same steps as before. To generate a disturbing emotion during the first step, we try to recall feeling low self-esteem, self-hatred, or self-importance, and then try to feel these emotions again. Lastly, we repeat the procedure while looking at the series of photos of ourselves and then looking away and imagining ourselves at each of those periods in our life. When generating various emotions, we try to recall moments of feeling self-hatred or self-importance regarding ourselves as we were then.

9   Accessing the Natural Talents of Our Mind and Heart

In Exercise Two, we relied on a line of reasoning to generate one of the ingredients of balanced sensitivity. In Exercise Three, we imagined our mental activity containing all the necessary qualities. In Exercise Four, we accessed a basis level of some of these qualities through memories of experiencing a certain degree of each. Now, we are ready to work with another source for the elements of balanced sensitivity.

Exercises Seven and Eight have given us the background. The former accustomed us to the general features of mental activity, while the latter familiarized us with the qualities of its clear light nature. To gain the ingredients for balanced sensitivity, we can now tap the natural talents of our mind and heart.

Clear Light Talents

According to the explanation of other-voidness, clear light mind is naturally resplendent with all enlightening qualities. These include the two main ingredients of balanced sensitivity: attentiveness and responsiveness. The fact that each moment of our mental activity engages with its object means that some level of attention is always operating. Otherwise, mental engagement would be impossible. Paying attention to something means taking it as an object of focus, whether that be through seeing it, hearing it, thinking it, feeling it, and so on. Therefore, we have the first prerequisite for balanced sensitivity:

attentiveness. This basic activity is the framework on which to hang other required factors such as interest and concentration.

Further, the fact that in each moment our mental activity produces an appearance of its object—whether that object be something visible, audible, thinkable, or "feelable"—means that some level of responsiveness is part of that activity. In other words, part of the mental activity that naturally occurs in response to looking at someone's face, for example, is the production of the sight of it that we see. Since we are responding to our encounter at least in this reflex manner, we automatically have the second prerequisite for balanced sensitivity: responsiveness. We can add other essential qualities to it, such as warmth and understanding.

Natural Concern to Take Care of Someone

Other qualities that balanced sensitivity requires also naturally endow our clear light mind. Noteworthy among them is concern to take care of someone. As a mental activity, it may not be functioning at its highest level now. Accompanied by selfishness and greed, our concern may be directed primarily at ourselves. Moreover, when low self-esteem also accompanies it, our concern for ourselves may not be particularly warm. Nevertheless, concern is present. Otherwise, we would do nothing to further our self-centered interests.

When we remove confusion from the basic mental activity of concern, we discover that naturally warm and caring feelings radiate to all. Selfish worry and altruistic concern are different forms of the same mental activity.

The Relation between Concern and Appearances

From the point of view of biology, the instincts for self-preservation and survival of the species automatically lead to various activities to support life. The dzogchen system describes the same phenomenon when explaining that mind's natural concern automatically leads to the activity of producing appearances.

The appearances that arise due to concern for taking care of someone may be of sights, sounds, smells, tastes, physical or tactile sensations, thoughts, or emotional feelings. Specifically, these are appearances of ourselves engaging in various physical, verbal, and mental activities. Moreover, warm concern gives rise not merely to the sight, sound, or feeling of these activities, but also to the actions themselves.

These points relate to the development of balanced sensitivity. When we direct our concern primarily at ourselves and mix it with self-importance, it does not function at its highest level. When freed from selfishness, however, our concern naturally translates into the appearance of balanced and sensitive words and actions.

Natural Warmth and Joy

The Sakya system of other-voidness focuses on the "natural bliss" of the subtlest clear light mind and calls this joy the "youth of the mind." This is the bliss of that level being naturally free of conceptual thoughts and disturbing emotions. Specifically, it is the blissful joy of its being free of the work of these coarser levels. That work is to fabricate fanciful ideas and impossible roles that we feel compelled to fulfill. When our mental activity stops spinning webs of preconceptions, we experience relief and joy naturally filling our heart and mind.

Conceptual thoughts and disturbing emotions tie up our innermost energy, often manifesting in tension and nervousness. On the subtlest clear light level, this energy flows freely. When we reach this level, we regain, in a sense, the forgotten youth of our mind. The clarity, freshness, and joy that were always there naturally translate into sensitive attention and warm responsiveness.

Many Sakya adherents of self-voidness also speak of natural bliss as the source for the appearances we manifest. These masters focus, however, on the blissful joy that characterizes the realization that clear light mind is naturally free of all absurd modes of existence.

This presentation of natural bliss is also relevant for gaining balanced sensitivity. Many people suffer from low self-esteem. Some even feel guilty if they are happy. Such self-deprecation blocks sensitivity to their own true qualities and prevents attentiveness to those of others. We do not exist, however, in the damning manner our confusion projects. Therefore, we have no reason to feel guilty about feeling comfortable and happy with ourselves. Happiness, in fact, is the natural state of the mind. When we comprehend this point, we automatically feel relief and joy. Feeling good about ourselves naturally leads to feeling comfortable with others, being sensitive to their situation, and being confident to help in whatever way needed.

EXERCISE 9

Accessing the Natural Talents of Our Mind and Heart

The first phase of this exercise begins with looking at a picture or simply thinking of someone with whom we have a close relationship. This may be a friend, a relative, or a colleague at work. Using the breathing technique of letting go and the image of writing on water, we try to relax our muscular tension and quiet our mind of verbal thoughts and images.

We then try to become conscious of the preconceptions we have about the person, about our relationship, and about ourselves. We try to bring to mind any associated judgments we make, such as: "You are so lazy and inconsiderate," "You are not relating to our relationship," or "I am always right." Realizing that no one remains forever the same—the contents of experience are ever-changing—we try to drop these preconceptions and judgments. We imagine them slowly leaving us with our breath as we gently exhale. Alternatively, or in addition, we may picture them automatically dissolving like writing on water.

Next, we try to become conscious of the roles we feel that each of us must play toward the other. These may include: "You have to be the efficient secretary," or "I have to be a perfect mother to you." We also try to become aware of the expectations that we have, such as: "You must always be available for me," or "I always have to clean up after you." We then remind ourselves that living up to a fixed role is impossible. No one exists in terms of simply a role. Everyone is simply a human being. Realizing this, we try to release this person and ourselves from these projected roles and associated expectations. We do this again by trying either to breathe them out or to let them naturally dissolve like writing on water. During the process, we try to feel ever-deeper levels of physical, mental, and emotional tension releasing themselves and ever-subtler levels of stress slowly lifting. We enter a state of profound and quiet relief.

Lastly, we try to notice how we naturally feel in this state that approximates one of clear light. If we have successfully brought to the surface and at least partially released our major preconceptions, we automatically feel warm, joyous, and open to the person. We are naturally attentive, concerned, and feel no hesitation or anxiety in responding with whatever words or actions seem appropriate. We try to bask for several minutes in this state. Tibetan masters call it the "resting place of the yogis."

Next, we repeat the exercise while looking at a picture of a stranger or while looking at a photo or thinking of someone we hardly know. We try to bring to consciousness and then to dismiss the public image we feel compelled to maintain, especially when meeting someone new. Trying also to drop our preconceptions about foreigners or strangers, we try to rest in the naturally balanced sensitivity toward the person that this relaxing process automatically brings. Then, we follow the same procedure while focusing on someone we dislike.

We practice the second phase of the exercise while facing a succession of partners. We try to release the various preconceptions, judgments, roles, and expectations that are specific to the relationship we have with each. Practicing with as broad a spectrum of people as possible is particularly important here. Best is to work with persons of each sex from three generations: our own, a younger, and then an older one. For each category, we try to practice with someone from the same and then a different social background, nationality, or race than ourselves. Moreover, within each subcategory, we try to work first with someone we know and then with a stranger. We may even practice with a dog or a cat. We need to sweep ourselves thoroughly of all fixed ideas. If we lack such diversity in our group, we may use pictures from a magazine.

During the third phase, we aim the practice at ourselves, first while looking in a mirror and then after putting the mirror aside. Trying to bring to the surface the preconceptions and expectations we have of ourselves and the roles and games we play in our life is crucial here. We need to release them all. We conclude by focusing on the series of photos of ourselves. When we let go of our judgments, we find that we are naturally more warm, open, and sensitive toward ourselves as we were in the past, as we are right now, and as we shall be in the future.

10   Applying the Five Types of Deep Awareness

The Five Types of Awareness

An additional asset of subtlest clear light mind is that five types of deep awareness naturally endow it. These five are a topic discussed primarily in the highest class of tantra, *anuttarayoga*. The Nyingma and Kagyü traditions correlate them with Buddha-nature and provide the most detail. As crucial ingredients for balanced sensitivity, the five comprise what we have so far been calling "understanding." They are (1) mirror-like awareness, (2) awareness of equalities, (3) awareness of individualities, (4) accomplishing awareness, and (5) awareness of reality (*dharmadhatu*).

Like mind, the five are mental activities directed at an object. More specifically, each is a manner of engaging with an object. Thus, more fully, the five are: (1) perceiving the details of an object in the way that a mirror does, (2) perceiving how the object is equal to others in various regards, (3) perceiving the object as something individual and unique, (4) perceiving how to accomplish some purpose concerning the object, and (5) perceiving the object's reality.

Like other natural talents of our clear light mind, the five types of awareness have basis, pathway, and resultant levels. To develop balanced sensitivity, we need to recognize within our experience their basis level and then cultivate pathway levels to achieve at least an approximation of their resultant state.

Mirror-like Awareness

Everyone has a basis level of mirror-like awareness. This is because everyone's sensory or mental consciousness takes in all the details of the object at which it aims. The word "mirror" in this technical term does not imply that this type of awareness is limited to the visual sphere. Mirror-like awareness also functions with our senses of hearing, smelling, tasting, and feeling physical sensations, as well as with our "mental sense" of feeling emotions.

The term "mirror" also does not imply that our sensory or mental consciousness reflects information. It merely takes in information, like a video camera or a microphone. Thus, whenever we focus on a particular item in a sensory or mental field, we not only perceive that item, we also take in all its details. When we look at people's faces, for example, we also see their eyes and nose. Moreover, this mental activity does not require verbalization. We see all these features without needing to say, either aloud or silently, "eyes" or "nose."

Although we take in all the information of our sensory and mental fields, our mirror-like awareness does not currently produce the fullest results that it can. This is because the supportive mental factors accompanying it, such as attention and concern, also do not currently work at their optimal level. This, in turn, is due to little interest or weak concentration. Our attention, for example, may be divided because of self-absorbed thoughts or emotion. Further, our interest and concern may be merely curious or academic. The frequent result of these deficiencies is that we are insensitive to what we see, hear, or feel. We neither respond to it nor even remember what we have perceived.

To benefit others and ourselves more fully, we need to notice, with loving interest and concern, all the information that our senses and mind naturally take in with mirror-like awareness. Noticing means to understand the presence of a particular feature or detail of something. It is a mental factor—or mental activity—that may accompany seeing, hearing, smelling, tasting, or physically or emotionally feeling that feature.

Seeing people and noticing the presence of various aspects is an important component of balanced sensitivity and leads to further understanding. For example, we can tell a lot about people when we notice their facial expression, the lines on their face, how they hold their body, how calm or fidgety they are, and whether or not they look at us during a conversation. We can also learn a lot about them by noticing how healthy or unhealthy they look, how fresh or tired they seem, how clean or dirty they are, how they dress, how they keep their hair, and how much makeup and jewelry they wear. Whenever we look at people, we see all these details. We need merely to pay attention and notice them.

Similarly, when we listen to people speaking, we can tell much about them, not only by hearing the words that they say, but also by noticing the emotional tone in their voice and the volume, speed, and clarity of expression. The person's grammar, style, and accent also reveal information. Moreover, we can learn much about ourselves by trying to notice the complex emotions and feelings that comprise our moods.

On a pathway level, we can work with our mirror-like awareness to derive the most benefit from it. We do this through extending the scope of this awareness and through enhancing our interest and concentration. Consequently, we notice increasingly more information about whatever we see, hear, or feel. On the resultant level, a Buddha notices, with all-loving concern, every detail of information that his or her mirror-like awareness naturally takes in. We aim for this ideal.

Awareness of Equalities

When we perceive something, we not only take in information, we naturally organize that information into patterns so that we can process, comprehend, and react to it. Organizing information into patterns is the function of awareness of equalities, or equalizing awareness. We all have this awareness on its basis level. For example, when we look at people, our mirror-like awareness takes in the shape of their body. When we are aware of this physical feature, we compare it with previous knowledge and understand that this shape is similar to others we have seen. Consequently, we see people with the understanding that they fall in the common category of being thin or fat. We do not need to verbalize this fact to see people with this understanding.

Equalizing awareness functions similarly whether we focus on one person or on several people at a time and whether we look at, listen to, or think about them. However, when more than one person is involved, we are also aware that they are equal to each other in sharing some feature. We may also be aware of them and ourselves as equal in some regard. Furthermore, awareness of equalities may concern obvious physical facts, such as weight, or less obvious ones like being on a diet.

Awareness of equalities does not operate at peak level when its scope is limited. Its scope varies according to how much detail we notice and how many facts we know about someone or something. It also depends on the range of persons or objects we consider as sharing these features. For example, suppose we are standing in line at a checkout counter behind several people. When we look at them, we see that each of them is equally waiting their turn, just as we are. If, however, we do not note that each of us probably also has other things to do, we might think that we are the only one in a hurry. Thus, we become impatient and annoyed. Awareness of equalities allows us to see what we have in common with others so that we can relate more sensitively.

Other facts about people are more basic than their being in a hurry, and they apply to everyone. Ordinarily, we do not see everyone as equal regarding his or her wish to be happy and not to suffer. Nor do most of us see everyone as equal in having the same right to be happy and not to suffer. Consequently, we do not regard everyone with equal concern, attention, love, or respect. A Buddha sees everyone as equal in that everyone shares the same wishes and rights, everyone has the same potentials for growth, and everyone exists in the same manner. If we wish to achieve perfectly balanced sensitivity, we need deep awareness of all beings, including ourselves, as equal in these profound and extensive ways.

We also need to direct our awareness of equalities to seeing patterns in our own and others' destructive behavior. If we cannot recognize the patterns of disturbing attitudes that fuel our recurring emotional turmoil, we cannot begin to respond sensitively with appropriate steps to becoming more balanced.

Awareness of Individualities

When we perceive people or objects, we not only are naturally aware of how they are equal to others in certain regards, we are also aware of their individuality. For example, we can see a class of undisciplined teenagers as all being rowdy. Simultaneously, however, we can also see each person in the class as an individual: John, Mary, or Fred. We do not need to verbalize or even know their names to see them as individuals.

Awareness of individualities, or individualizing awareness, is essential for balanced sensitivity. Standing in a crowded subway, for example, we often lose sight of this awareness and become insensitive to others. People, however, do not exist as just another face in the crowd or as just another member of an ethnic minority whom we need to fear. Everyone on the subway is an individual. Each has a family, a private life, a business life, and a personal history. Seeing each with this understanding allows us to respect them all as individuals. This, in turn, allows a more balanced and sensitive response to each. As a Buddha, we would see all people in this way, everywhere and always.

When we are aware of the patterns in others' and our own neurotic behavior, we need also to see the individuality of each manifestation. Otherwise, we may react with a stock response that does not fit the particular occasion. Though two events may share a pattern, they are never identical. Different situations call for distinct responses.

Accomplishing Awareness

The fourth type of awareness is of what to do to accomplish something and of how to do it. We all have a basis level of this awareness. When we are hungry and see food on our plate, for example, we automatically know what to do and how to do it. We do not need to verbalize this knowledge to accomplish our goal.

With this type of awareness, we also know how to relate to various persons and situations. When we take care of a baby, for instance, we know how to act and speak. We also know how to comport ourselves when with adults. Not relating identically to babies and to adults, we are naturally flexible. We respond differently according to what is appropriate.

Now, however, this awareness is not working at its highest level. We may sometimes treat our grownup child as if he or she were twelve years old. At other times, we may be at a loss how to connect with someone at all. As a Buddha, we would know how to relate perfectly to everyone.

Accomplishing awareness becomes more proficient the more we enhance the scope of the previous three types of awareness. For example, when we meet a friend and notice, with mirror-like awareness, that he or she has a troubled expression, we would see the pattern of emotional upset with awareness of equalities. With individualizing awareness, we would respect this as an event in its own right and take it seriously. We would not regard it as yet another scene. Based on this and on loving concern, we would respond fittingly with accomplishing awareness, for instance by comforting and calming the person.

Awareness of Reality

Every phenomenon has two facts, or natures, that constitute its reality. These are usually called the "two truths." They are the conventional fact of what a phenomenon is and the deepest fact of how it exists. On a basis level, awareness of the reality of something or someone is awareness of what or of who it is. For example, when we see our little boy acting disruptively, mirror-like awareness and awareness of equalities provide information and patterns. These allow for the fifth awareness that he is a boy, that he is a child, and that he is being naughty. Depending on how much information we notice, we may also be aware of his reality as someone who is overtired. Despite his horrible behavior, he wants love, not scolding, just like us. Our awareness of his individuality and of how to accomplish something meaningful may allow us to relate fittingly and put our son to bed. However, to be of continuing help we need also to be aware of the deepest sphere of his reality.

As we learn more about reality, we see that the boy does not have a fixed identity as a naughty child. The situation is open. He may act differently tomorrow and, after all, he will not always be a child and need supervision. Such awareness allows total flexibility to relate to the boy creatively as he grows up, without the constrictions of preconceptions or outdated modes of response. If we aim for balanced sensitivity, we need to expand the scope of our awareness of reality. As a Buddha, we would know every fact about the boy, on all levels, and remain conscious of each of them, simultaneously and at all times.

The Necessity for Integrating the Five Types of Deep Awareness

Anuttarayoga tantra explains that the five types of deep awareness comprise each moment of a Buddha's experience. This suggests that balanced sensitivity also requires the five functioning together harmoniously. For example, when we are depressed, we need to take in, like a mirror for emotions, all the details of what we feel. Using awareness of equalities, we would compare this information with what we have previously experienced and identify the pattern. With awareness of reality, we would know that we are upset about something.

Not discounting the scene as yet another time we are upset and depressed, we would note the unique features with individualizing awareness. This would allow us to react appropriately with accomplishing awareness. Lastly, with awareness of deepest reality, we would know that although we may be depressed now, this is not our inherent, lasting identity. Understanding this, we are nonjudgmental in trying to change our mood.

EXERCISE 10

Applying the Five Types of Deep Awareness

As it is difficult to direct mirror-like awareness at thoughts of someone, we practice the first phase of this exercise only while looking at photographs. We begin by focusing on a family photo or on a picture of a group of our friends. As in the previous exercises, we try to quiet our mind of mental chatter, preconceptions, and nonverbal judgments. Being in a subtler, quieter state, we may automatically feel a certain amount of warm concern. We need to enhance that feeling. It forms the context for applying the five types of awareness. Best is to repeat Exercise Two and try to generate loving compassion through a line of reasoning: "Everyone wants and deserves to be happy and not to suffer neglect, just as I do. Each of these persons is a human being. Therefore, all of them have the same wishes and rights as I do."

Once we sincerely feel warm concern for the happiness of these people, we try to focus on each with mirror-like awareness. Like a video camera, we try to take in all the information that we see, without commenting in our mind. Following this, we try to look at several of them together, in different combinations, with equalizing awareness. Specifically, we try to see them all as equally wanting to be happy and never to suffer. Based on this caring regard, we try to feel equal love, compassion, and concern for them all. Next, we try to look at each with awareness of his or her individuality. We try to accompany this with respect for each as an individual, without voicing even his or her name.

Then, we try to focus with accomplishing awareness. Specifically, we try to look with the understanding of how to relate to each person. For example, we may imagine being at a dinner table with the entire group. We would have no difficulty turning from one to the next and knowing how to talk to each according to his or her age, interests, and personality. Next, we try to apply awareness of reality. We try to see each not only as our sister, parent, child, or friend, but also as open to being many things. Although the person may now be a child with certain interests, he or she will grow and change over the years ahead. We try to see the child as open to all possibilities.

Lastly, we try to familiarize ourselves with these states of mind and types of awareness, by using the seven key phrases: "no mental comments," "loving compassion," "camera," "equal," "individual," "relate," and "open." First, we work with one state of mind or one type of awareness at a time, as we repeat the sequence several times. Then, we try to combine an increasingly larger number of these states, by using first two phrases, then three, and so on, until we can hold all seven mental states simultaneously.

Next, we place beside the photo of our loved ones a magazine picture of a stranger and repeat the exercise. Although we do not know the stranger personally, yet based on our mirror-like awareness of his or her appearance, we have some idea of how to relate with accomplishing awareness. In any case, we know how to relate to strangers in general. As a final step for this first phase, we place next to these two photos a picture of someone we dislike and again repeat the procedure.

During the second phase of the exercise, we sit with our group in a circle. For each step, we try to look at each person in turn with either loving compassion or one of the five types of awareness, by using the seven key phrases as before. Here, repeating the key phrase also for the initial generation of each type of awareness, and alternating it with "no mental comments," is especially helpful. For equalizing awareness, we look at two or three persons at once. When we try to combine the seven states of mind, we no longer look around the circle. Instead, we focus on a particular set of two or three people for the entire round. When we repeat this step for integration, we may choose another set of persons.

We begin the third phase by sitting with several people before a large mirror. Seeing our image in a group and realizing that we are equal to the others can be a powerful and valuable experience. We go through the steps of the exercise as before.

Next, we sit alone without a mirror. After trying to generate mental silence and a warm, gentle feeling of loving compassion toward ourselves, we direct mirror-like awareness at the feelings and emotions we are currently experiencing. We try to become aware of the complex factors that comprise the moment, but without mentally commenting. This part of the exercise is more effective when practiced at the start of a new session when the feelings of the day still color our mood. We need to include as part of what we notice any judgmental feelings we might currently have toward ourselves. We also need to include feeling nothing, if that is our present state.

With equalizing awareness, we then try to see the patterns in our feelings and emotions. Nevertheless, with individualizing awareness, we acknowledge the uniqueness of what we are experiencing now. With accomplishing awareness, we try to see how to relate to what we are feeling. Perhaps we need to be kinder to ourselves, or perhaps we need to be more firm and lift ourselves out of depression. Lastly, with awareness of reality, we try not to identify solidly with our mood of the moment. We see that our moods and ourselves are open to change. We use the seven key phrases to assimilate and combine these states of mind and kinds of awareness.

As a final step, we arrange before us the series of photographs of ourselves spanning our life. First, we direct mirror-like awareness at the feelings and emotions that each elicits. Then, we repeat the procedure we used for focusing on our mood of the moment, working through the other four types of awareness. We conclude by trying to direct equalizing awareness to regard ourselves with equal warmth throughout our life.

PART III
Dispelling Confusion About Appearances

11 Validating the Appearances We Perceive

Statement of the Problem

The most basic mental activity during each moment of our experience is to produce mental objects and simultaneously to engage with them. If, however, the actual object we perceive with mirror-like awareness is merely an appearance our mind creates, this raises a serious question. How do we know that the interpretation that our awareness of reality makes of what we see or hear is true?

For example, suppose we notice an expression on our friend's face and our mind makes it appear as though he or she is upset with us. How do we know that what we perceive is accurate so that we can properly respond with accomplishing awareness? After all, paranoia may make someone appear disapproving of us when he or she simply has an upset stomach. This can easily cause us to make a fool of ourselves.

Confirming the Conventional Validity of What We Sense

The sixth-century Indian Buddhist master Chandrakirti explained three criteria to validate any perception. First, what we perceive needs to be well known in the world. For example, when people are upset and disapprove of someone, they may knit their brows and twist their mouth askew. This convention, however, is not universal. In some societies, people show disapproval by raising their eyebrows and making the sound "tsk." Dogs, on the other hand, growl. With awareness of equalities, we need to correlate what we see or hear with the appropriate social convention. We need also to apply awareness of equalities to compare what we see with the individual's personal pattern of behavior. This tells us if our friend usually expresses being upset this way.

Second, what we perceive must not be contradicted by a mind that validly sees the conventional facts of reality: what things are. Therefore, even before applying the first criterion, we might need to come nearer or to put on our glasses. We need to make sure that what we see is not a distortion due to distance or poor eyesight. If nothing is wrong with our mirror-like awareness and what we perceive fits the right pattern, we then need to corroborate our conclusion with other evidence. We may rely on further observation and on conversation with our friend and those close to him or her.

Anger arises from a broad array of causes and circumstances. These include someone's emotional makeup, his or her personal, family, and societal backgrounds, and an incident that sparks the anger to arise. Anything that arises from causes and circumstances produces effects. Therefore, if our friend is upset with us, he or she is likely to do this or that and respond to us in this or that manner. This will happen whether or not our friend is conscious of his or her anger and whether or not our friend is willing to discuss it. We need to look for further evidence with mirror-like awareness and to identify the patterns with awareness of equalities.

In short, the ability to produce an effect distinguishes whether or not what we conventionally perceive is a total figment of our imagination. By these first two criteria, then, we discriminate between accurate and distorted appearances and between correct and distorted understandings of what accurate appearances conventionally signify. This, however, is still not enough.

Suppose the appearance we perceive of our friend's knitted brow is accurate, not a distortion of weak vision or insufficient lighting. Suppose also that the person is from a society that shares the custom of showing this expression when upset. Moreover, following this convention is our friend's normal behavior when in such a mood. Furthermore, suppose that we have checked other evidence. Our friend glared at us when we arrived and remained silent when we said hello. Thus, our understanding and labeling of the significance of the sight are correct. Our friend actually is annoyed with us and does not merely have an upset stomach. Still, our friend may appear to us as a truly ridiculous person who is always becoming upset and angry. Consequently, we may overreact and we too become annoyed. To confirm the validity of this appearance, we need a third criterion. The appearance our mind produces must not be contradicted by a mind that validly perceives the deepest fact of reality: how things exist.

Validating the Deepest Fact of Reality According to the Self-Voidness Position

According to the self-voidness position, as explained by the Gelug tradition, the deepest fact of reality is that everything exists devoid of fantasized, impossible ways of existing. Unless we are an enlightened being, however, our mind automatically creates a deceptive appearance of how our friend exists. It then mixes an appearance of a mode of existence that does not correspond with reality with one that does. In other words, our mind fabricates an appearance of an impossible mode of existence—as a truly ridiculous person. It then projects it onto the appearance of our friend existing as he or she actually does—as simply a person who is presently annoyed with us due to causes and circumstances. When we believe that our projected fantasy refers to something real and that our friend actually exists in the way our mind makes him or her deceptively appear, we may overreact. Therefore, we need to employ the third criterion to validate the mode of existence that we perceive.

Let us examine this point more closely. The confusing appearance our mind produces when we see the sight of our friend's frowning face is that he or she is *really* an angry and ridiculous person. Our friend appears to be someone who *always* becomes furious at the most trivial things and who is hopeless and will *never* change. It does not appear as though we are simply correctly labeling the expression we see as signifying that our friend is now upset. Nor does it simply appear that our friend as presently upset is merely what this label signifies based on the various aspects of his or her facial expression and on various causes and circumstances. Instead, it appears as though we can point to some inherent feature in our friend that is giving him or her the seemingly concrete identity of a *really* angry and ridiculous person, for example a permanent character flaw.

Suppose our friend actually existed with some inherent findable feature that rendered him or her a *really* angry person. It would make our friend upset continuously, forever, despite what might happen or what we might do. This is preposterous. No matter how angry or upset someone might presently be, no one exists inherently like that.

Therefore, if our confused mind produces an appearance of our friend as inherently immature—which provokes our seeing him or her with disapproval, impatience, and anger—what we perceive is invalidated by a mind that correctly sees self-voidness. Such an appearance does not refer to anything real. Though our friend may be upset with us now and may be acting immaturely, no one exists as an inherently and incorrigibly oversensitive person. No one exists with some permanent flaw making him or her, when upset with anger, always hold an eternal grudge. People's upset and immature behavior arises dependently on causes and circumstances. When we change the variables affecting the situation, the person's behavior also changes.

Validating the Conventional and Deepest Facts of Reality According to the Other-Voidness Point of View

According to the other-voidness explanation given in the Karma Kagyü tradition, the subtlest clear light mind gives rise to our experiences. The contents of each moment of experience consist of two inseparable aspects: perceiving something and something being perceived. When instincts of confusion accompany our experiences, our mind produces "dualistic appearances." "Dualistic appearance-making" causes the perceiving aspect of an experience and the perceived object at which it is directed to appear as if they were two totally separate, unrelated phenomena. It seems as if our mind is somewhere "in here" looking out, and the sight or appearance we see is sitting "out there," waiting for us to see it. Such a mind and mental object are totally imaginary phenomena. A mind that validly perceives the conventional facts of reality contradicts such a confusing appearance.

Dualistic appearances are also contradicted by a mind that validly perceives the deepest fact of reality, namely a mind that realizes other-voidness. Other-voidness is the subtlest level of clear light activity. Such activity is devoid of all grosser levels, such as those that produce these dualistic appearances and those that believe in them. The deepest fact of reality is that the pure activity of this subtlest level is merely to produce nondualistic experiences. Such mental activity contradicts all appearances of dualism.

Let us consider our previous example. When we meet our friend, our clear light mind gives rise to an appearance of the sight of his or her face and to the seeing of it. Under the influence of the instincts of confusion, a slightly grosser level of mental activity then produces a dualistic appearance. The object and mind in the experience seem split into two opposing forces. The upset face seems to be some truly annoying thing "out there," which we, the innocent bystander "in here," have had the misfortune to see. We identify the appearing object as a concrete "you" and the mind perceiving it as a concrete "me," confronting each other. Believing this appearance to correspond to reality, we feel we cannot relate to our friend. We think that he or she is a truly hopeless person who is always angry and upset. We also feel sorry for ourselves as a truly innocent victim who is forever unjustly tormented by this ridiculous person. Totally disgusted with these confrontations, we decide never to see our friend again.

If we check this appearance of two solidly opposing factions, one "in here" and the other "out there," we realize that it does not conform to reality. All that has occurred in the incident was the arising of an experience—the seeing of a sight—and this sight appearing as our friend's upset face. Of course, this sight has arisen dependently on our friend, our mind, and our eyes. Nevertheless, if we are to react in a balanced and sensitive manner, we need to understand that experience is not composed of some tragic hero facing the onslaught of overwhelming forces sent by the gods. Such a view of experience is a total fantasy.

Accepting the Conventional Facts of Reality That We Validly Experience

Let us consider the implications of the above points for developing balanced sensitivity. Suppose, for example, we look at our face in the mirror first thing in the morning and we see ourselves as fat and old, with a pimple on our nose. We feel disgusted with our appearance. What options do we have?

We need to validate the accuracy of what we see. Is it totally imaginary? We check the image and our evaluation of it with several criteria. Putting on the light, we look closer at the mirror. Is it just poor lighting that is making us look fat? Have we included a shadow as part of our face? We touch our nose. If a pimple is there, it should produce the effect of giving a certain physical sensation that we can feel with our finger. Further, we consider whether in our society the appearance of white hair definitely signifies that we are old, even if someone begins to gray in his or her thirties. We may be old compared with a child, but are we old compared with our grandmother?

Suppose we discover that what we see in the mirror is accurate and not just a figment of our imagination. We have no choice but to accept its reality. Denying what we see, never looking at ourselves in the mirror again, or cleverly applying makeup and dyeing our hair cannot change the fact that we have experienced now an accurate appearance. Our face is fat, old, and has a pimple on its nose. Does the appearance we see of our face after we apply cosmetics change what we saw when we looked at our face in the mirror when we first woke up?

After we have determined that what we see is not a total fantasy, we are left with only one reasonable option. Whether we like it or not, we need to accept what we see. Our mind has given rise to a conventionally valid appearance of a fat, old face with a pimple on its nose and to the experience of accurately seeing it. That is all. Only based on calm acceptance of an actual situation can we deal with it sensitively and respond with balance.

Rejecting the Appearances That Contradict the Deepest Facts of Reality

Normally, our mind does not give rise to the appearance of our face as merely fat and old. It superimposes an image of us as *really* fat and *really* old. Seeing our appearance like that in the mirror and believing it to be true, we overreact. We become depressed and disgusted with ourselves. The sight of the face we see does not appear to be "me" and we want to deny it.

If, however, the person we see reflected in the mirror is not us, who is it? It is certainly not someone else. Nor is it nobody. We have no alternative but to accept the fact that based on the appearance we see of this fat and old-looking face, we have to admit this is "me." However, when we project onto the mere appearance an inflation of its way of existing and think, "This is a *really* fat, *really* old person, how disgusting!" and when we identify "me" with someone having the shape of a sexy young movie star, we have plunged into the realm of fantasy. We identify with the person looking in the mirror and commenting in our head. We regard this horrified person as solidly "me"—the one about whom we are vain and worried about being really fat and old. In addition, we identify the horrifying figure we see in the mirror as something that is certainly not "me" and we reject it completely.

It feels as if there were two concrete people present: (1) an outraged person sitting in our head looking out our eyes and concretely existing as "me" and (2) some old, fat, horrible thing looking back from the mirror and concretely existing as someone having nothing whatever to do with "me." This dualistic feeling does not refer to anything real. We do not exist as Beauty looking at the Beast, despite what we might think or feel.

This does not mean that we need to be the martyr and resign ourselves to being the Beast. That would only cause us either to feel sorry for ourselves or to repress our emotions. Just as we do not identify with Beauty, we also do not identify with the Beast. Beauty and the Beast are characters of fiction. No one could possibly exist as either of the two. A correct understanding of self-voidness corroborates that fact. When we comprehend this point, we reject the appearances and feelings we perceive as utter nonsense. Our insight pops the balloon of our fantasies. Consequently, we avoid or stop overreacting. This happens even if our family or society has taught us to regard ourselves as a Beauty or as a Beast, and even if others have treated us as such. Our conviction in reality dispels our belief in their shallow opinion.

A mind that correctly focuses on other-voidness also invalidates the dualistic appearance of Beauty and the Beast. Our clear light mind is merely producing the experience of seeing a sight. When we focus on that pure mental activity, we can reject the dualistic appearance of the seeing and the sight being Beauty and the Beast. The imagined dualism here is like the two covers of an opened book of fantasies. Our insight closes the book, ends the fairy tale, and returns us to reality. Thus, we also avoid or stop overreacting.

We can understand the process of rejecting fantasy by considering the example of seeing someone dressed as Santa Claus. When we realize that Santa Claus is just a myth, we can easily dispel our belief that the person exists as who he or she appears to be. By focusing on the absence of a real Santa Claus, we can see the person beneath the costume as who he or she actually is. Consequently, we can relax and have fun during an encounter. Dismissing a delusion, however, requires kindness, understanding, and forgiveness. Otherwise, we inflict serious self-damage by thinking of ourselves as having been an idiot and by then feeling guilty about how we felt or behaved.

EXERCISE 11

Validating the Appearances We Perceive

We begin the first phase of this exercise by imagining that after dinner we see our sink full of something. It seems like a pile of dirty dishes, but we wish it were something else. We picture using various criteria to validate what we see. For example, we turn on the light and check whether the sink is actually full of dirty dishes or full of packages of frozen food that are defrosting. After confirming that they are in fact dirty dishes, we have no choice but to accept as accurate what we see. We imagine looking at the dishes with calm acceptance, trying to see them for what they are—simply dirty dishes in the sink, no more and no less.

Next, we recall seeing such a sight and try to remember how the dishes looked and how we felt. They might have seemed like a disgusting mess and, in our reluctance to wash them, we might have felt like a prima donna, too good to get our hands dirty. Thinking of such a scene now, we try to revive that feeling. We then reflect that we are inflating the situation. They are merely dirty dishes in the sink and we are merely a responsible adult who needs to wash them. Dirty dishes are not inherently disgusting; we are no prima donna; and washing the dishes is no big deal.

Realizing the absurdity of our melodramatic view, we reject it by imagining the sharpness of our insight bursting the balloon of our fantasy. Then, we try to focus on the absence of anything findable inside. An inherently disgusting mess and an immaculate prima donna cannot be found, simply because they are not real.

We need to be sure that when we reject our fantasy, we do not dismiss it as though switching to a different station on the television. If we dismiss our fantasy like this, we may shortly return to the same program. Dismissing it, instead, with the image of a balloon bursting helps us to stop reinflating our fantasy. We need to feel that the story is over forever.

Moreover, if we conceive of the fantasy of a seemingly concrete "me" being vanquished by an even stronger "me" wielding an even more powerful "insight," we have merely switched to another level of dualistic appearance and fantasy. The balloon bursting is a form of mental activity and, as such, it occurs without a concrete agent in our head making it happen.

We reinforce our rejection of fantasy by noting that basically we merely saw a sight. Our imagination has inflated this event by creating and projecting onto it the dualistic appearance of a seemingly concrete "me" and seemingly concrete dishes. This appearance is a fantasy. Realizing this, we imagine that the covers of our storybook abruptly shut. The fairy tale "The Prima Donna Faces the Disgusting

Mess" is over. Picturing the storybook dissolving into our mind, we try to focus on the fact that the dualistic drama was merely a production of our imagination. After rejecting our fantasy in this way, we try to imagine calmly washing the dishes, without identifying ourselves as a martyr or as a servant.

Next, we look at a picture or simply think of someone we live with who might often leave dirty dishes in the sink overnight. If we live alone, we may focus on someone we know who is like this and imagine that we live together. First, we imagine seeing the sink filled with dishes in the morning. Before jumping to conclusions, we picture checking whose turn it was to wash up last night. If it was this person's responsibility, we try to imagine calmly accepting the fact that he or she did not wash them. That is all that happened, nothing more.

We then examine how the person appears to us and how we feel. Most of us can recall such an experience and remember the other person appearing as a lazy slob and us self-righteously feeling like an overtaxed victim who can no longer put up with this nonsense. We remind ourselves that no one exists as a lazy slob who is incapable of ever washing up, or as a victim who must always clean up after others. Realizing the exaggeration of our fantasy, we reject it by picturing the balloon bursting. We try to focus on the absence of these fictional characters inside.

We reinforce the dismissal of our fantasy by trying to realize that we are overreacting to a dualistic appearance. Picturing the storybook of "The Lazy Slob and the Self-righteous Victim" shutting and dissolving into our mind, we focus on the fact that the fairy tale came from our imagination. All that occurred was that we saw the person and that he or she left the dishes overnight.

After clearing away our fantasy, we can now deal rationally with the reality of the situation. For example, we try to picture remaining quiet and patiently waiting for the person to wash up after breakfast, if that is his or her habit. Alternatively, if we need to remind the person or to redistribute the housework, we try to imagine doing so calmly, without making accusations.

Next, we turn to other disturbing scenes from our personal life—in the home, in the office, or in our personal relationships. We follow the same procedure for validating and accepting the accuracy of what we have seen or heard. Once we have accepted what actually happened, we examine, recognize, and try to relinquish the inflated, dualistic appearances that our judgmental mind might have projected. We do this by reminding ourselves that our fantasies about oppressors, victims, and so forth, are simply nonsense that comes from our imagination. Picturing the balloons of these fantasies bursting and the storybook shutting and dissolving into our mind, we try to return to seeing the situation as it actually is.

The second phase of the exercise begins with sitting in a circle with a group and focusing on each person in turn. We look carefully in order to confirm the conventional appearance that we see of the person—for example, someone who colors his or her hair, someone who wears one earring, and so on. Without mental comments, we try to accept as accurate what we see. We then try to notice how the person appears to us and how we feel. For example, the person may look like someone totally vain, or like an absolute fool who mindlessly follows fashion, or like the most enticing or threatening thing in the world. Moreover, we may feel like the self-appointed judge or like the shipwrecked survivor on a desert island desperate for company. We try to dismiss these images and feelings by picturing the balloon bursting and the storybook shutting and dissolving into our mind. Then, we try to look at the person acceptingly, without feeling guilty or foolish for what we felt.

Next, we repeat the procedure while sitting facing a partner and working with his or her appearance. Then, going deeper, we note any feelings of nervousness or fear we might have. Specifically, we try to notice and dismiss any feeling we might have of ourselves as a seemingly concrete "me" in our head confronting a seemingly concrete "you" sitting behind this person's eyes. Using the images of the balloon popping and the storybook shutting and dissolving into our mind, we note the deep feeling of relief and the natural warmth and openness that this rejection of fantasy brings.

The third phase of the exercise begins with looking at ourselves in the mirror. Checking the accuracy of what we see, we try to accept it without making judgments. We try to relinquish any feelings we might have of Beauty and the Beast, again by bursting the balloon of fantasy and by shutting and dissolving the book of fairy tales. If we are practicing at home and have the facilities, we may repeat the exercise while listening to our voice on a tape recorder and then while watching a video of ourselves.

During the second part of this phase, we sit quietly and try to notice what we are feeling. Then, we check the accuracy of our assessment. Is what we sense simply what we have decided beforehand that we are feeling or is it how we actually feel just now? If we really are feeling lonely or content, or even if we really are feeling nothing, we try to accept what we feel without making judgments. If we accurately sense that, in addition, we are feeling sorry for ourselves, feeling guilty about what we are feeling, or feeling totally incapable of feeling anything, we try to accept the presence of these impressions too. Otherwise, we may feel guilty for feeling guilty. We try to recognize, however, that we may be inflating and making too much of our feelings. Realizing this, we reject the inflated impression we have of our feelings. We burst the balloon, shut and dissolve the storybook, and notice how much more comfortable we feel. We are able to deal with our feelings now with more balance.

Lastly, we look at the series of old photos of ourselves and repeat the exercise. Directing our analysis toward the appearances that we see and the feelings they elicit, we try to accept ourselves as we actually were then. If we are inflating the feelings we remember from those periods or the feelings we still have regarding those times, we burst the balloon, close the storybook, and dissolve the book into our mind. We then continue calmly looking at the pictures.

12   Deconstructing Deceptive Appearances

The Need for Deconstruction Techniques

Sometimes, we discover that we are overreacting to what we see, hear, or feel because we are mistaken about what we perceived. We thought, for example, that our friend was angry with us because he or she did not call for days. In fact, our friend had no time because of extra work at the office. A telephone call easily clears up such misunderstandings.

When we discover, on the other hand, that our overreaction is due to belief in an inflated dualistic appearance, it is not so simple. Suppose, for example, that whenever we think about our friend it feels as though we cannot live without hearing from him or her each day. We believe that this person is the key to true happiness. Even if we know intellectually that this is sheer nonsense, such strong emotions are involved that we find it difficult to dismiss the feeling when it arises.

Using the images of the balloon bursting and of the storybook shutting and dissolving helps us to reject invalid appearances. Yet, the haunting feelings still return. We need additional techniques to handle such situations. Let us look at three methods to deconstruct the deceptive appearances and feelings that arise out of habit. Each uses a visualization to enhance our awareness of reality.

Focusing on Life's Changes

Many people are frightened, for example, to visit the hospital wards of nursing homes, even if a relative suffers from Alzheimer's disease and lives there. Convinced that they are too sensitive to handle the visit, such persons are, in fact, rationalizing their insensitivity. Remembering impermanence and visualizing life's changes may help to deconstruct their fear. The traditional meditation to overcome infatuation by picturing someone young and attractive as withered and old suggests this technique.

First in imagination and then during actual encounters, we need to take a deep and compassionate look, for example, at our senile, emaciated mother. Her present appearance slumped in the wheelchair is not a distortion. She looks like this now. However, when we inflate this appearance into something dreadful, it gives the impression that she has always been like that. This is a deceptive appearance. Although our mind makes her look awful and it upsets us enormously to see her this way, we know that she did not always look like this. We can easily remember what she looked like when she was younger and healthier. We can use this ability to deconstruct her present upsetting appearance.

The practice is to see her not as if gazing at a static portrait, but as if flipping quickly through a stack of photos spanning her life. We need to keep in mind, however, that our mother is not a photograph, but the person to whom that picture refers. When we see her present appearance as merely another snapshot in the sequence—admittedly, a sad and unfortunate last one—we stop inflating it out of proportion. Consequently, we stop cementing her into an identity based solely on the horrifying sight of her as a terminal Alzheimer's patient.

According to the Gelug presentation of the *prasangika* (absurd conclusion) teachings concerning self-voidness, things exist as what they are in relation to the names or labels used validly to refer to them. For instance, based on the assembled and functioning parts of a vehicle, we label something a "car." The car is the object that the label "car" refers to based on all its parts. Moreover, we do not use this label to refer to this object based on its parts only at the moment they are first assembled. We validly label the object as a car from its manufacture to its demolition. The same process is true of our mother.

Spreading before us an extensive basis for using the label "mother," we understand her reality more clearly. Although she became our mother only when she conceived us, yet when we look at a photo of her taken as a child, we conventionally say that this is our mother as a child. Thus, "mother" refers to her throughout her life, not just to her as she appears now. This realization helps us to continue treating her sensitively and lovingly. Imagining additional photos of her in the future, extending to her death, enables us to respect her dignity until she dies.

Seeing our mother throughout her life's changes also helps to eliminate and prevent another form of insensitivity. We may see the decrepit figure in the wheelchair and deny that this is really our mother. Identifying her exclusively with how she was in her "better days," we want to remember her only like that. The fault is attaching the label "mother" to merely part of the valid basis for her labeling. Just as "mother" does not refer to her simply as she looks now, it also does not refer to her simply as she looked five years ago. Viewing our mother in light of a stack of photos spanning her life brings us back to our senses. It enables us to deal sensitively with the person before us. Although she may have no idea who we are, she is still our mother.

When discussing awareness of reality, we noted conventional and deeper facts concerning everything and everyone. These facts are inseparable from each other. They are not like different levels of reality, with some that we can dismiss as less real than others. Therefore, our mother's conventional appearance as she is now and the composite of scenes spanning her life are equally valid bases for labeling her "mother." When deconstructing our mother's horrifying appearance, then, we need to take care not to ignore her as she is now. Correct deconstruction leaves both her objective appearance and the deeper fact of her life's changes. Seeing the two as equally valid is imperative for relating to her sensitively in her present condition.

Past and Future Lives

An advanced level of seeing life's changes is to view people not only in light of a series of portraits spanning this lifetime. We try to see them also in the context of past and future lives. In doing so, however, we need to be careful not to fall to one of two extremes—either giving people eternal concrete identities or depersonalizing them completely.

From the Buddhist point of view, everyone—including animals and insects—has assumed all possible forms of animate life at one time or another. Although each stream of continuity of lives is individual, none has the seemingly concrete, lasting identity of any one particular lifetime. In other words, this view does not regard a particular animal or Neanderthal man as a previous incarnation of someone with the concrete, lasting identity as our mother. It sees all three as constituent lifetimes in a particular stream of continuity of lives. It calls each stream a "mind-stream." Mind-streams, however, are not anonymous. They do not lack any identity at all. Particular mind-streams serve as the basis for labeling individual beings.

This view does not contradict the fact that conventionally this is our mother that we see in the wheelchair. Our mother does not exist as an impersonal mind-stream. She is, after all, our mother in this lifetime and, at the moment, happens to be old and decrepit. Again, we need to keep in mind both facts about her—her conventional identity as our mother now and her deeper identity as an individual taking different forms in myriad lifetimes.

This understanding enables us, for example, not to be squeamish about giving our mother an injection if we are a nurse. We can relate to her not only as our mother, but also as an individual who happens to be a patient in our ward. It also enables us to treat other patients with as much compassionate sensitivity as we show our mother. We do not see them merely as people unknown to us earlier in this lifetime. Since they might have been our mother in some previous life, we can also relate to them as "mother." This realization forms the foundation for many of the Mahayana meditations on universal love and compassion.

Raising Awareness of Parts and Causes

The Gelug approach to self-voidness explains that everything is devoid of existing in fantasized, impossible ways. This does not mean that things do not exist at all. They exist in ways that are not preposterous. One such way is that everything exists as what it is depending on its parts and causes and depending on its correct names and their meaning. This mode of existence is called "dependent arising."

The view of dependent arising suggests a second way to deconstruct deceptive appearances. Often, situations or people deceptively appear to exist with a seemingly concrete identity established without depending on anything but their own nature. A person may appear, for example, as someone inherently impossible to cope with. He or she may in fact be difficult to deal with right now, but this situation has arisen from innumerable factors. When we dissect the situation into its components and visualize them in an exposed form, it becomes less daunting.

Consider the example of being kept up at night by loud music a teenage boy is playing next door. Our mind makes the sound seem to be a solid, piercing, horrible noise that shatters both our sleep and our nerves. It also makes the teenager appear as "that rotten kid next door who should be shot." We become so angry that even after he shuts off the music we still cannot sleep. To stop this hypersensitive reaction and prevent recurrences, we need to dissect our experience.

The teenager is playing music loudly. Our experience of hearing its sound is the result of a vast assortment of parts and causes. This experience arose from a complex interaction between a compact disc player, a compact disc, an amplifier, and speakers. It also depended on the vibration of air between the speakers and our ears, the sympathetic vibration of our inner ear, our nervous system translating those vibrations into electrochemical messages and transmitting them to our brain, and so forth. Further, the teenager turned on the player, requiring the use of his hand, which consists of a collection of atoms—as do his sound system, our ears, and our brain. Moreover, a variety of physical, psychological, and social reasons may have combined to make him play his music loudly. He may be hard of hearing, high on drugs, or depressed. He may have friends visiting whom he wishes to impress with his fancy equipment. Past life causes and simply his youthful age may also contribute to his lack of consideration. Actually, his playing music loudly has arisen dependently upon a huge conglomeration of factors.

To dispel our hypersensitive reaction, we need to deconstruct the deceptive appearance of the situation as an ordeal. Dissecting the teenager, his music, and our hearing of it into their component factors accomplishes this. We imagine the event opening into a network of interwoven physical parts and psychological, social, and karmic causes. We do this by visualizing the seemingly solid event becoming like a threadbare sock with holes between its weave. We see behind it a collage of parts and causes. Although we do not deny that the teenager is a person or that the music is loud, we look at him and his playing music on a different level. After all, when we look at a blood sample under a powerful microscope, we do not deny that it is still blood, despite its unusual appearance.

The relevance, here, of applying microscopic vision is that when we depersonalize the sound of the music and the hand of its player, we also divest the noise and the teenager of being demons. This helps us to deal nonaccusingly with our lying awake. Remaining calm, we can put in earplugs and, if necessary, call the police. We may still be unable to sleep until he shuts off the music, but at least we do not become upset.

Using the Image of Waves on the Ocean

Suppose we have prepared dinner for a mutually agreed time and, an hour past it, our guest has still not arrived. We call and hear that our friend met someone a short while ago who invited him or her for a meal. They are now in a restaurant. We feel extremely hurt and become furious.

The Karma Kagyü approach to other-voidness suggests another technique for calming our hypersensitive reaction. First, we need to examine what has happened. The original experience was that we heard our friend's voice on the telephone saying that he or she was not coming for dinner. Had we left the experience at that and accepted its contents, we would have simply eaten our meal and put his or her portion in the refrigerator. We might have felt sad that we missed having dinner with our friend, but we would not have felt personally hurt or angry. However, we did not do that. Our mind tore the experience into two alienated parts. It created an appearance or feeling of an "inconsiderate scoundrel" out of the words we heard and one of an affronted, victimized "me" out of the hearing of them. Believing in this deceptive, dualistic appearance, we became upset for hours, unable to get thoughts of the insult out of our mind.

We need to deconstruct this deceptive appearance and return to the experience of merely hearing our friend's words. Remembering that experience, we need to focus on the clear light activity that produced it. In doing so, we do not divest the experience of all emotion, feelings, or meaning. However, what happened need not disturb us. Experiences are like waves on the ocean of the mind. Visualizing the event of hearing these words as a wave of clear light activity, we picture that wave naturally settling without ever disturbing the depths of the ocean. This helps us to calm down.

To avoid extremes, we need to experience the wave nondualistically from the viewpoint of the entire ocean, from its depths to the surface.

In so doing, we neither avoid the wave, like a submarine hiding from the enemy, nor do we let it batter us like a ship on the surface. A wave is merely a movement of water. It does not constitute the entire ocean.

Three Forms of Compassion

Chandrakirti explained three types of compassion: compassion aimed at suffering, aimed at phenomena, and unaimed. With the first, we look at animate beings in light of their suffering and develop the wish for them to be free from both that suffering and its causes. One source of their suffering is their unawareness that they even have any problems, let alone their not knowing the causes of their problems. For example, our friend becomes upset at the slightest thing that goes wrong and sees this as normal. He or she does not understand that hypersensitivity is to blame and that something can be done to remedy this. When we see this sad situation, our compassion for our friend becomes even stronger.

Compassion aimed at phenomena looks at beings in light of their moment-to-moment changes. With it, we wish others to be free of suffering and its causes based on the understanding that these both are impermanent. We also see that others are unaware of this fact and so, when depressed, for example, they make their sufferings worse by imagining that they will last forever. Realizing this further enhances compassion for them.

Unaimed compassion looks at beings in terms of their voidness. It has the same wish as the other two forms, but is based on not identifying others concretely with their suffering. Seeing that others do not have this insight and that consequently they identify themselves with their problems intensifies our compassion for them even more.

The deconstruction techniques we have outlined highlight the impermanence and voidness of the person in focus and reveal the causes of his or her suffering. Practicing them provides the insight needed for developing the three types of compassion. Therefore, after gaining familiarity with the three exercises in the next chapter for deconstructing deceptive appearances, we complete the sequence with a practice for combining compassion with them. Balanced sensitivity always requires the joint development of wisdom and compassion.

Developing Compassion for Ourselves to Avoid Overreacting to Slow Progress

Deconstructing the deceptive appearances our mind creates does not instantly prevent our mind from ever fabricating and believing in them again. Both our instincts and these appearances are compelling, and can only be weakened by our development of a total familiarity with seeing reality. Familiarity, however, grows through stages. It does not come instantly. When we understand this, we gain more patience and compassion for ourselves as we mature in our development.

Suppose, for example, we are possessive of our computer. Despite knowing that our partner can competently use the machine, we instinctively lack confidence. Whenever he or she uses it, we hover nearby waiting for disaster to strike. Our mind makes our partner appear as though he or she will surely break it.

When we deconstruct this appearance and our reaction to it, we are able to exercise self-control. We do not stand over our partner and we do not yell even if he or she does something wrong. Yet, we still get angry if something happens. With familiarity, we do not become angry, but we still feel nervous. Only after a great deal of practice do we stop feeling nervous at the thought that something could go wrong. Until we completely rid ourselves of this syndrome, however, we might still automatically yell, "Don't touch that," if our partner makes a sudden move to the computer, catching us by surprise.

We pass through similar stages when working with our response to accusations from our partner that we do not trust him or her. First, we do not yell back, although we feel angry and hurt. Then, we do not even become angry, but our energy becomes upset. Again, it requires a long time for our energy not to become disturbed when our partner yells at us. We need a longtime commitment to gain total balance.

13   Four Exercises for Deconstructing Deceptive Appearances

EXERCISE 12

Visualizing Life's Changes

The first exercise for deconstructing deceptive appearances helps us to dissolve faulty impressions we might have of situations or persons as permanent. We need to deconstruct our feelings that a person's appearance or mode of behavior, or our reaction to them, is fixed. We begin by looking at a photograph or by simply thinking of someone with whom we have a close daily relationship, for example a relative. We notice how the person appears to exist permanently as one age, either the present one or an outdated one, and how we treat the person insensitively because of this. For example, our parents may seem always to have been old and our children may seem always to be kids.

To deconstruct this deceptive appearance, we try to visualize portraits of our relative spanning each year of life from birth to death, projecting what he or she will look like in the future. Picturing these images in a vertical stack, like a deck of playing cards, we imagine those from infancy to the present standing on one side of the person. Those extending to old age and death stand on the other. Flipping through the stack, we try to see the present image as just one in a series.

Despite the truth of our deconstructed vision, we need to keep sight of our relative's present stage in life in order to relate meaningfully. Therefore, we try to alternate focusing on the person through two "lenses." Through the first, we see only his or her accurate current appearance. Through the other, we view his or her changing image spanning a lifetime. After switching back and forth between our restricted and expanded perspectives, we try to perceive the two simultaneously, like seeing Venetian blinds and the view of a busy street behind them. We may do this by looking at the photo while projecting life's changes onto it or by visualizing the two images superimposed. Lastly, we let the feeling sink in that our relative's appearance as concretely one age does not represent his or her lasting identity. When advanced in this practice, we may repeat the procedure, extending the visualization to include images of hypothetical past and future lives, or at least a feeling for their existence.

The same technique can help us to deconstruct the deceptive feeling of someone having a permanent, singular identity, based on an upsetting incident. For example, when a relative yells at us in anger, we often regard the person for days exclusively in the light of this event. We lose sight of our other interactions with the person. In this exercise, however, we work only with our conception of our relative. We may use a photo as a reference point to help us return to the exercise if our mind wanders. However, a photograph often locks us into the scene in which it was taken and is not conducive for representing how we regard the person now.

First, we focus on our conception of our relative based on the incident and note how fixed it feels. Our conception may take the form of a mental image or a vaguer impression of the person yelling in anger, or it may take the form of a pejorative term for the person. In each case, we usually accompany our fixed conception with a strong emotion. Then, we recall other encounters in which the person acted differently. Often, he or she was affectionate, humorous, astute, and so on. Representing these scenes also with mental images or vague impressions, we imagine them and a variety of possible future scenes like stacked slides on either side of our fixed conception. We then follow the rest of the procedure as before.

In the end, we let the realization sink in that our relative's seemingly fixed appearance as an upsetting person is a limited and deceptive view. From the perspective of an entire life, any difficult emotional scene wanes in importance. Even if upsetting behavior is a recurrent pattern in the person's life, other modes of behavior also comprise it. Nevertheless, we need to deal appropriately with what has happened now.

To deconstruct our seemingly set feelings toward the relative who upset us, we may follow the same technique, by using a mental image or a vaguer impression of the person as a focal point for representing each feeling. As before, we may use a photo as a point of reference. When our feelings seem fixed, they may cause us to forget other emotions we have felt toward the person over our history together. They may also obscure the fact that we may feel differently in the future. We need to see what we presently feel in a larger context. Yet, at the same time, we need to respect what we feel and not repress it. When we deconstruct annoyance, for example, it no longer seems like our only feeling toward someone. Still, we need to deal with it until even its residual traces are gone.

We practice the second phase of the exercise while sitting in a circle of men and women from as wide a variety of ages and backgrounds as possible. Looking at each in turn and following the procedure as before, we first deconstruct their deceptive appearance as people who have always been and will always be their current age or weight. Then, to deconstruct their appearance as having a seemingly permanent, singular identity, we look away and work with our impression of each. To help maintain our point of reference, we may occasionally look back at the person. Practicing while facing a partner is not conducive for deconstruction. The force of looking in each other's eyes is too compelling.

For persons we do not know, we try to work with the superficial impression we gain by merely looking at them. Either a positive or a negative one will do. Having a positive impression of someone, for example as a pleasant person having no problems, can render us as insensitive to his or her reality as having a negative one. When such a person tells us about some difficulties in his or her life, we often trivialize them or do not take them seriously. They do not fit in with our image of the person. If we learn of hidden dark sides of his or her behavior, especially if we believed the person to be spiritually advanced, we may overreact and lose all faith.

During this part of the exercise, we picture each person in the circle within a cluster of images of other known or hypothetical aspects of his or her personality and behavior. Traditional Buddhist meditations for gaining equanimity similarly enable us to see everyone potentially as a friend or an enemy. When properly practiced, such training does not lead to a loss of trust in everyone. It brings, instead, a realistic attitude and emotional balance. We conclude this phase of the exercise by similarly deconstructing any seemingly permanent feelings toward each person, including indifference, also while looking away and only glancing back for reference.

The third phase of the exercise follows the same procedure. We skip, however, working with the mirror for the same reason as not practicing while facing a partner. First, we focus on our current self-image. To deconstruct its deceptive appearance as our permanent, singular identity, we try to see it in the context of other aspects of our personality and behavior, both in the past and hypothetically in the future. Then, we repeat the procedure to deconstruct any seemingly fixed emotions we might feel toward ourselves as we are now.

Next, to deconstruct our identification with our present physical appearance or with how we looked at one stage in our life, we follow the same procedure by working with a series of past and present photos of ourselves. We add to them projected images of how we might look in the future. Lastly, using the photos merely as a reference, we deconstruct any fixed conceptions and feelings we might have of ourselves at particularly difficult periods in our life. Since we base such conceptions and feelings on selective memories, we need to view ourselves then in the perspective of a wider range of recollections.

EXERCISE 13
Dissecting Experiences into Parts and Causes

The first phase begins with thinking of someone we know very well who recently upset us, for example the relative from the previous exercise who yelled at us in anger. We mentally picture the person acting like this. If we wish to use a photo of the person as a point of reference to help us visualize, we choose one with a neutral expression. Thinking of our yelling relative, we notice how concretely he or she seems to be an upsetting person. Our relative seems to have a solid identity as an upsetting person that is an inherent feature to his or her very being and which has come about independently of anything.

To deconstruct this deceptive appearance, we need to change our focus. We try to see the person and the incident as dependently arisen phenomena. When we are sensitive to the factors that contributed to the existence of our relative and the incident, we find the person and his or her behavior understandable. Consequently, they seem less threatening and less upsetting. This enables us to deal with our relative and our feelings with more balance.

First, we try to imagine the seemingly concrete image of our relative dissolving into a collection of atoms. After alternating between picturing his or her body as a whole and picturing it as a collection of atoms, we try to perceive the two simultaneously as in the previous exercise. After all, our relative is not merely a mass of atoms. He or she is also a person.

Next, we dissect our relative's upsetting behavior to appreciate the causal factors that led to what happened. We consider previous actions and experiences since early childhood, relevant persons with whom our relative has interacted, and social, economic, and historical factors that played a role. For example, our relative's parents or classmates might have treated him or her in a certain way and this occurred during wartime. Our analysis need not be exhaustive and our knowledge of these factors need not be specific. A few examples and a feeling or appreciation for the rest will suffice.

Once we have made a brief analysis, we try to imagine the seemingly concrete image of our angry relative becoming threadbare like an old sock and then dissolving into a collage of these causal factors. Our conception of these factors may take the form of a mental picture of a few of them with a vague impression of the rest, or it may be merely a feeling for the existence of these factors. Again, we try to alternate and then combine picturing our relative yelling, simply as an accurate representation of what occurred, and picturing a collage of causal factors that led to this occurrence, or merely feeling the existence of these factors.

The next lens for further deconstructing our seemingly concrete impression provides a view of past generations. Following the same procedure, we now consider that our relative's parents treated him or her the way they did because they, in turn, were affected by their own parents, family, and acquaintances, their historical period, and so forth. The same is true for everyone else with whom our relative has interacted throughout his or her life and for everyone in each generation. Spending too much effort analyzing the details, however, is distracting. We limit our analysis to what we know about our relative's genealogy and try simply to have a feeling for the rest. The important point is to have an appreciation for how the person's behavior arose dependently on these factors.

We can add a further deconstruction. We also consider the past lives of our relative and of everyone involved in the current and previous generations. We also try to take into account the karmic factors that have affected each of these people.

To begin integrating our appreciation of the many factors that have interdependently given rise to our relative's upsetting behavior, we repeat several times the sequence of views. We do this by focusing on our relative while alternating the key phrase "simply what the person did" with each of the phrases "atoms," "past causes," "past generations," and "past lives." Lastly, we try to see the person from an increasingly larger number of views simultaneously, by alternating "simply what the person did" with two, then three, and lastly all four phrases. For initial practice, we may use merely a feeling for each of the four factors when trying to be aware of them simultaneously. Alternatively, we may use a mental image of one example to represent each.

Defusing an upsetting incident or our memories of it requires working not only with the upsetting image of the other person involved, but also with the deceptive appearance of us and of our upsetting feeling. We need to apply the same technique to deconstruct our identification with our emotion and our resulting feeling of being someone who, by inherent nature, becomes upset when others yell at us. When we are sensitive to the myriad factors that have interdependently given rise to our becoming upset, our emotion feels less solid. Because we consequently do not hold on to the emotion or to our identification with it, our feeling of upset quickly passes.

First, we try to feel our sense of seeming solidity dissolving into the lightness of atoms. Looking next at our upbringing, our previous behavior, and our encounters with others, we try to focus on the various causes that led to our experiencing the upsetting incident and to our disturbing emotional reaction to it. Although analyzing possible causes makes this vision more meaningful, we need not spend much time on details. We can work on these separately. During the exercise, we try to recall scenes representing merely a few causal factors and then work primarily with a feeling for a network of causes.

Next, we try to add the contributing factors from previous generations and, lastly, the karmic factors from previous lives. Alternating each vision with an acknowledgment and feeling of ourselves as a person who became upset when our relative yelled—as an objective description of what happened—is important. It helps us not to lose sight of the conventional existence of our emotion and ourselves. At the end, we try to combine the visions by using the five key phrases as before.

During the second phase of the exercise, we try to apply the same dissecting vision to the members of a group, while sitting in a circle. We look at each person briefly, then look away and work with our impression of the person, glancing back only for reference. Here, we try to deconstruct the deceptive appearance of each as having a seemingly inherent, concrete identity independently of anything. For strangers or persons we hardly know, we try to work, as before, with the superficial impression we gain of who they are, by merely looking at them. Even if we have no idea of their past or family, we try to work with an abstract feeling for them. After all, everyone has a past and a family. With people we know, we can fill in more detail. We then repeat the procedure to deconstruct our deceptive feeling of being someone who, by inherent nature, experiences a certain emotional response toward each type of person, including indifference.

During the third phase, we turn our attention back to ourselves. Skipping the practice of looking in a mirror, we repeat the procedure as above. First, we use it to deconstruct the deceptive appearance of our current self-image as our seemingly inherent, concrete identity, independent of anything. Then, we apply it to deconstruct the deceptive feeling of being someone who, by inherent nature, feels a certain way about him or herself as he or she is now.

Next, we place before us the series of photos of ourselves. Using them merely as a point of reference, we repeat the procedure to deconstruct the deceptive appearance of the self-images we hold about our past as constituting our inherent identity then. Lastly, we similarly deconstruct the deceptive feeling of being someone who, by inherent nature, feels a certain way about him- or herself as he or she was in the past.

EXERCISE 14
Seeing Experiences as Waves on the Ocean

The first phase of this exercise begins with thinking about someone close to us who recently upset us with his or her words. Let us continue with the example of the relative who yelled at us in anger. Suppose our reaction was to feel, "How dare *you* say that to *me*." Even if we did not react like that, we imagine feeling this now. We note the impression we have of ourselves standing concretely on one side as the victim or judge and of our relative standing concretely on the other as the offender.

Analyzing, we try to see that during the first moment of our experience we merely heard the sound of our relative's words. Subsequently, we projected the dualistic appearance of victim and oppressor onto the contents of the experience. Believing in the truth of this appearance, we might have overreacted with disturbing emotions. Alternatively, we might have suppressed our feelings and said nothing.

To deconstruct this dualistic appearance, we recall our bare experience of the arising and hearing of a sound and try to imagine it as a wave on the ocean of our clear light activity. Without mentally picturing the wave as an object that we see below or before us, we try to experience merely a mental feeling of a wave coming from our heart. As the upsetting experience evolved, the wave swelled, filling first with a dualistic feeling and then with a disturbing emotion.

Broadening our perspective, we try to experience a nondualistic feeling of the entire ocean from the floor to the surface. This means neither identifying concretely with the ocean nor imagining ourselves as a concrete entity separate from it, either in or out of the water. We try to feel simply like a vast and deep ocean, with waves on the surface. We recall that no matter how huge and terrifying a wave may seem to be, it is only water. It can never disturb the depths of the sea.

Without feeling like a concrete entity being battered by the wave, we now try to feel the wave naturally subsiding. As it gets smaller, the disturbing emotion and then the dualistic feeling quiet down. We return to the bare experience of merely hearing the words. In the end, this movement of mind also stills. We feel like the placid yet vibrant sea.

In going through this process, we do not deny the occurrence of the event, our original experience of it, or our experience now of remembering it. We do not become like a submarine and try to escape the storm by submerging into our clear light mind. We try to stop, however, tearing any of these experiences into two opposing forces and inflating them with seemingly concrete, lasting identities. No longer upset, we can better handle the situation by responding calmly and sensitively.

Suppose that in our emotional turmoil we spoke cruelly in return. Regretting what we said, we might have felt guilty afterwards. In feeling guilty, our mind produces a dualistic appearance of a seemingly concrete idiotic "me" and the seemingly concrete stupid words we said. This occurs from tearing in half our clear light activity of producing words and perceiving their sound. We try to deconstruct this dualistic experience of guilt, by using the same technique as before.

Next, we apply the technique to hearing pleasant words from our relative. Dualistic experiences are not limited to unsavory events. When we hear someone say, "I love you," for example, we may similarly tear the experience in half. On one side stands a seemingly concrete "me," who perhaps we feel does not deserve to be loved. On the other, stand the seemingly concrete words as something unsettling that the person could not possibly mean. Alternatively, we may feel ourselves concretely the beloved and the other concretely the one who loves us. Consequently, we project unrealistic hopes and expectations onto the person and become lost in fantasy. This inevitably leads to disappointment. We deconstruct the event and our recollection of it by trying to imagine them also as waves on the ocean of mind.

Dispelling Nervous Self-consciousness with Others

We practice the next phase of the exercise, first while sitting in a circle with a group, and then while facing a partner. During it, we work with our experience of seeing someone dualistically, with a seemingly concrete "me" over here and a seemingly concrete "you" over there. Disturbing emotions such as hostility or longing desire may or may not accompany our experience. A sure sign of a dualistic feeling, however, is nervous self-consciousness. We may be worried, particularly with strangers, that the person might not like us. Hypersensitive, we may even be worried about how our hair looks. Further, we may be uncertain of ourselves and of how we should act or of what we should say. Emotional blocks and fear may even cause us to experience the other person as an inanimate object without any feelings. Consequently, we react insensitively. In an unexpected encounter, for example, we may be overwhelmed with thoughts of how to escape.

To deconstruct dualistic feelings of nervous self-consciousness evoked by looking around the circle or at a partner, we apply the wave analogy as before. Our unsettling experience is due to the feeling of a confrontation between what seem like inherently nervous and inherently unnerving beings facing each other from opposite sides of a fence. To calm ourselves, we try to regard our experience of discomfort as a wave of mental activity. As it settles down, the experience of merely seeing the sight of the person remains. We try to experience this process of settling from the perspective of the entire ocean, from the depths to the surface.

While experiencing an encounter nonjudgmentally and unself-consciously, we still relate to the other person. Nondual does not mean that you are me or I am you. In the previous deconstruction exercises, we tried to keep in mind both the conventional and deeper appearances of someone by using the image of simultaneously seeing Venetian blinds and the view out the window. We were working, however, primarily with feelings rather than images. Here, we also try to keep two things in mind. While viewing the conventional appearance that this is a person before us, we simultaneously try to feel that there are no solid barriers between us. Our deconstruction removes nervous self-consciousness. It does not eliminate positive feelings.

Becoming More Relaxed with Ourselves

During the final phase of the exercise, we focus on ourselves, first while looking in a mirror and then after putting it aside. Now, we try to deconstruct any feelings of discomfort we might have with ourselves. Such feelings arise from the dualistic impression of what seems like two "me"s: a "me" who is not comfortable with "myself." Self-consciousness, judgments, and general nervousness usually accompany the disturbing feeling. We may intellectually dismiss two "me"s as preposterous, but to become more relaxed with ourselves, we need to deconstruct what we feel.

To deconstruct our nervousness, we try to view our deceptive feeling as a wave on the sea and let it settle. Remaining beneath is the calm oceanic experience of focusing on ourselves with warm understanding. In other words, we discover that nervous self-consciousness is merely a confused distortion of self-concern and self-awareness. Ridding ourselves of self-worry does not eliminate warm feelings for our welfare. It allows them to function without obstruction.

Lastly, we focus on the past photos of ourselves and observe any unsettling judgmental feelings that these elicit. Discomfort with ourselves as we were then also arises from a dualistic appearance. We try to deconstruct this feeling by focusing once more on the ocean from the floor to the surface. Realizing that our deceptive experience is just made of water, we do not get caught in it. We try to let it naturally subside like a wave. This allows us to make peace with those times

EXERCISE 15

Combining Compassion with Deconstruction

We begin the first phase of this exercise by thinking of someone who recently upset us, for instance the relative used in the last three exercises. First, we picture our relative acting in a way that upsets us. Then, we try to imagine his or her changing physical appearance, from infancy to old age, as in Exercise Twelve. We make sure to include past and future lives, at least in the form of a feeling for their existence.

Following this with trying to imagine a collage of our relative acting in a variety of other ways, we return to the image of him or her acting in an upsetting manner.

We think how sad it is that our relative does not understand impermanence. Our relative believes in the deceptive appearance his or her mind creates of every situation as permanent. Consequently, he or she suffers greatly by imagining that difficult situations will last forever. Keeping impermanence in mind and focusing on our mental picture or now on a photograph of our relative, we try to generate compassion. We sincerely wish for him or her to be free from suffering and from this cause of suffering. The more rid we are of fixed impressions of our relative, the more deeply felt our compassion becomes.

Putting down the photo, if using one, we focus once more merely on the mental picture of our relative acting disagreeably. As in Exercise Thirteen, we try to view the person sequentially in terms of atoms, causes for his or her behavior from this lifetime, from past generations, and from past lives, and then his or her appearance now, acting in this upsetting way. Then we supplement these vistas with a feeling for the explosion of repercussions that his or her behavior will have in the future. We try to view these in three progressive levels: the consequences on the rest of our relative's present life, the repercussions for future generations, and the impact on his or her future lives and on the future lives of everyone involved. After focusing on these levels one at a time, representing each with a collage of images or with a feeling for its existence, we return to the relative's present appearance.

Our relative is unaware of the dependently arising nature of his or her behavior and has no idea of the future consequences it will have. Realizing this, we try to generate compassion. Again, we direct our feeling toward our relative through either our mental image or a photograph.

Lastly, putting down the photo, we recall the bare experience of the arising and hearing of the sound of our relative's upsetting words. We try to imagine that experience like an ocean wave of our clear light activity. As the wave of experience swelled, it filled first with the dualistic feeling of a seemingly concrete "me" as the victim and a seemingly concrete "you" as the oppressor, and then with a feeling of emotional upset. Imagining now the wave subsiding, we try to picture first the disturbing emotion, then the feeling of dualism, and finally the arising and hearing of the sound settling back into the ocean of our mind.

Returning to our mental picture of our relative acting disagreeably, we reflect on how he or she does not see this. Our relative still is caught in a recurring syndrome of projecting and believing in dualistic appearances. Consequently, he or she suffers greatly and will continue to experience anguish. Trying to generate compassion and the wish that our relative be free of this suffering and this cause of suffering, we direct these feelings at him or her while focusing on our mental picture or a photograph.

During the second phase of the exercise, we repeat the procedure while sitting in a circle with a group and focusing on each person in turn for each of the three deconstruction sequences. If we have never encountered the person acting in an upsetting manner, we may work with an imagined scene of him or her behaving this way. We look at each person only briefly to gain a point of reference, look away while imagining the collage of his or her life's changes and so forth, and then look back while directing compassion. Although the other members in our group are also doing the same exercise, we pretend that they are not.

We focus the third phase on ourselves, first with a mirror and then without one. We follow the same procedure used while we were sitting in a circle, but recall an incident in which we acted destructively. Lastly, we repeat the practice while working with the series of photographs of ourselves. When generating compassion, we wish that we could have had these insights then.

14 Grasping at Mind's Natural Qualities for Security

Statement of the Problem

Because of the deeply rooted habit of confusion about reality, our mental activity instinctively and constantly produces a dualistic appearance of a seemingly concrete "me" and a seemingly equally concrete "non-me." It unconsciously projects this appearance onto every moment of our naturally nondualistic experience of things as they are. The confusion that automatically accompanies this mental activity causes us to believe in the deceptive appearance. However, because the alienated "me" we create and identify with is totally imaginary, we naturally feel insecure about its seemingly solid existence.

Hoping to gain a sense of concreteness and security, we feel compelled to establish or to prove the existence of the imaginary "me" in our mind. Alternatively, we feel driven to lose this "me" and to find security by becoming nonexistent. We focus our futile efforts on assorted facets of our experience. The Kalachakra literature explains how we do this particularly with clear light mind's natural qualities, such as warm concern.

The *abhidharma* (special topics of knowledge) analysis of poisonous attitudes then suggests three ways in which we try to find security. Inflating these qualities into concrete entities, first we may hope that possessing them will make us secure and more real. Second, we may fear and wish to avoid the qualities. They seem to threaten or compromise this supposedly concrete "me." Third, we may hope to lose ourselves in them. In all three cases, our attitude and consequent behavior make us both insensitive and hypersensitive to others and to ourselves.

Seven Natural Qualities That We Grasp for Security

According to the Kalachakra system, clear light mental activity naturally leads to four waves of experience. These are physical expression, subtler forms of expression, being quiet, and experiencing pleasure. Each of these waves consists of sensory or mental awareness, warm concern, and energy. This trio corresponds to the three invisible factors that produce experiences: mental activity, "creative drops" (*bindu*, *tigley*), and "winds" (*prana*, *lung*). The drops and winds are features of our energy system and have varying degrees of subtlety. Mental activity is like a painter of experience, creative drops are like a palette of colors, and winds are like a brush. Similarly, seeing, hearing, thinking, and so on create the images that we perceive. Different levels of warm concern color our experience of them, by using our energy as the brush.

When confusion and its instincts dominate our life, waves of clear light activity pass through one or another of four subtle creative drops. These subtle drops resemble floodgates into four domains of ordinary experience—physical activity and being awake, verbal activity and dreaming, rest and being asleep with no dreams, and experiencing peak moments of pleasure. At these drops, "winds of karma" agitate the waves to create the confusing dualistic appearances of these experiences. This confusion may concern the sensory or mental awareness, the warm concern, or the energy involved during any of the experiences. Belief in these confusing appearances then brings disturbing emotions and problems.

When unmixed with either confusion or its instincts, natural waves of clear light activity associate simply with the subtlest creative drop and the subtlest wind. Working together, they give rise directly to the four Buddha-bodies. The Buddha-bodies also encompass waves of physical expression, verbal expression, quiet experience, and joyous pleasure. They also consist of awareness, loving concern, and energy. Here, however, these seven qualities of clear light mind bring us and others only benefit.

The scheme of four waves and three aspects of clear light activity producing either confusing experiences or Buddha-bodies suggests that balanced sensitivity comes from removing confusion from seven factors. These are (1) our physical activity, (2) our verbal expression, (3) our sensory and mental experience, (4) our expression of warm concern, (5) our expression of energy, (6) our rest, and (7) our expression of pleasure. Let us therefore focus on identifying and removing dualistic appearances specifically from these seven qualities.

A Linguistic Scheme for Identifying the Forms These Problems May Take

The Kalachakra system also describes the external, internal, and spiritual or alternative worlds as parallel in structure. An important aspect of our internal world is the structure of language. Kalachakra texts present this structure in terms of Sanskrit grammar. This suggests a powerful tool for analyzing and remedying problems associated with mind's natural qualities.

Sanskrit verbs generate active and passive, simple and causative, indicative and subjunctive, and past, present, and future forms. They also occur in the affirmative and negative. For example, we speak to someone, are spoken to by someone, make someone speak to us, would speak to someone, spoke to someone, will speak to someone, or do not speak to someone. Since each of the seven natural qualities of mind involves an activity, each of these activities may take some or all these forms. Sensitivity disorders arise from grasping at, fearing, or trying to lose ourselves in any of them.

EXERCISE 16

Identifying the Syndromes of Grasping at Mind's Natural Qualities for Security

To help identify these disturbing syndromes, let us survey some common illustrations of each. As in Exercise One, we need to discover the disorders that pertain to us. First, we try to recall incidents in which either we or others have experienced these forms of behavior. Then, we need to think about how such behavior may arise because of grasping at one of mind's natural qualities for security or because of fearing it as a threat. Reflecting on how this confusion causes insensitivity or hypersensitivity to ourselves or to others, we try to recognize and to acknowledge the problems that may result. When we begin to understand the psychological mechanism underlying our sensitivity problems, we have opened the door to leave them behind us.

In illustrating the assortment of disorders that crystallize around each of the seven qualities, we shall restrict ourselves to four categories. These are problems regarding (1) expressing these actions, (2) being afraid or uncomfortable to express them, (3) receiving these actions, and (4) being afraid or uncomfortable to receive them. If we keep in mind the linguistic scheme of variations, we may recognize various subcategories from our own or others' behavior.

For abbreviated practice, we may choose one example for each of these categories of mind's seven qualities, or just one illustration for each quality. Alternatively, we may work only with personally pertinent examples.

Grasping or Fearing Physical Activity

(1) Mental activity naturally leads to physical actions. Nevertheless, we may hope to gain security by being the concrete agent who makes these actions occur. For example, believing that being productive justifies our existence, we may become a "workaholic," unable to cope if we lose our job. Alternatively, we may try to lose ourselves in work so that we do not have to think about our personal problems. This renders us totally insensitive to ourselves.

Because of nervous insecurity, we may feel the need to keep our hands forever busy. Wanting to feel needed, we cannot let others do anything for themselves, like tidy their desk. Doing things for others to gain a feeling of self-worth, however, is merely a form of insensitive exploitation. This is especially true when others do not want our help. Moreover, immersing ourselves in trying to help others often becomes a way to avoid helping ourselves.

Sometimes, we may try to prove our existence by producing effects. For example, we may be unable to pass an electronic gadget without pressing the buttons, even if we have no idea how to use the machine. If someone tells us to leave it alone lest we break it, we take this as a threat to our competence and value as a person. We overreact with hostility.

A causative form of the syndrome is to grasp at giving others work to do. This is the classic "power trip." To assert our existence, we boss people around. In doing so, we are insensitive to the fact that no one appreciates being ordered to do something. Subjunctive forms include feeling that if only we could find the perfect job, we could cope with life. We might also feel that if only we could be in control of everything in life, we would feel secure. Lost in such dreams, we lose touch with reality.

Focusing on the past or on the future, we may hope to achieve security by resting on the laurels of our achievements, or to establish our worth by planning innumerable projects. Such thinking often renders us insensitive to the moment. Adding a subjunctive element to this form of the syndrome, we may feel that we would now be secure if only we had accomplished something earlier in life. A negative form of the same is to think that we would now be secure if only we had not committed certain mistakes in our youth. We overreact by feeling sorry for ourselves.

We may also combine forms of this syndrome with grasping at other natural functions of the mind. For example, we may grasp for security by seeing others being active. Hoping to feel more alive or to lose ourselves by becoming anonymous, we may live in a bustling city. Similarly, we may need to go every day to the shopping mall to watch the people. Insensitive to our family's preferences, we may insist that they come with us.

Lastly, we may compulsively run from one activity to the next, because of fear of missing out on something. Making this causative, we may feel that our children should not miss out on anything either. Consequently, as an individual or as a society, we push them into a grueling schedule of sports and lessons after school. In doing this, we make our youngsters' lives as speedy and as full as those of adults working in a high-pressured office. Even the computer games that our children play are hyperactive.

(2) Grasping at being the recipient of others' actions may also take several forms. Hoping to gain a sense of self-worth from receiving others' service or to lose ourselves by not having to deal with a domestic scene, we may compulsively eat in restaurants. Our insensitivity to our partner's feelings may make the person feel that we do not think he or she can cook.

A causative form is feeling unsure of ourselves and always asking others what we should do. If the person tells us to use our judgment, we become even more insecure and nervous. Subjunctive forms include feeling that we would be better able to cope with life if we could find a partner to do everything for us. Such thinking makes us insensitive to feeling true love.

(3) Fear of being the agent of physical actions, fueled by low self-esteem and lack of self-confidence, may make us "technophobic." We

may feel incompetent to handle the latest electronic equipment. Convinced that we are hopelessly clumsy, we may even feel insecure about changing a lightbulb. When faced with such tasks, we overreact with anxiety.

(4) We may also be uncomfortable with being the recipient of others' actions. For example, if someone drives the car instead of us, we may feel insecure because we want to be always in control. If someone does something for us or pays our bill at a restaurant, we may feel robbed of our dignity. Causative forms are being unable to bear someone telling us what to do or even asking us to do something, because we feel it threatens our independence.

Grasping or Fearing Verbal Expression

(1) Mental activity naturally creates waves of words to express itself. However, when we conceive of our mind as a concrete "me," we may grasp at this natural occurrence in the hope of it establishing and proving our existence. For instance, we may talk compulsively. Unable to endure silence when with someone, we may nervously chatter even if we have nothing to say. We are insensitive to anyone's need for quiet. Inflating the significance of our words, we may imagine that everyone is interested to know what we think. Consequently, we may always have to voice our opinion. Moreover, we may feel that we must always get in the last word. We have to be right. If someone says the shirt is blue, we automatically reply no, it is dark blue.

(2) When we grasp at receiving verbal expression, we may always need to hear others speaking. We may insensitively insist that someone talk to us, otherwise we feel ignored and nonexistent. Delighting in others' conversations, we may also be addicted to listening to talk shows or to following chat groups on the Internet. These forms of escape may be symptomatic of insensitivity to our own life problems.

A variant form is hoping for more security if someone else conducts business or obtains information for us on the telephone. If the person makes a mistake, however, we inevitably overreact with accusations of his or her incompetence.

(3) When we fear verbal expression, we feel nervous to tell someone what is on our mind. Afraid that the person might reject us, we do not want to jeopardize our security by proving ourselves an idiot. For similar reasons, we might also feel nervous to speak before an audience.

(4) We may also feel discomfort at being the recipient of verbal expression. For example, we may be unable to accept criticism. Whenever

someone points out our shortcomings, we may immediately throw it back to the person, accusing him or her of the same fault. We may also feel personally threatened when someone says something politically incorrect, such as "waitress" rather than "waitperson." Similarly, we may feel our existence negated if someone tries to make a reservation for us over the telephone. Insensitive to the person's feelings, we snatch the receiver from his or her hand. We may also be unable to bear someone typing for us, without hovering and waiting for the person to make a mistake.

Grasping or Fearing Sensory or Mental Experience

(1) We may grasp for security by accumulating sensory or mental experiences. For instance, when we go abroad as a tourist, we may feel compelled to visit and photograph every site. Unconsciously, we think that this will somehow make the tour worthwhile and prove that we were there. Alternatively, we may try to lose ourselves in sightseeing in order to forget our problems at home. Our insecurity and frenetic pace drive our travel companions insane.

Regarding the other senses, we may need to have music or television playing from morning until night. Otherwise, we feel lost in a frightening vacuum of silence. We prefer deliberately losing ourselves in music instead. Or, insensitive to anyone else's comfort, we may insist on having all the windows open, even in subzero temperature. We feel that we must always smell fresh air in order to feel alive. Moreover, when we go to a buffet, we may compulsively need to taste every dish. Otherwise, we feel we are not really there. We take no account of what others might think of our display of greed.

Insensitive to other shoppers, we may mindlessly touch every item of clothing in the store as we walk past the rack, to ground us to reality. Or, needing frequent body contact to reassure ourselves of our existence, we may give each person a hug when we enter or leave a room, even if this is inappropriate. Wanting to know all the latest news, we cannot bear to be uninformed about our family, our friends, or world affairs. Having information somehow makes us feel more real. Similarly, we may never know when to stop asking questions. Not knowing what is happening, or where we are going when someone takes us out makes us feel completely insecure.

Teenagers act under the influence of this syndrome when they play music at an ear-shattering volume, enhance their senses with recreational drugs, and endure the pain of body-piercing. The more intense their sensory experiences are, the more they feel that somehow they exist despite the impersonal, deadening world around them. Alternatively, the more intense their experiences are, the more they hope they can lose themselves in them.

(2) We may also grasp for security by being the object of other people's experience. For instance, we may feel the need to be seen at the right parties and the right places, wearing the latest fashions. If someone else is wearing the same shirt or dress, we feel shattered. We may also need others to hear us singing at karaoke bars to affirm our existence, even if we make a fool of ourselves. Feeling that our experiences become real only if others know about them, we indiscriminately tell our personal affairs to people sitting beside us on the plane. We are insensitive to the possibility that they may not be interested. Alternatively, we may constantly complain about our problems to others as an unconscious mechanism to avoid dealing with them ourselves.

(3) We may also fear having sensory or mental experiences. We may be frightened to make eye contact during a conversation, despite the unsettling effect our looking at the floor may have on the other person. Looking away is often an unconscious way of trying to avoid someone seeing the real "me." Being overly sensitive, we may feel threatened by the unfamiliar odors of a foreign market or be afraid to taste something new. We may also be frightened to feel our emotions. Feeling nothing seems more secure. Similarly, we may be uncomfortable even to be in the same room with someone who is terminally ill, because of unconsciously feeling our own existence threatened. Therefore, we may insensitively treat such people as if they were no longer human beings with feelings.

(4) When we feel uncomfortable with being the object of other people's sensory or mental experience, we may overreact if anyone sees us undress. We do not want them to see the real "me." We may also feel self-conscious if someone records our voice during a speech, because of feeling that now what we say actually counts. If others' bodies touch ours on a crowded subway, we may feel threatened. Physical contact with someone may seem like a more real encounter than being merely one inch away. Obsessed with privacy, we may also be paranoid about giving information about ourselves to anyone.

Grasping or Fearing Expression of Warm Concern

People often grasp at mind's natural warm concern for a sense of security, mostly in combination with grasping at one of the previous three qualities. The object of our concern may be a partner, a friend, a child, or a family member.

(1) When we grasp at warm concern for security, we may feel that life is not worthwhile or that we are unreal unless we are in an intimate relationship with someone. We may also long for a baby so that we will feel needed. We may do this even if we are not ready to be a responsible parent. Alternatively, we may wish for a baby so that we can lose ourselves in taking care of it.

Combining this syndrome with grasping at physical or verbal activity, we may compulsively feel the need to show our affection. We may do this by perpetually hugging, kissing, or doing things for someone, or by constantly verbalizing our love. It feels as if our affection does not exist unless we express it. Moreover, our feelings are completely hurt if the person shuns our advances or responds with passivity or silence.

Similarly, to confirm the reality of our love, we may compulsively have to see or touch our beloved or to look at his or her photo on our desk. Insensitive to other demands on the person's time, we may incessantly call him or her on the telephone, for similar reasons. We may feel insecure unless we share every aspect of our life with a partner—intellectual pursuits, sports interests, business matters, and so on—despite this being an unreasonable expectation or demand. This comes from thinking that sharing everything will make our relationship more real. Here, we are grasping at both mind's natural warmth and its leading to sensory and mental experience.

(2) Grasping at being the recipient of warm concern, we may feel unsettled unless we hear, "I love you," or receive a kiss when parting from our loved one. It feels as if, without it, the person's love for us is unreal. We may similarly feel insecure and overreact unless we know every detail about our beloved's day.

(3) When we are afraid of feeling warm concern, we may fear losing control if we fall in love. We may also feel uncomfortable to show our love by giving someone a good morning kiss, by saying "I love you," or by calling him or her each day from work. When our loved one asks us to do any of these, we overreact, as if it would kill us. This aggravates the person's insecurity in our relationship.

(4) We may also feel afraid of being the recipient of warm concern. For example, we may fear losing our independence if someone falls in love with us. Someone hugging or kissing us, telling us he or she loves us, or calling us at work may also make us feel uncomfortable. Saying,

"Don't be stupid," we react insensitively, either by rejecting the person's expression of love or by offering a passive martyr's response. Acting as if the hug or kiss were an attack on our sovereignty, or some childish indignity we have to endure, devastates the person who loves us.

Grasping or Fearing Expression of Energy

This syndrome usually underlies the previously listed sensitivity disorders.

(1) When we grasp at expressing our energy to feel more secure, we may feel the compulsive need to assert our will to prove our existence. We might also insensitively push ourselves on others, so as to confirm our existence by their response.

(2) When we grasp at receiving others' energy, we may insensitively demand that everyone focus their attention on us, to make us feel significant and real. Hypersensitive to people ignoring us, we may make a fool of ourselves to gain notice. We may even pretend to be sick or may act horribly, to force others to accept or reject our existence.

(3) We may also be afraid to express our energy. We may fear that if we assert ourselves, others will reject us. Such oversensitivity blocks our emotions and makes us insensitive to our feelings. Moreover, we may fear that exerting ourselves will leave us with no energy or no time. We resent demands that others make on us and feel them as a threat to our existence.

(4) Fear of receiving energy from others may make us self-conscious and uncomfortable if others show us attention. We may feel undeserving. Or, if we need to visit someone who always complains, we might be afraid that his or her negative energy will infect us. Consequently, we put up emotional barriers to defend ourselves.

Grasping or Fearing Rest

(1) When we grasp at taking a rest in order to feel more secure, we may constantly need to take breaks at work so as not to lose sight of being a person. Hypersensitive to noise, we may feel that we need peace and quiet to maintain our composure. We may long for sleep or even for death to escape our problems.

(2) Grasping at receiving a rest from others, we may feel that if others would give us a break and leave us alone, everything would be all right. Coupling this syndrome with previous forms of grasping, we may feel that we cannot fall asleep unless our loved one is lying next to us, unless we make love, or unless we read a book.

(3) When we are afraid to take a rest, we may feel that we will no longer be a person if we stop being active. We may be unable to relax or to fall asleep from fear of missing something or of not being in control. We may also insensitively feel that no one can handle our job if we retire or go on vacation.

(4) We may also be afraid of receiving a rest from others. If people do not call or ask us to do something for them, we may overreact by feeling unloved, unneeded, and unwanted.

Grasping or Fearing Expression of Pleasure

(1) Investing the experience of pleasure, happiness, or joy with the imagined power to establish our existence, we may grasp at it. This usually occurs in conjunction with fearing or grasping at one of the previous qualities. For example, terrified of boredom or wishing distraction, we may feel the need for sensory experience to provide us pleasure. Thus, feeling a need for constant entertainment to feel alive, we may compulsively roam the shopping malls or play computer games. Unable to watch a television program for fear that we may be missing something better, we drive everyone insane by incessantly switching channels.

We may experience a similar restlessness with our sexual life. Never satisfied with what we have, we endlessly seek something more exciting to make life feel worthwhile. Moreover, we may hope to lose ourselves in the pleasures of sex. People who are psychologically dependent on recreational drugs, cigarettes, or alcohol may feel that they cannot enjoy a meal, a movie, or making love unless experiencing the effects of their favorite substance of abuse.

We may grasp at pleasure by measuring it with physical activity or verbal expression. For example, we may feel that we have to *do something* in order to have "fun." We cannot simply enjoy someone's company without having to run with the person from one activity to the next. We may also feel that our happiness with someone is not real unless we verbalize it. This may make the other person feel uncomfortable and, inevitably, it ruins the mood.

When we grasp for pleasure from rest, we may look forward all day to coming home after work or to putting the children to bed. Only then do we feel that we can relax and be our "real selves." It seems as if during the rest of the day, we are not ourselves. This makes us overreact if anyone deprives us of the pleasure of our "private time off."

A causative form of this syndrome is compulsively feeling that we have to please everyone or just someone special. Insensitive to our needs or emotions, we sacrifice everything in this quest. For example, we may feel ourselves worthless as a lover unless we bring our partner and ourselves to orgasm.

Moreover, when someone comes to see us, we may feel that we have to entertain the person. Otherwise, he or she will not enjoy the visit. We may also feel that we always have to be the clown and make others laugh. Otherwise, people will not accept us as we are. Even if we joke to try to lighten people's moods, we need to remember that Buddha himself was unable to make everyone happy. How can we possibly succeed in his place?

(2) When we grasp at receiving pleasure, happiness, or joy from others, we may be obsessed with winning others' approval. We may feel that unless others approve, we either cannot or must not be happy. Thus, insensitive to our needs and goals, we may "do good deeds" to try to justify our existence and worth in people's eyes. Another form of this syndrome is feeling that we need others to entertain us or simply to be with us. We feel incapable of being happy on our own.

(3) We may be afraid to express joy or to feel pleasure or happiness. For example, we may not "allow ourselves to be happy" because we feel that we do not deserve it. We may also find it difficult to relax and have a good time because of fear that others will disapprove. Some people with this syndrome may even have the irrational fear that a severe parent will punish them for having pleasure, as if catching them masturbating as a child. A causative form of this problem is feeling uncomfortable to give someone physical pleasure, because of fear of inadequacy or that we have nothing to offer. Consequently, we become a passive lover.

(4) Lastly, we may feel uneasy receiving pleasure or accepting expressions of others' joy or happiness. For example, we may feel discomfort at someone trying to give us physical pleasure. It feels as if we were being invaded and so we are frigid. Moreover, we may feel frightened or threatened if someone tries to derive physical pleasure from us, as if it would deprive us of something. We may also be uncomfortable at others' being pleased with us and offering us praise, because we feel we do not deserve it.

15   Relaxing Dualistic Appearances of Mind's Natural Qualities

Dispelling Insecurity through Deconstruction

To dispel the problems of insecurity that our confusion and its instincts create regarding mind's natural qualities, we need to identify the dualistic appearances that fuel these problems. Recognizing the absurdity of our fantasies, we then need to deconstruct these deceptive appearances. Techniques such as seeing experiences as waves on the ocean help with the process.

Clear light mental activity is like an ocean. Its natural qualities, such as verbal expression, are also activities. They naturally arise like waves on the ocean. Circumstances, motivation, and an intention—for instance, seeing the flight attendant coming down the aisle, wanting something more to drink, and deciding to ask—affect when waves of certain activities arise and what form they take. Nevertheless, the waves repeatedly arise as characteristic features of everyone's clear light mind.

When we project a dualistic appearance onto these activities, the winds of our karma churn the waves. Our mind becomes agitated and we experience the naturally arising waves as monstrous. They throw us off balance: we become self-conscious and nervous. Indicative of insecurity, these two unsettling feelings drive us to grasp at, fear, or try to drown ourselves in waves of activities. For example, we feel too shy to ask for some orange juice. We suffer greatly.

When we stop projecting dualistic appearances onto these waves, or we at least stop believing in these deceptive appearances, the winds of our karma automatically die down. Waves of clear light activity still naturally arise, but they no longer seem monstrous. The problem is not with the waves. Waves consist merely of water and do not disturb the depths of the ocean. The problem lies with the dualistic appearances of them. Experiences, such as asking the flight attendant for something to drink, are not disturbing in themselves. They disturb us only when we mix them with confusion.

To deconstruct our disturbing experiences correctly, we need to understand that we do exist. We do not exist, however, as a concrete "me" in our head that we need to make secure. We do not need to prove, justify, or defend our existence. Nor do we need to drown it in something. The vain attempt to do so just brings us battering from the waves of our disturbing experiences. Further, we need to divest words, deeds, and so on of the unrealistic power we imagine that they have to grant us security if we express or avoid them.

The deconstruction process does not leave us with sterile relationships with others or with ourselves. What remains is the automatic functioning of mental activity's seven talents. No longer on an endless quest for elusive security, we can act, speak, experience sensory and mental objects, love, be energetic, be quiet, and enjoy life with balanced sensitivity.

EXERCISE 17

Relaxing Dualistic Appearances of Mind's Natural Qualities

During the first phase of this exercise, we try to recall situations in which we grasped for security based on projecting and believing in dualistic appearances of our mental activity's seven natural qualities. With each quality, we consider the four forms this syndrome may take—grasping to express the quality, clutching to receive expressions of it, being afraid to express it, and being uncomfortable at receiving it. We also try to recall any insensitivity to others' feelings or hypersensitivity to the situation that may have accompanied our experience.

During the exercise, we work with common illustrations of each syndrome. Later, we may explore other forms on our own. If we have never experienced some of the examples, we may try to empathize with someone we know who suffers from these syndromes and imagine what it must be like. To abbreviate the practice, we may choose one illustration for each syndrome. Alternatively, we may work only with personally pertinent examples.

Regretting the suffering our imbalance may have caused and resolving to avoid recurrences of it, we deconstruct the dualistic appearance. First, we need to recognize our fantasy. The imagined dualism consists of (1) a seemingly concrete "me" who hopes to gain security by grasping at, avoiding, or drowning in (2) a seemingly concrete activity that can provide that security in one of these ways. We have projected this fantasy of dualism onto a wave of our experience; and the winds of our karma have churned the experience into something monstrous.

Recognizing the absurdity of our fantasy, we picture the projector in our mind shutting off and dissolving. The bad movie ends. Imagining the winds of our karma becoming still, we try to relax our grasping or our fear. The wave of the experience no longer seems monstrous. It begins to settle. We arrive at the underlying nondualistic experience of a wave of one of mind's natural qualities.

From the perspective of the entire ocean, waves of activity are surface events. They can never disturb us: they naturally pass. Realizing this, we imagine engaging nondualistically in the deconstructed activity, without self-consciousness, tension, or worry. We try to experience the imagined action as a wave naturally arising from clear light mind and naturally settling back into it.

As a final step, we recall someone else acting in each disturbing manner, particularly toward us—imposing unneeded help, constantly speaking, and so forth. To defuse our hypersensitive reaction, we try to understand that he or she was overlaying one of mind's natural talents with a dualistic appearance. The person was either grasping at the quality in order to gain security, or fearing it as a threat. With this insight in mind, we deconstruct our own dualistic experience of being the recipient of the person's action. Again, we use the images of the projector of the fantasy shutting off and dissolving, the winds of karma stilling, and the wave of the experience settling. As with Exercise Fifteen, we then direct compassion at the person, by wishing him or her to be free of the suffering that his or her confusion creates. Lastly, we try to imagine reacting appropriately and nondualistically with balanced sensitivity.

Physical Activity

(1a) To dispel the feeling that we always need to keep busy, we recall a wonderful conversation at the dinner table. Feeling too tense to continue talking when people had finished dessert, we jumped up and immediately washed the dishes. We might have felt out of place in the conversation and unconsciously hoped to escape our insecurity and discomfort by losing ourselves in the task. Our insensitivity in fussing with the table killed the conversation. Regretting our action, we see through the dualistic feeling of "me" and the dirty dishes and imagine handling the scene differently. Letting our tension settle, we try to picture enjoying the rest of the conversation, without feeling uneasy. We clean up only when the talk is over.

Recalling someone else who suffers from this compulsive "washing up" syndrome, we think how tense and miserable it must make the person. Instead of intolerance, we wish for him or her to be free of this pain. We imagine telling the person it is all right to do the dishes later.

(1b) To overcome our need to order others around, we recall seeing a relative or friend sitting idly in front of the television. We try to imagine not being drawn into the dualistic appearance of "me" and this "lazy bum." Instead, we try to feel our tension settling and no longer feeling compelled to tell the person to get up and do something. We imagine asking him or her to do something only if there is an urgent task, otherwise we are patient. With understanding and compassion, we imagine similarly releasing dualistic feelings of outrage at someone telling us what to do. We picture calmly telling the person that we are enjoying the program, or simply getting up if there is something urgent.

(2) To stop expecting someone always to do things for us, we recall sitting at the table and noticing that we do not have a napkin. Letting go of the dualistic feeling of "me" and a "you" whom I expect to fetch one for me, we try to relax our tension and imagine getting it ourselves. Thinking of someone who expects us to wait on him or her, we also try to calm our dualistic reaction of outrage or servitude. We imagine politely telling the person that we are in the middle of eating, or simply getting what the person wants if we are finished.

(3) To overcome feeling afraid to do something, we remember needing to change the ink cartridge in our printer. Releasing our tension of

an incompetent "me" and a computer nightmare, we try to imagine facing the task nondualistically. Even if we do not succeed, that does not make us a worthless person. We picture trying to figure out how to do it ourselves and only seeking help if all else fails.

Then, we think of someone who always asks us to do things for him or her because of lack of self-confidence. We try to imagine not feeling this as an imposition on a seemingly concrete "me" whose kindness everyone abuses. Instead, we imagine patiently guiding the person through the task. If the person cannot do it, we picture helping him or her without resentment.

(4) To dispel feeling uncomfortable to accept someone doing something for us, we recall sharing the driving with someone on a long motor trip. Letting go of the dualistic feeling of a "me" who is not in control and a "you" who has all the power, we try to imagine sitting in the passenger seat without any tension. We also try to picture not making the other person feel nervous by commenting on his or her driving throughout the journey. Then, we try to imagine reacting nondualistically, with balanced sensitivity, to someone finding it difficult to be a passenger while we are driving. We make sure that we are driving safely.

Verbal Expression

(1) To overcome insisting on having the last word, we recall listening to someone say something that we disagree with. Dualistically conceiving of a "me" and these words challenging my identity, we felt threatened and became defensive. We remind ourselves that voicing our opinion cannot make a supposedly solid identity more secure. In this way, we try to relax. Without making the person feel that we can never accept what he or she says, we imagine only adding something if it is constructive. Recalling someone who forever feels compelled to disagree with us, we try to imagine listening silently with understanding, patience, and compassion.

(2) To quiet the insecurity behind our insistence that someone talk to us when he or she has little to say, we remember someone visiting us and hardly speaking. The person's silence did not mean that he or she did not love us. It did not invalidate the visit. Relaxing our expectations, we try to imagine enjoying someone's silent company.

Similarly, we recall a loved one complaining that we never talk to him or her. Viewing this remark nondualistically, we try to calm our overreaction to the implied accusation that we do not care for the person. There are many ways to show love.

(3) To dispel shyness at speaking up, we recall having to make a report to our organization. We were afraid that we would make a fool of ourselves and that the audience would laugh at us. Realizing that the world does not end even if others criticize us for being a poor speaker, we try to picture delivering the report so that people can hear us, without feeling nervous.

Similarly, if someone is too self-conscious to speak audibly when we ask a question, we imagine gently excusing ourselves for being unable to hear. Demanding with annoyance that the person speak louder only makes him or her feel more insecure.

(4) To stop feeling uncomfortable with others' words, we recall someone saying something politically incorrect. Even if he or she directed these words at us, we realize that they do not have the power to rob us of our self-dignity. Without taking personal offense or accusing the person of being a bigot, we try to relax. If he or she is receptive, we imagine suggesting a more sensitive way of speaking. If the person thinks we are too touchy, we try to imagine holding our tongue.

We then recall ourselves unwittingly using a politically incorrect term and someone taking offense. Without feeling annoyance or guilt, we try to imagine accepting the person's correction nondualistically, with patience and gratitude.

Sensory and Mental Experience

(1) To overcome the compulsive drive to indulge our senses, we recall being at a buffet and tasting every item. We acted as if we would never have the chance to eat again and here was a "last meal" that could somehow make our life worthwhile. Relaxing such a preposterous feeling, we try to picture leaving several dishes behind once we are full, and not feeling deprived. We then recall someone with us stuffing his or her plate. With compassion and understanding, we view the person without disapproval or disgust.

(2) To stop feeling that we need others to know everything about us, we recall sitting next to someone on an airplane and telling the person all our problems. Understanding that others knowing what we are doing does not establish or confirm our reality, we try to relax our dualistic feeling of a "me" and someone I simply have to inform about everything. Exercising discrimination, we try to picture telling

others only what is necessary for them to know and confiding only in those whom we can trust. Remembering someone who compulsively tells us every detail of his or her day, we understand the person's insecurity and try to imagine gently changing the topic of conversation.

(3) To dispel feeling uncomfortable with sensory experience, we recall feeling shy and nervous to look directly at someone during a conversation. Realizing that looking in someone's eyes does not expose a "me" in our head whom the other person will surely chastise, we try to relax. Instead of making the other person feel bad by looking at the wall while we are speaking, we picture maintaining normal eye contact during the conversation.

Recalling someone not looking at us while speaking, we try to understand the person's dualistic feelings and not take it personally. Instead, we try to feel compassion for the person's self-consciousness and discomfort. When we scold a child, for instance, if we insist that he or she look at us, we do not allow the child any self-dignity.

(4) To dispel our fear of being the object of others' sensory experience, we recall having close body contact with a crowd on a subway. Realizing that a stranger's body touching ours is not equivalent to rape, we do not wince and make the person feel terrible. We try to relax and picture merely experiencing the sensation and letting it pass. Recalling when our body inadvertently touched someone else's on the crowded subway and the person grimaced, we try to imagine shifting positions without feeling offended.

Expression of Warm Concern

(1) To overcome compulsively expressing affection, we recall seeing our partner or child and feeling that we simply must voice our love. Doing so in front of his or her friends embarrassed and annoyed the person. Understanding that saying "I love you" does not make our love or us more real, we try to relax and not make the person feel uncomfortable. We imagine saying it only at appropriate times—not too often and not too rarely, but especially when he or she needs to hear it. When overused, the words "I love you" lose their meaning. Then thinking of someone who compulsively tells us he or she loves us, we try to relax our dualistic feeling of being embarrassed. We imagine responding warmly and sincerely, "I love you, too."

(2) To overcome grasping at receiving affection, we recall seeing our partner or child and asking for a hug. He or she told us not to be stupid. Although receiving a comforting hug may make us temporarily feel

better, it cannot make us more real. Realizing that our need for someone constantly embracing us is like that of a small child for a security
blanket, we relax our demands. We try to imagine asking for a hug
only at appropriate moments and otherwise feeling secure in our relationship and in ourselves. Recalling someone who makes such spoken or unspoken demands on us, we try to relax our dualistic feeling
of protest at someone having expectations of what we should do. We
picture hugging the person if the time and place are appropriate and,
if they are not, telling the person we will hug him or her later when
the situation is more comfortable.

(3) To dispel feeling uncomfortable at expressing affection, we recall
seeing a loved one who needed reassurance of our feelings. We had
difficulty telling the person we love him or her. Saying "I love you,"
however, or giving someone a hug, is not a sign of weakness. It does not
deprive us of anything. Nor does it mean that we have become a slave
to our passions or to this person and that we are no longer in control.
Understanding this, we try to relax and not let the person feel unloved,
especially when he or she is depressed. We imagine saying "I love you"
and sincerely meaning it. Then we give him or her a reassuring hug.
Recalling a loved one who has difficulty expressing affection, we try to
understand that the person does not have to verbalize his or her love in
order for us to be reassured of its existence. Instead of feeling unloved
or rejected, we try to feel compassion for the person.

(4) To dispel discomfort at receiving affection, we remember feeling threatened and stiff when a loved one kissed us. Receiving physical shows of affection, however, does not rob us of our independence.
It cannot render us into a baby who is no longer in control. Realizing
this, we do not make the person feel like a fool by saying something
nasty or by being passive. We try to relax and imagine accepting the
show of affection warmly and responding in kind. If our discomfort is
due to feeling that we do not deserve to be loved, we remind ourselves of the natural good qualities of our mind and heart. In this way,
we try to banish our low self-esteem as absurd. Then, recalling someone who feels uncomfortable receiving displays of affection, we imagine compassionately restraining from embarrassing the person. We
can show our love in other ways.

Expression of Energy

(1) To stop feeling it necessary to assert our will, we recall going out
for dinner with our friends and insisting that we go to the restaurant of

our choice. Getting our way does not prove that we exist. We do not have to feel insecure if we are not in control of everything that happens. No one can control everything anyway. Remembering this, we try to imagine being relaxed when discussing where to eat and being open to other suggestions. If a friend insists on getting his or her way and there is no good reason to object, we try to imagine graciously accepting if only the two of us are going out. We do this without feeling defeated or hurt. If we are with a group of friends, we picture asking their opinion and going along with the majority choice.

(2) To overcome feeling the need for others to focus on us, we recall feeling frustrated when visiting or living with someone engrossed in the television or in the computer. Feeling insignificant and unloved, we insisted that the person shut it off and pay attention to us. Our insecurity caused resentment and no one enjoyed the encounter. We try to imagine seeing the person engrossed like this and not taking it as a personal rejection. Even if the person is trying to avoid us, we reflect that perhaps we are contributing to the problem by being too pushy and demanding more attention than is reasonable. We try to relax.

If we have nothing else to do and want to spend time sharing something with this person, we can try to develop interest in the television program or in the computer. Why do we feel that quality time with someone is restricted to sharing only what we like? Sometimes, however, we may need to remind someone addicted to television or to the computer that there are other things in life. But, we need to do this nondualistically, without haughty disapproval or fear of rejection.

Recalling someone who demands our attention when we are engrossed in something or having a conversation, we try to imagine not feeling invaded. We picture warmly trying to include the person, if appropriate. Suppose the person is a small child and is not content if we merely hold him or her on our lap. We picture leaving what we are doing or excusing ourselves for a moment. Without dualistic feelings of resentment, we imagine taking care of the child's needs.

(3) To overcome feeling afraid to assert ourselves for fear of rejection, we recall silently complying with someone's will or submitting to his or her outrageous behavior. If we wish to avoid confrontations, we need to remove our feelings of dualism, not our active input into the relationship. The passive contribution of our resentful silence shapes the relationship just as much as if we say something. We try to

picture being more assertive without feeling nervous or tense. Even if the person becomes angry and rejects us, this does not reflect our worth as a human being.

We then recall someone who is afraid to assert him or herself with us. Dismissing any dualistic feelings that may lead us to take advantage of the person's docility or to become exasperated with it, we try to imagine gently encouraging him or her to speak up. We let the person know that even if we momentarily become angry at his or her words, this will not lead to our abandoning the relationship. Instead, this change in his or her attitude will enhance our respect and improve the relationship.

(4) To dispel our fear of others' energy, we recall dreading to visit a relative who always complains. We were afraid that his or her energy would infect us. Quieting our dualistic feeling, we try to imagine listening to the complaints and letting the energy pass through us. Depression or annoyance comes from making an invading force out of the person's energy and from putting up walls to defend us from it. The energy itself is just a wave of clear light activity, as is our experience of it. We take our relative seriously, but do not take the complaining personally.

We then recall someone who found our energy too threatening and shut him or herself off from us. Perhaps it was our teenager who rebelled at us being an overbearing parent. We try to imagine easing off without feeling anxious. Playing a more removed role in our teenager's life does not mean that we are no longer a caring parent. We can still be involved, but at a distance that the teenager finds more comfortable.

Rest

(1) To overcome grasping for a break, we recall feeling overwhelmed with work. It feels as if we are not really ourselves at the office. We can only feel like a person on the weekend. This dualistic view is clearly absurd. We are equally a person on the weekdays and the weekend. Both are equally valid parts of our life. We may need a rest after a hard week of work, but a break cannot make us real again. We try to imagine calmly looking forward to the weekend, without resentfully feeling trapped at work.

Recalling someone who takes frequent coffee breaks, we try to imagine reacting calmly without dualistic feelings of disapproval or annoyance. If the person is lazy, we may need to speak with him or her about it. On the other hand, if the person's workload is unreasonable or the working atmosphere is unpleasant, we may need to do something to improve the situation.

(2) To quiet our grasping at receiving a break from others, we recall our parents, for example, pressuring us to find a job or to get married. We feel that if they would only leave us alone, we would be all right. Trying to release our dualistic feeling of concrete parents pressing down on a concrete "me," we acknowledge and try to appreciate their concern. When we build emotional barriers to an onslaught from parents, we can never rest or relax. We are always defensive and become hypersensitive to any remark they make.

Suppose our parents' concern is valid and we have avoided doing anything because of childishly wanting to be independent and not liking someone to push us. We try to relax our tension. Imagining taking steps to improve our situation, we try to feel reinforced, not bullied, by our parents' concern. If we have been trying to find work or a partner, but have not succeeded, we imagine gently explaining this without feeling guilty. If we have valid reasons for not finding a job or getting married, we try to imagine calmly explaining them without being defensive or apologetic.

Suppose our parents become melodramatic. We try to experience their words and energy nondualistically and reassure them that we are happy the way we are. We will be all right. If our parents are facing ridicule from their friends about our lack of a job or a spouse, we need to show sympathy. However, this does not mean that we need to be insensitive to ourselves. We may ask them, for instance, without arrogance, which is more important, their child's happiness or their friends' satisfaction.

We then recall someone who feels that he or she needs a break from us in order to feel like an independent, real person. Without taking this as a personal rejection, we try to imagine giving the person the time and the space to be alone. Everyone needs a rest sometime.

(3) To overcome being afraid to take a rest, we recall feeling uneasy about going on vacation. Then, we think how no one is indispensable. Suppose we were to die. Everyone's life would still go on. We try to imagine leaving our work without the unsettling feeling of an irresponsible "me" and concrete work piling up that no one else can do. Recalling someone else at work who does not want to take a vacation for the same reason, we imagine reassuring the person that everything will be fine while he or she is away.

(4) To quiet our fear of abandonment, we recall no one calling or visiting us when we were sick. We felt that nobody loved us. People, however, are busy and perhaps they thought that we needed a rest. We try to imagine regarding their silence nondualistically and picture enjoying the peace and quiet. Recalling someone who would feel abandoned if we did not call or visit, we imagine telling the person of our intention to let him or her have a total rest.

Expression of Pleasure

(1) To overcome grasping for pleasure, we recall switching endlessly through the television stations out of boredom or dissatisfaction. We never give any program a chance because we compulsively search for something better. A black hole will not swallow us, however, if we find nothing to watch. Realizing this, we try to relax. We picture putting on the television only when we actually want to watch something. If we find something interesting, we try to imagine enjoying it, without clutching the remote control in case the program suddenly displeases us. We also picture shutting off the set when the program is finished. If nothing interesting is on, we imagine accepting that fact and turning off the television without repeating the search.

We then recall watching television with someone who compulsively switches channels. Feeling compassion for this person who can never enjoy anything, we try to experience his or her restlessness nondualistically, without feeling it as an attack on our pleasure. In this way, we defuse the situation from becoming a battle of wills. This enables us to find a reasonable compromise.

(2) To quit compulsively striving to win others' approval, we recall doing something just to please someone, such as taking a prestigious but boring job. Pleasing others is of course very nice, but not at the expense of what is beneficial for others or for ourselves. Realizing that we do not need to justify our existence by gaining others' approval, we try to relax. We try to imagine making choices that feel comfortable and that are right for us. If others approve and are pleased, that is very good. If they do not approve, we feel secure enough that it hardly matters.

Then, we recall someone who always tries to win our approval. We try to relax our dualistic feeling of a "you" who is trying to place responsibility for the success or failure of his or her decisions on "me" and my approval. We try to imagine encouraging the person to decide for him- or herself and assuring the person of our love no matter what choice the person makes.

(3) To stop being afraid to have a good time, we recall being at an office party and thinking that we will lose our dignity if we dance. Realizing that having a good time and dancing are expressions of our human qualities, not a denial of them, we try to relax. Without making everyone feel uncomfortable by sitting with a frown of disapproval, we try to imagine dancing and enjoying ourselves like everyone else.

Thinking of someone who is afraid to relax and have a good time in our presence, we try to drop our dualistic feeling of impatience and disapproval of his or her shyness. It only makes the person feel more nervous and insecure. We then try to picture accepting the person no matter what he or she does.

(4) Lastly, to dispel feeling uncomfortable to accept others being pleased with us, we recall someone expressing his or her pleasure with our work. We protested, feeling that what we had done was inadequate and that we are no good. There is no harm, however, feeling good about what we have accomplished. It does not render us vulnerable or conceited. Understanding this, we try to imagine accepting the approval graciously, saying thank you, and feeling happy.

We then recall someone being unable to accept our pleasure with him or her. The person is convinced that no matter what we say or do, we do not love him or her and we disapprove. We try to imagine quieting our dualistic feeling of outrage at the person not believing us. This enables us to relax and be more compassionate so that the person feels more secure in our approval.

Feeling Comfortable with Others and with Ourselves

During the second phase of the exercise, we practice with a partner. We try to experience the seven waves of natural activities without a dualistic feeling of a seemingly concrete "me" encountering a seemingly concrete "you." This means engaging in and receiving the actions without feeling self-conscious, without being nervous of the person, and without worrying about our performance or about being accepted. To do this, we ourselves need to be totally receptive and accepting of the person and of ourselves. Being nonjudgmental and being free of mental comments are the keys to this practice.

If dualistic feelings of nervousness or self-consciousness arise, we try to deconstruct them as in the first phase of the exercise. We imagine the projector of fantasy in our mind shutting off and dissolving. Then, we try to picture the winds of our karma stilling, the wave of the experience seeming no longer monstrous, and lastly the wave set-tling back into the ocean of our mind. If various positive or negative feelings arise while doing this exercise, we also try to feel them pass like an ocean wave, without grasping at or fearing them.

Holding our own hand for a few moments to accustom ourselves to nondual sensations, we begin by massaging the person's shoulders. We then experience being massaged. Following this round, we sit face to face and massage each other's shoulders simultaneously. Without worrying about how well we are doing and without judging the person's performance, we simply experience the wave of the physical activity and let it pass. We enjoy the wave, but do not inflate it into something concrete to grasp at, to fear, or to lose ourselves in.

Next, we speak to the person from our heart for a few minutes about how we have been the last few days and what we have been feeling. Then, we listen to the other person do the same. When speaking, we try not to worry about the person accepting or rejecting us. When lis-tening, we try to be totally attentive, receptive, and nonjudgmental.

We follow this with gently looking in the person's eyes, without feeling we have to say or do anything. The other person does the same. We completely accept each other. When it feels right, each of us ex-presses our warmth to the other, without forcing it or feeling self-con-scious or nervous. We may take the person's hand, give him or her a hug, or say, "I really like you," or "It's nice to be with you"—which-ever feels natural. We then try to feel and accept each other's energy, without being nervous or putting up defenses. Then, we completely relax and sit quietly with each other. In the end, we just feel the joy of being in each other's presence.

First, we practice this sequence with someone of the opposite sex, then with someone of the same gender. If possible, we practice with persons of each sex who are our own age, then younger, then older—first all three of the opposite sex and then all three of the same gender as ourselves. Including among these persons people from different cultural or racial backgrounds and alternating people we know with those who are new to us is also helpful. We try to note the different levels of self-consciousness and nervousness we experience with people in each category. In each case, we try to deconstruct our feel-ings of dualism and just be relaxed and accepting.

We practice the third phase while focusing on ourselves. Since look-ing at ourselves in a mirror or at pictures from our past often supports a feeling of dualism, we work without props. We try to experience the seven natural actions directed at ourselves without a dualistic feeling of there being two "me"s present—the agent and the object of the action. This means being nonjudgmental, fully relaxed, totally accepting of ourselves, and verbally silent in our mind.

First, we smooth our hair without feeling like either the doting parent or the child enduring the insult of being groomed. Next, we speak to ourselves in our mind about how we need to work harder or to be more relaxed. We do this without identifying as either the disciplinarian or the naughty child. Without feelings of self-hatred, disgust, or guilt, we simply say what we need to do.

We now hold our hand reassuringly, trying not to feel the dualism of someone doing the touching and someone else feeling the touch. Then, we show ourselves warm concern by stretching our legs if we are sitting cross-legged or by loosening our belt. We try to do this without feeling we are rewarding someone or being allowed to relax. Next, we try to feel our own energy, without being frightened. Totally accepting ourselves, we try to relax fully and to sit quietly without feeling lost, restless, or bored. Lastly, we try to feel the joy of simply being with ourselves. We enjoy our own company, nondualistically and fully at ease. Practicing this phase of the exercise immediately after the second one makes the process of relaxing much easier.

16 Dispelling Discomfort at the Eight Transitory Things in Life

Eight Transitory Things in Life

The *lamrim* (graded stages) literature speaks of eight transitory things in life. These "eight worldly *dharmas*" are praise or blame, good or bad news, gains or losses, and things going well or poorly. We may be either the recipient or the agent of each of the eight. In either case, we usually overreact and lose our balance. We become excited, depressed, or uncomfortable at receiving or giving any of them. In things going well or poorly, we feel similarly unbalanced when we are the recipient or agent of these passing occurrences.

A traditional way to overcome hypersensitivity to receiving or giving these ephemeral things is to see the relativity of what we experience. For example, although some may praise us, others will always find fault, and vice versa. Thus, we may deconstruct a scene of receiving criticism by recalling the thousands who have praised or blamed us throughout our life and who will do so in the future. When we need to criticize someone, we may similarly recall the myriad times we have had to praise others or to offer them constructive criticism. We will undoubtedly have to do the same in the future. Such thoughts and the equanimity they grant us put our experiences into perspective and help us not to overreact. We still feel appropriately happy or sad when we receive or need to give any of these things, but we do not become emotionally overwhelmed or upset by the event.

When we receive these transitory things in life, we may also consider what makes a person's present words seem to reflect his or her true feelings toward us. When someone yells at us, for example, why do we immediately lose sight of all the pleasant things he or she has said before? When the person calms down and again speaks lovingly, why do we sometimes deny the significance of the previous upsetting scene? Why, on the other hand, do we sometimes cling to the memory of the wound as having more reality, no matter how much the person reassures us? Praise, blame, and so forth are perishable entities. None of them lasts.

Deconstructing Dualistic Appearances of Receiving or Giving Any of the Eight

Another method for maintaining balance in the face of gains, losses, and so forth is to deconstruct the dualistic appearances our mind projects onto receiving or giving them. For example, when we receive a thank- you or lose someone's friendship, our mind creates the feeling of a seemingly concrete "me" and a seemingly concrete gain or loss. Believing that this deceptive appearance corresponds to reality and feeling insecure, we take this experience as an affirmation or as a denial of our worth as a person. Not only do we overreact to the present experience by becoming elated or depressed, we grasp for more gains and fear more losses in the elusive quest to make this imaginary concrete "me" more secure.

Overreacting to the eight transitory things derives from grasping at or feeling uncomfortable with mind's natural qualities. Receiving or giving praise, criticism, or good or bad news entails receiving or giving verbal expression, sensory experience, and energy. Being the recipient or agent of gains or losses involves the same qualities, physical activity, and sometimes warm concern. Being the recipient or agent of things going well or poorly requires receiving or giving joy or its absence.

To stop overreacting to these things in life, we need to deconstruct our experiences of them. Receiving or giving something pleasant, for example, does not prove that an imaginary concrete "me" is so wonderful. Nor does it threaten the independence of such a "me." Likewise, receiving or giving something unpleasant does not prove that this seemingly concrete "me" is a terrible person. Nor does it establish a seemingly concrete "me" or "you" as deserving pain.

Because our confusion makes us feel that if something is verbalized it is real, our mental comments and worries reinforce such dualistic feelings. Therefore, we can begin to dispel our belief in these myths by not verbalizing or commenting before, during, or after receiving or giving these things.

Correct deconstruction enables us to relax when receiving or giving the eight transitory things in life. Without denying that they are directed at us—not at thin air or at someone else—we do not take them personally. Without denying that we, not anyone else, are aiming them at others, we do not give them self-consciously. We experience these events as waves of our clear light mind's natural activities, such as receiving or giving verbal expression.

Moreover, correct deconstruction does not rob these events of the happy or sad feelings that naturally accompany them. It simply divests the events of any power to upset us. Consequently, we avoid hypersensitive reactions and prevent insensitive behavior. By accepting the reality of the situation at hand, we can deal with it sensibly. For example, we can calmly evaluate the praise or the criticism and learn something from it.

EXERCISE 18

Dispelling Discomfort with the Eight Transitory Things in Life

During the first phase of this exercise, we work with each of the eight transitory things in life, one at a time, considering first receiving it and then giving it to someone. We begin by recalling a situation in which we overreacted to one of the eight. Whether our pattern is to grasp at the transitory thing or to feel uncomfortable with it, we regret any pain that our loss of balance might have caused the person or us. We resolve to try to prevent this from happening again, and then deconstruct our disturbing syndrome.

Tantra practice sometimes employs forceful imagery to shock us out of habitually neurotic emotional patterns. In the previous exercise, we accustomed ourselves to a gentle form of deconstruction with the imagery of the projector, wind, and so forth. Now, let us try a stronger image to dispel the dualistic appearance and our belief in it that made us overreact. We shall use the image of the balloon of our fantasy popping, introduced in Exercise Eleven.

A concrete "me" sitting in our head and a gain or a loss so absolute that it establishes the worth or the worthlessness of such a "me" are preposterous fictions. They do not refer to anything real. When we picture our realization of this fact popping the balloon of our fantasy, we try to experience the burst shocking us out of our daydream. We try to feel our attachment, aversion, and confusion disappearing in an instant, leaving no trace. The popping of our fantasy leaves us only with the wave of experience that served as its basis.

Trying to feel this wave from the oceanic perspective of clear light activity, we next try to imagine receiving or giving each of the eight transitory things in life without tension or internal commentary. Without denying either the experience of this wave or the feeling of happiness or sadness that it naturally brings, we let it settle and pass.

We then recall feeling tense at someone overreacting when he or she received from us or gave to us the same transitory thing. Understanding the confusion behind the person's hypersensitivity, we deconstruct our dualistic response by imagining it abruptly popping like a balloon. Then, compassionately accepting, for example, the person's depression or anger when receiving our constructive criticism, we try to imagine reacting nonjudgmentally with balanced sensitivity. We neither ignore the person's emotions, nor become upset and feel guilty. Instead, we imagine feeling sad at the event and letting the person know what we feel. Although we are calm, if we show no emotion the person may only become more upset.

Receiving or Giving Praise or Blame

(1) We recall either gloating or feeling unworthy when receiving praise from someone. For instance, our supervisor might have told us that we are a good worker who is kind to the rest of the employees. Dismissing our feeling of seemingly concrete words proving a seemingly concrete "me" to be a saint or a hypocrite, we try to imagine listening to them without tension or internal comment. They are merely waves of verbal expression and sensory experience, no more and no less. We naturally feel happy if they are true or feel sad if they are false, but we do not make a monumental event out of receiving the praise. Out of modesty, we may politely deny the recognition, but we do not make a disturbing scene of protest.

We then recall feeling annoyed at or awkward with someone who boasted or protested too loudly when we commended him or her for good work. Understanding the confusion behind the person's overreaction, we deconstruct our dualistic response to it and try to imagine listening patiently. We feel sad at his or her lack of maturity and balance. However, without saying anything aloud or to ourselves, we imagine letting the experience of hearing this pass. Next time, we will consider more carefully the value of praising the person to his or her face.

(2) We repeat the procedure remembering when we praised someone, such as for a job well done. We might have felt condescendingly gracious, compromising, or uncomfortable when saying the words. These feelings arose from believing in a concrete "me" who could prove its existence by bestowing concrete words of praise or who felt its superiority threatened by their utterance. All that happened, however, was the arising of verbal expression from our clear light mind. Remaining mindful of this fact, we try to experience the arising of our words nondualistically and let them pass. We then recall and deconstruct feeling suspicious of or embarrassed by someone who was uneasy while praising us.

(3) Next, we work with feeling anger, mortification, or low self-esteem when receiving criticism or blame, such as for working poorly. Suppose we successfully deconstruct the experience so that we do not overreact to hearing these words. We may still be hypersensitive to the person's negative energy. To avoid upset, we need to let that energy pass through us without aversion or fear, as we learned in Exercise Seventeen. When we relax and see the person's energy as a wave of clear light activity, it cannot harm us. Then, we recall and deconstruct feeling guilty or cold with someone who overreacted when we constructively criticized him or her.

(4) Lastly, we deconstruct feeling self-righteous, nervous, or upset at offering someone constructive criticism, for example concerning his or her performance at work. We need to let go of the feeling of a seemingly concrete "me" standing on a pedestal asserting its existence through uttering seemingly concrete words, or quivering in fear of reprisal and loss of security because of these words. Again, we try to experience offering criticism as a wave of clear light activity. Similarly, we recall and then deconstruct being annoyed or disappointed with someone who felt too timid or too polite to point out our mistakes when we asked for a critical evaluation of our work.

Receiving or Conveying Good or Bad News

(1) Following the same procedure, we recall receiving good news, such as that we passed our exam. We might have reacted by becoming so overexcited and falsely self-confident that we did not study hard

enough for the next test and failed. Alternatively, we might have felt that it was just a lucky accident. Superstitious, we became too nervous to do well the next time. Relaxing our dualistic view, we try to imagine hearing the news as a wave of sensory experience. We feel happy that we passed and then continue studying hard for future exams. We also recall and then deconstruct condescendingly feeling that someone was acting like a child when the person became overexcited at our conveying good news.

(2) Next, we remember giving someone good news, for instance that he or she passed the exam. Possible overreactions include self-importantly taking credit for the person's happiness or becoming more excited than the person did so that he or she felt uncomfortable. Alternatively, we might have jealously felt that the person did not deserve to pass. Quieting down the feelings of dualism behind these reactions, we try to imagine conveying good news as a wave of clear light verbal activity. We naturally feel happy at the news, but do not inflate our role. Then, we recall and deconstruct feeling embarrassed or disgusted at someone's seemingly inappropriate show of emotion when the person became more excited than we did when conveying good news.

(3) Next, we recall receiving bad news, such as that we failed the exam. We might have felt sorry for ourselves, protested that the test was unfair, or become angry with the person who conveyed the news. On the other hand, we might have felt that this event proves us a failure and that we deserve punishment. We might even think to punish ourselves. We dismiss these dualistic impressions as absurd and try to imagine hearing the news with sober equanimity. Accepting the facts, we resolve to study harder.

We then recall feeling emotionally stiff or awkward when someone cried at receiving bad news from us. Deconstructing the dualistic response we had, we try to imagine reacting instead with quiet sadness and sympathy.

(4) Lastly, we remember giving someone bad news, such as that he or she failed the exam. Possible overreactions include feeling guilty or gloating self-righteously that the person deserved it. Sometimes, we are so afraid of hurting the other person that we do not convey bad news at all. Quieting our dualistic feelings, we try to imagine breaking the news without tension. Then, we recall and deconstruct feeling uncomfortable or impatient when someone felt awkward or reticent when giving us bad news.

Being the Recipient or Agent of Gains or Losses

(1) Continuing as above, we recall gaining something, such as a gift of money from someone. On the one hand, we might have become overexcited or we might have felt that this proved how wonderful we were. Alternatively, we might have felt undeserving or robbed of our independence and now obligated to the person. We deconstruct either reaction and try to imagine receiving the money with appreciation, happiness, and grace.

We then recall feeling rejected or frustrated when someone felt uneasy with our offer to help with some money. Deconstructing the dualistic response that we had, we do not insist. Honoring the person's need for self-dignity, we imagine trying to find anonymous ways of helping.

(2) We follow the same procedure remembering giving someone financial help, for instance our elderly parent living on an inadequate pension. We might have felt, because of prior guilt, that our gift made us a more worthwhile person and proved us a good son or a good daughter. On the other hand, we might have felt deprived and uncomfortable with parting with the money. Deconstructing each of these feelings, we try to imagine offering the money unself-consciously, with warmth and respect.

Then, we recall and deconstruct feeling outraged when someone had expectations of us or made unreasonable demands because of our accepting a gift. We try to imagine politely refusing or returning the present without making a fuss.

(3) Next, we recall losing something, such as someone's friendship. Taking this as a personal rejection, we might have overreacted by feeling devastated, by feeling indignant that we did not deserve this loss, or by convincing ourselves that this proved that we are no good. Deconstructing the dualistic feelings behind our response, we try to imagine experiencing the loss as a wave of clear light activity. Life goes on. Feeling sad not only at our own, but also at our friend's loss, we send the person thoughts of compassion and wishes for happiness.

We then recall feeling guilty or cold when someone became depressed or angry when we ended an unhealthy relationship. Deconstructing the dualistic response we had, we try to imagine experiencing the person's upset as a wave of clear light energy and words. Respecting the person's feelings, we also try to increase our compassion.

(4) Lastly, we remember depriving someone of something, such as when needing to say no to a request. We may have felt afraid beforehand to hurt the person and uncomfortable while speaking. Alternatively, we might have delighted in our action and felt that the person deserved it. Having to say no is never easy or pleasant but, deconstructing the experience, we try to imagine saying it nondualistically.

Then, we recall feeling stupid or annoyed for even asking for a favor when someone felt terrible at having to refuse it, for example when he or she was unable to help. Deconstructing the dualistic response we had, we try to imagine warmly reassuring the person that we understand. We will find someone else or manage on our own.

Receiving or Fulfilling Expectations or Demands

As a supplement to the issue of being the recipient or agent of gains or losses, we may work with three levels of increasingly stronger hypersensitivity to giving something to someone. We may overreact to giving something on our own initiative, to giving it because someone expects us to give it, or to giving it upon demand. Here, we work specifically with saying thank you and with apologizing to someone. Since thank-yous and apologies seem to require giving something of "ourselves," rather than merely a possession such as money, we are often particularly hypersensitive to expectations and demands for them.

We start with the issue of saying thank you. First, we recall simply thanking someone. If our appreciation was insincere, we may have felt patronizing. On the other hand, we may have thought that thanking someone placed us in a subordinate, vulnerable position and now we felt obligated to return the favor. Deconstructing the experience, we try to imagine thanking someone without these dualistic feelings. Saying thank you, after all, is just verbal expression. Even if we do not appreciate someone else's actions, or if what he or she did was unhelpful, still the person may appreciate thanks. We need to be sensitive, however, to the person's ethnic background. In some cultures, thanking someone for showing courtesy or kindness is an insult. A thank-you implies that we did not expect this from him or her.

We need to remember these points when trying next to dispel our overreaction when someone expects a thank-you from us. Belief in a seemingly concrete "me" undoubtedly lies behind feeling indignant, insulted, or guilty. The same is true with our overreaction of feeling condescending, resentful, or demeaned when thanking someone because of an expectation that we do so. If thanking someone will just inflate his or her pride, or the person was merely being helpful to gain our praise or to make us indebted, then not saying thank you may be more helpful. Even in such cases, however, we need to deconstruct any dualistic feelings of moral superiority.

Lastly, we consider possible overreactions when someone demands a thank-you from us. We may self-righteously refuse, feeling outrage, or we may feel guilty for not having thanked the person earlier. Being hypersensitive, we may then feel arrogant, scornful, or defeated if we choose to thank the person upon demand. Deconstructing these disturbing emotions and attitudes, we try to imagine saying thank you graciously and sincerely, apologizing for not having previously said it.

We repeat the procedure with apologizing to someone. First, we recall apologizing on our own initiative. If we viewed our experience dualistically, we may have felt condescending or embarrassed. Deconstructing the dualistic feeling behind these reactions, we imagine apologizing simply as a wave of verbal expression, accompanied by sincere regret and consideration for the person's feelings.

Then, we try to dispel feeling incensed, indignant, or guilty when someone expects an apology, and subsequently feeling unrepentantly smug, resentful, or humiliated when apologizing. Such overreactions come from confusion. Lastly, we recall someone demanding an apology. We may have refused, feeling self-righteous and outraged, or we may have felt extremely guilty. If we give in to the demand, we may apologize feeling arrogant, scornful, or defeated. These overreactions bring us only aggravation and pain. We need to deconstruct them. Even if someone expects or demands an apology from us, the experience of being the recipient or fulfiller of expectations and demands is still just a wave of clear light activity.

Suppose we were not at fault and someone's demand for an apology is unjustified. The traditional training in cleansing our attitudes recommends giving the victory to others. If we say we were sorry, even if we were not at fault, the dispute and hard feelings are finished. If, however, we do this with a dualistic feeling, we again feel defeated or resentful. Apologizing nondualistically allows us to maintain our balance. Moreover, if we acknowledge that undoubtedly both of us were at fault and then apologize for our part in the problem, we leave the door open for the person to acknowledge his or her part too. This helps to prevent the person from taking advantage of our forgiving nature.

Being the Recipient or Agent of Things Going Well or Poorly

(1) We next recall being on the receiving end of things going well, for example in a relationship with someone. The person was acting lovingly and all was going smoothly. We consider overreactions we might have had of being elated or perhaps smugly feeling that this proved how wonderful we were. On the other hand, we might have worried that it was too good to be true and therefore clutched to the relationship in fear of losing it. We might even have convinced ourselves that the person would soon discover our true self as a terrible person and would then abandon us. In addition, we might have felt that we would inevitably ruin the relationship by our usual stupid behavior. Deconstructing such dualistic feelings, we try to imagine simply enjoying our happiness with the relationship, without making something monumental of it.

We then recall feeling impatient or annoyed when someone felt insecure in a good relationship with us. Deconstructing the dualistic response that we had, we try to imagine extending our understanding and compassion. We do not make the person feel even more nervous by scolding him or her for acting like an idiot.

(2) We then remember being the agent of things going well in a relationship. We had been trying our best to be a loving friend or partner and our efforts had succeeded. Recalling any feelings of being the self-sacrificing martyr or worries that we would inevitably slip and show our true nature, we deconstruct these tensions. We try to imagine continuing to act kindly, without being self-conscious, and regarding this as a wave of physical activity, warm concern, and positive energy. Then, we recall and deconstruct feeling exasperated when someone felt low self-esteem despite acting perfectly well in a relationship with us.

(3) We follow the same procedure recalling being the recipient of things going poorly in a relationship. Possible overreactions include having felt sorry for ourselves that nothing ever works out or having felt relieved that the person found out the truth and was treating us the way we deserve. We deconstruct these feelings and try to imagine accepting the situation and seeing what we can do to salvage the relationship.

We then recall feeling disappointed or irritated when someone constantly complained about things going badly in a relationship with us, but did nothing constructive to try to improve the situation. Deconstructing the dualistic response that we had, we try to be patient.

(4) Lastly, we remember being the agent of things going poorly in a relationship. We had been acting inconsiderately and were picking fights with the person. Now, we deconstruct any dualistic feelings we might have had of hopelessness, depression, guilt, or self-satisfaction. Trying no longer to imagine ourselves as a terrible person or as the self-righteous avenger, we nevertheless accept responsibility for our behavior. It arose as a wave of clear light activity, but it need not continue. Without being tossed by this wave, we resolve to change our ways. Then, we recall and deconstruct feeling callous or unforgiving when someone felt awful at having hurt us in a relationship.

Avoiding an Emotional Roller Coaster When Directly Relating to Someone

The second phase of the exercise entails giving and receiving from a partner the eight transitory things in life. Without feeling tense, self-conscious, silly, elated, glorified, depressed, or hurt, we try to experience each action nondualistically as a wave of clear light activity. If any of these disturbing emotions arise, we may follow the previous procedure to deconstruct the dualistic appearances behind them—imagining the balloon of our fantasy popping, and so forth. We need to take care, however, to avoid "over-deconstructing" the experience and consequently divesting it of all feeling. Therefore, when we spontaneously feel happy or sad, we try to relax with these feelings and to resist inflating them. We also need care to avoid depersonalizing these experiences. Otherwise, we may become insensitive to the person.

First, we praise our partner by remarking, for instance, that his or her hair looks pretty. We try to do this without being patronizing or flirtatious. Then, we receive a similar compliment, trying to resist any feelings of being sexually harassed. Next, trying to avoid being intrusive or cruel, we offer constructive criticism by suggesting, for example, that our partner needs to go on a diet. We try to offer this advice gently, without being afraid to hurt the person's feelings and without feeling insecure that he or she will reject us for what we said. We then receive a similar suggestion and deconstruct feeling insulted or hurt.

Next, without the exaggerated enthusiasm used when speaking to a two-year-old, we tell our partner good news, such as we are having ice cream after the session. We then receive similar good news trying to avoid becoming overexcited with anticipation. Without being afraid to upset the person, we then convey the bad news that his or her flight has been canceled. We receive the same news and try to accept it without becoming annoyed or depressed.

Turning next to gains and losses, we try to avoid feeling any dualistic tension in the face of either of them. First, we experience giving and receiving money from each other and then taking it away and having it taken away from us. Then, we thank the person on our own initiative, demand a thank-you in return, and receive that thanks. Correspondingly, we receive a thank-you from the person's own initiative and a demand for a thanks in return, and then we fulfill that demand. Next, we apologize to the person on our own initiative, demand an apology in return, and receive that apology. We end this sequence by receiving an apology from the person's own initiative and a demand for an apology in return, and then we fulfill that demand. We try to do all this without disturbing emotions or attitudes.

Next, without gloating, we acknowledge to ourselves and feel happy at our efforts to improve the relationship and that it seems to be working. Then, trying to resist feeling solely responsible for the success, we admit to ourselves and feel happy that he or she has been working hard too. We repeat the process, acknowledging with sadness, but trying to avoid feeling guilty, that the relationship has degenerated because we have been acting poorly. It might also have not developed because we have made no efforts. Lastly, we think how the relationship has sunk or not evolved because the person has been behaving terribly or has ignored our show of friendship. We try to do this nonaccusingly, yet feeling sad.

Avoiding Emotional Extremes When Relating to Ourselves

During the third phase of the exercise, we skip practicing with a mirror and begin by sitting quietly without any props. We direct the eight transitory things to ourselves and try to experience them without feeling the presence of two "me"s: one the agent and the other the recipient. We may use the previous deconstruction procedure if needed. Through this process, we divest the experiences of any tension or feelings of self-consciousness.

First, we encourage our positive efforts by praising ourselves. We try to do this without feeling self-patronizing, uneasy, or undeserving. Then, we criticize ourselves for mistakes we are making, trying to avoid being accusatory or feeling low self-esteem or guilt.

Next, we tell ourselves good news, such as that there is only one day left until the weekend. We try to do this without feeling like a parent holding out hopes for a reward to a child or like a child being goaded to behave nicely. Then, we tell ourselves bad news, such as we have to go back to work tomorrow. We try to avoid feeling like either a taskmaster or a slave.

Following this, we try to imagine experiencing a gain, such as figuring out the solution to a personal problem, without feeling like either a brilliant psychologist or a dense patient. Then, we imagine experiencing a loss, such as being unable to remember someone's name or unconsciously saying the wrong word when we mean something else. This frequently happens as we grow older and can be especially unnerving during the first years. We try to imagine experiencing this without becoming annoyed with ourselves or feeling that we need to reserve a place at the nursing home.

Also helpful is deconstructing the experience of actively giving ourselves a gain or a loss. For example, we picture doing something nice for ourselves, like taking a hot bath. We try to imagine relaxing and enjoying it without feeling like a self-satisfied master who has rewarded someone or like a beast of burden that has been rewarded. Similarly, we picture restricting ourselves, for instance not taking dessert because we are dieting. We try to imagine doing this without feeling like a disciplinarian or a naughty child being punished.

Next, we think about the things that have been going well in our life, without feeling proud as the agent of this achievement or undeserving as the recipient. Then, we conclude by thinking about the things that have been going poorly. We feel sad, but try to avoid feeling like either the guilty perpetrator or the helpless victim.

During the second part of this phase, we turn our attention to the series of past photos of ourselves and try to experience nondualistically the eight transitory things as they relate to those periods of our life. We praise ourselves for our strong points during those times and criticize our mistakes. Next, we tell ourselves both the good and bad news of what happened because of our behavior then. We follow this with thinking of the gains and losses we have experienced because of those actions. Lastly, we acknowledge and feel happy about the things that went well and acknowledge and feel sad about the things that went badly at those times.

17 Dissolving Disturbing Emotions into Underlying Deep Awareness

Both grasping at mental activity's natural qualities for security and fearing them as a threat arise from projecting and believing in dualistic appearances. Deconstructing these appearances leaves us with merely the experience of these natural qualities. Similarly, disturbing emotions also arise from projecting and believing in dualistic appearances. Under their influence, we become insensitive or hypersensitive. Upon deconstruction, we find underlying them the key for gaining balance—the five types of deep awareness.

The following presentation derives from the abhidharma discussion of the five major disturbing emotions: naivety, pride, longing desire, jealousy, and anger. Other-voidness teachings provide the most detail about their deconstruction into deep awareness.

Naivety

Naivety (*moha*) is the confusion, either about cause and effect or about reality, that accompanies destructive behavior or thought. Such confusion may arise because of not knowing about these matters or because of apprehending them in an inverted manner. When we are naive about cause and effect, we may believe that our insensitive actions have no effects. We might also imagine that they bring happiness when in fact they cause harm. When we are naive about reality, we do not realize that the dualistic appearances our mind creates are merely waves of clear light activity. They do not refer to anything real. Consequently, we overreact.

Distorted, antagonistic thinking often accompanies naivety, making us closed-minded. This leads to stubbornly denying the existence of cause and effect or refusing to accept the existence of, or facts about, a situation, or the facts about someone. It also makes us defensively or aggressively insist that our dualistic experiences correspond to reality.

Since naivety, especially in its closed-minded forms, is a common ailment that most people do not even detect, let us list some examples:

Naively denying the existence of our feelings, we alienate ourselves from them.

Although upsetting thoughts or images obsessively come to mind, we do not want to think about them.

We imagine that by not thinking about our problems, they will go away.

Believing that we are the center of the universe, we do not want to consider another's view.

We insist that someone do something for us even if the person has no time.

Convinced that we are incapable of relating, we are frightened of others and close ourselves off from meaningful contact.

Refusing to accept the reality of a loved one as an independent person, we become overprotective.

When we recognize the dualistic appearances behind our naivety, we can deconstruct them. For example, suppose we have a sixteen-year-old and our mind has been creating the feeling of a threatened "me" versus a threatening thought, such as: "You no longer need me in the same way you did as a baby." According to the other-voidness view, when we relax the grip of insecurity, we find awareness of reality. In other words, we know that our child is sixteen years old. Nevertheless, we do not wish to think about what this fact implies, and so we feel anxious. Naively believing that treating our child like a baby will create no problems, we are overprotective. Anxiety and naivety, then, obscure our awareness of reality.

Further beneath our tension lies the awareness that constitutes the deepest sphere of reality, namely the clear light mental activity that gives rise to experience. When we fully relax, we experience thoughts as merely waves on the ocean of the mind. Thus, thinking of our child as an independent person is no longer a threatening experience.

The self-voidness position explains that when we relax the grip of frightened naivety, we find underlying it mirror-like awareness. We have taken in the information of our child looking, acting, and speaking like a sixteen-year-old, but either have not paid attention or have chosen to ignore it. When we open our mind and our heart, we reach the underlying experience that was there all along—merely taking in information like a mirror or a microphone.

In short, naivety is not like producing and engaging with objects, taking in information, or knowing what things are. This disturbing emotion is not a fundamental feature of mental activity. It arises only when we overlay these basic activities with dualistic appearances and believe in them. Only when we conceive of a concrete "me" facing a concrete "object" do we become frightened of our experiences. Consequently, we naively shut ourselves off as if we could avoid reality. When we release our feeling of dualism, or at least our belief that it refers to what is real, we discover the mirror-like awareness of reality that was there all along as the structure of our experience.

Pride and Miserliness

Pride or arrogance is the feeling that we are better than others in all or just certain ways. For example, we are proud that we are wealthier, more clever, or better looking. It may be conventionally true that we have more money than someone else has. However, when we project and believe in the dualistic appearance of a seemingly solidly wealthy "me" and a seemingly solidly impoverished "you," we feel that this makes us a better person. Thus, we feel proud. An inverse form of pride is to feel humiliation at others being better than we are in all or in just some respects.

The dualistic appearance of ourselves as concretely superior or inferior to someone, or to others in general, is nonsense. No one exists in this fantasized way. We all share the same fundamental features of mind and heart that allow us to become a Buddha. When we realize this, we relax the grip of our disturbing emotion. What remains is the underlying mental activity, namely awareness of equalities. We were merely considering others and ourselves in terms of a shared feature, how much money we have. Only when we overlay such consideration with a dualistic appearance and concrete identities do we regard one side as inherently better and the other as inherently worse.

Miserliness is the unwillingness to share something with others. It derives from the dualistic appearance of a seemingly concrete "me" as inherently more worthy of possessing something than a seemingly concrete "you." A nervous feeling that sharing with this "you" would threaten the security of this "me" often accompanies belief in this deceptive appearance.

Sometimes, miserliness takes the inverse form of destructive self-denial. Here, we do not allow ourselves a fair portion of something. This is because we believe in the dualistic appearance that our mind creates of a seemingly concrete "me" as truly unworthy and of a seemingly concrete "you" as inherently more deserving.

Pride and miserliness are similar disturbing emotions. With both, we consider ourselves better or worse than others are. Deconstructing the dualistic appearances that fuel our miserliness enables us to relax our insecurity and tension. Again, we discover underlying awareness of equalities, and simultaneously consider others and ourselves in terms of possibly sharing something.

Longing Desire or Attachment

Longing desire is the obsession to possess something, while attachment is the nervous insistence not to let go once we possess it. Both are based on the dualistic appearance of (1) a seemingly concrete "me" who cannot live without some person or object and (2) a seemingly concrete "you" or object that could make me secure if I only had it or if I never let it go. An inverse form of this disturbing emotion is the obsession to be possessed by or to belong to someone or to some collective group and not to be abandoned once we belong.

We need to see through the deceptive appearance fueling this disturbing emotion. Denying our ability to cope on our own, we are exaggerating the qualities of someone or something. Fooled by this, we become infatuated. When we deconstruct the appearance by understanding that it does not refer to anything real, we relax the grip of our insecurity. Underlying our inflation of the person, the group, or the object into someone or something truly special, we find individualizing awareness. We merely specified a particular person, organization, or thing. Only when we overlay that specifying with a dualistic appearance and concrete identities do we experience ourselves as inherently deprived and the person, group, or object as inherently alluring.

Jealousy

Jealousy is the inability to bear someone else's achievement, for instance his or her success. We wish that we could achieve it instead. A variation occurs when someone receives something from someone, such as love or affection; we wish that we could receive it instead. This disturbing emotion derives from the dualistic appearance of (1) a seemingly concrete "me" who inherently deserves to achieve or receive something, but did not, and (2) a seemingly concrete "you" who inherently did not deserve to get it. Unconsciously, we feel that the world owes us something and it is unfair when others get it instead. An inverted form is to feel that we are inherently undeserving of what we have, while others innately deserve it instead.

Naivety about cause and effect usually accompanies jealousy. For example, we do not understand and even deny that the person who received the promotion or affection did anything to earn it. Moreover, we feel that we should get it without having to do anything to bring it about. Alternatively, we feel that we did do a lot but still did not get the reward. Our mind makes things appear to happen for no reason at all, or for only one reason: what we alone did.

When we deconstruct these deceptive appearances, we relax our feelings of injustice. Beneath our jealousy is merely awareness of what has been accomplished. This makes us aware of a goal to achieve. If we do not begrudge someone else for achieving or receiving it, we can perhaps learn how the person accomplished the feat. This enables us to see how to accomplish it ourselves. We only feel jealous because of overlaying this awareness with a dualistic appearance and concrete identities.

Anger

Anger is the generation of a rough state of mind toward someone or something, with the wish to rid ourselves of it or to do it harm. This disturbing emotion derives from the dualistic appearance of (1) a seemingly concrete "me" who cannot possibly endure this person, group, or object and (2) a seemingly concrete "you," group, or object, which if I could eliminate would make me secure. Just as longing desire fixates upon and exaggerates the good qualities of someone or something, anger focuses on and inflates the negative qualities.

An inverse form of anger occurs when, for example, someone acts terribly toward us but, overestimating our own bad qualities, we blame ourselves. Insecure and afraid of rejection if we say something about the incident, we repress the anger we might feel toward the person. We direct it at ourselves instead.

According to the other-voidness presentation, when we deconstruct the deceptive appearances fueling our anger, we relax the tension of our hostile rejection. We find simply mirror-like awareness, for instance that someone is acting in a certain way. The self-voidness position explains that we discover awareness of reality. We are simply differentiating between the way that someone is and is not behaving and seeing nonjudgmentally that one is appropriate and the other is not. Only when we overlay this fundamental mental activity with a dualistic appearance and inherent identities do we react with violent emotion toward what we find unacceptable.

Worry and Complaint

Worry and complaint are two additional disturbing syndromes that arise from projecting dualistic appearances onto deep awareness and mind's other innate qualities. Worry comes from viewing ourselves as inherently helpless and regarding a person or a situation as something out of our control. When we relax our insecurity and tension, we find merely individualizing awareness and concern about someone or something. Our calmer view allows us to evaluate the situation to see what can be done, if anything, and then simply to do it. As Shantideva said, "If a situation can be changed, why worry about it? Just change it. If we cannot do anything to change it, why worry? Worrying does nothing to help."

When we realize that underlying someone's neurotic worries over us are warm concern and individualizing awareness, we can defuse our hypersensitive reaction. Instead of viewing the person's behavior dualistically as a threat, we focus on awareness of individualities. Being the object of this type of awareness coming from someone cannot possibly rob us of our individuality. Moreover, recognizing the person's concern for us reinforces our patient understanding.

When we complain about having to do something or haughtily protest when someone asks us to do it, we are also caught in a dualistic web. A seemingly concrete "me" appears to be facing an inherently distasteful task that we do not want to do. When we relax the grip of this compelling feeling, we find accomplishing awareness focused on a task that needs doing. Also present is reality awareness focused on the issues of our ability to do it and of the propriety of our doing it. We also see that someone asking us to do something does not threaten our freedom. In this way, we just do what needs to be done, if there is no harm, or we decline if the task is inappropriate. We may use a similar technique to avoid overreacting when we hear someone else complaining about having to do something.

EXERCISE 19
Dissolving Disturbing Emotions into Underlying Deep Awareness

During the first phase of this exercise, we look at a photograph or simply think of someone toward whom we have felt or are currently feeling disturbing emotions. For each emotion, we may need to choose a different person. Acknowledging and regretting the pain that our imbalance may have caused the person, we resolve to try to overcome these problems. Recognizing the dualistic feeling behind each disturbing emotion as based on sheer fantasy, we try to deconstruct it. We do this by first relaxing completely. As we feel our tension easing, we try to feel the fantasy and its accompanying disturbing emotion releasing themselves, by using the image and feeling of the clenched fist of our mind opening. We then try to feel that our mind, emotions, and feelings are now clear. In this state, we try to recognize and rest in the corresponding form of underlying deep awareness.

Next, we look at a photo or think of someone who has felt or is currently feeling the same disturbing emotion toward us. Similarly deconstructing our overreaction, we try to rest again in the underlying form of awareness. We conclude by trying to feel compassion for this person, who does not relax and contact his or her deep awareness. Disturbing emotions are bringing the person much pain.

(1a) First, we consider an example of naivety about cause and effect. We may choose a small child, for instance, on whom we naively felt that our words or actions had no effect. We insensitively felt that fighting with our partner in front of him or her did not matter. Viewing the experience dualistically, we imagined a concrete "me" acting in a vacuum and the child as a concrete entity unaffected by his or her surroundings. Our insensitivity has brought the child much unhappiness, which we now regret.

Realizing that such ways of existing are impossible, we drop our naivety about the situation. Suppose we knew about the effects of our actions, but had felt them too painful to admit or to deal with. We now try to drop the tension behind our naive assumption that if we do not think about or acknowledge something, it will disappear. From the other-voidness point of view, we find awareness of reality. We see the conventional facts of the situation. In other words, we see the effects of our actions on the child. They were there all along. We either did not notice them or ignored or denied them if we did. From the viewpoint of the self-voidness presentation, we find mirror-like awareness taking in the information that is clearly there.

We focus for a minute on these two mutually supportive types of awareness: awareness of reality and mirror-like awareness. Such vision allows us to deal soberly and sensitively with the situation now. We need to take care, however, not to feel guilty by overinflating the importance of our actions. As explained in Chapter Six concerning not being afraid to react, we have contributed to the situation but have not been the sole source.

Now, we focus on someone who insensitively said something painful to us and was naively unaware that his or her words would be upsetting. For example, perhaps the person said something about a loved one we had recently lost. Deconstructing the hypersensitive feeling of a "poor me" who has been hurt by a "cruel you," we try to relax. We try to discover the underlying mirror-like awareness of reality. Our loved one is gone. Whether or not someone reminds us, nothing can change this fact. This helps us to accept reality, although no one can deny that it is sad. Realizing how terrible the person must feel when others overreact to his or her insensitive remarks, we try to feel compassion. We hope that the person will soon overcome his or her naivety.

(1b) Next, we repeat the procedure with an example of naivety about reality. We choose, for instance, someone who told us something about him- or herself that we have difficulty accepting, such as that he or she is getting older and now tires more easily. Until now, we have denied or ignored this fact or have not taken it seriously. We have been relating to a "you" who matched our dreams. Our insensitivity has caused the person frustration, which we now regret. Trying to release the tension of our naivety, we find mirror-like awareness of the person's reality. Taking in the information and accepting it as true enables us to treat the person with proper sensitivity and respect.

Then, we focus on someone who has naively refused to accept the truth about us, for instance that we are not romantically interested in him or her. Deconstructing our dualistic feeling of a seemingly concrete "me" frustrated by an inherently blind "you," we try to remain with mirror-like awareness of our actual feelings about the person. This helps us to stop overreacting by being defensive. Feeling compassion for the person living under this illusion gives us the balanced sensitivity to impress the truth without being cruel.

(2a) We next look at a picture or think of someone to whom we arrogantly feel superior in one way or another or have felt this way in the past. This may be someone from our personal life or perhaps someone of a different race whose picture we saw in a magazine. Our conceit has led to hatred and pain, which we deeply regret. We notice that we have compared the two of us and judged ourselves inherently superior and the other inherently inferior. When we try to relax the tension and insecurity that compel us to make the comparison, we find equalizing awareness. We are merely considering the two of us as human beings. This allows openness and balanced sensitivity toward the person.

Turning to someone who arrogantly looks down on us, we similarly deconstruct our oversensitive feeling of outrage and insult. We may be poorer than he or she is, but that does not make us an inferior being. Calmly focusing on deep awareness of our equality as human beings, we try to feel compassion toward the person whose prejudice produces so many problems.

(2b) Next, we focus on someone with whom we did not want to share something. Our insensitivity hurt the person, which we now regret. We try to relax our dualistic feeling of a "me" who would be deprived if this undeserving person were to share what I have. When we loosen our tension, we find equalizing awareness of the two of us as people who could partake of something. This view of equality enables us to accept the fact that the person would also enjoy having a share. We try to imagine nondualistically giving him or her some of what we have. A traditional technique to overcome reticence to share is to give a portion of something with our right hand to our left.

Choosing someone who was unwilling to share something with us, we similarly deconstruct our hypersensitive feelings of "poor deprived me" and "selfish you." Trying to focus on our equality as human beings, we see that missing a share does not make us inferior. We then try to direct compassion at the person whose selfishness causes others so much resentment.

(3) Following this, we look at a picture or think of someone toward whom we have or have had longing desire. We may choose a person from our life or perhaps a magazine photo of someone scantily dressed.

We may also work with someone toward whom we are or have been attached, for instance a close family member. Acknowledging the pain that we caused by insensitively treating the person as merely a sex object or as a fledgling we tried to keep in the nest, we feel regret. We then try to relax the tense, insecure feeling of being inherently incapable of living without the person. This leaves us with individualizing awareness. Rather than grabbing after or tightly gripping the person, we are merely focusing specifically on him or her. This dispassionate view allows us to respect the person's individuality and to be sensitive to his or her personal needs.

Turning to someone who longs after or clings to us, we try to relax our dualistic feeling of being chased or oppressed. In place of being obsessed with escaping, we see the person with awareness of his or her individuality. This allows us to find a compassionate solution beneficial to us both.

(4) Next, we focus on someone toward whom we feel jealous, either now or in the past. Consider, for example, the new boyfriend or girlfriend of our previous partner. It feels as though we inherently deserve our old partner back and the person inherently does not merit the honor of enjoying her or his company. We regret the pain that our jealousy has brought. When we relax the tension of our bitterness, we discover underlying it awareness of what has been accomplished. We see that the person has accomplished having our old girlfriend or boyfriend as his or her partner. Our emotional sobriety allows us now to see our old partner's strong and weak points more objectively, with mirror-like awareness. Appreciating what the person toward whom we felt jealous now has to deal with, we know how to relate sensitively.

Choosing someone who has been or is currently jealous of what we have achieved, we deconstruct any feelings of annoyance or guilt we might have. We might feel, for example, that we inherently deserve what we have gotten and that the person inherently does not deserve the same. Trying to relax, we become aware simply that we have accomplished what we have through cause and effect. This enables us to wish, compassionately, that this person could find the causes to achieve the same.

(5) We then focus our attention on someone toward whom we are or have been angry. We may even choose a political figure whose policies annoy us. Our anger causes terrible scenes that disturb everyone around us, which we now regret. Thinking of the person or seeing his or her picture makes us self-righteously feel like an oppressed "me"

facing the onslaughts of an inherently terrible person. When we try to relax the tense impulse to destroy what we dislike, we discover mirror-like awareness. We are merely taking in the information about how the person is acting. We also discover awareness of the reality of the situation: we are differentiating that the person is acting like this and not like that. This understanding provides the calmness to see that although the person may be acting horribly now, he or she can change. This permits us to respond more appropriately.

Turning to someone who is angry with us, we deconstruct any dualistic feelings of rejection or outrage, such as "How dare *you* accuse *me*." Trying to relax leaves us with mirror-like awareness of what we have done and reality awareness to see its propriety. If what we did was wrong, we try to imagine calmly apologizing. If we were right, we try to imagine not feeling threatened. In either case, we try to feel compassion for the person who is obviously miserable while being upset.

(6) Next, we look at a picture or think of someone we obsessively worry about now or have worried about in the past. Acknowledging the discomfort we cause him or her, we feel regret. Noticing our dualistic feeling of a helpless "me" facing a "you" who is out of my control, we try to deconstruct it. Relaxing our tension leaves us with individualizing awareness of the person and with warm concern. Calmer now, we try to imagine what we can do to help, if anything, and then we try to picture simply doing it.

Focusing on someone who constantly worries about us, we try to deconstruct our hypersensitive feeling of being smothered. Relaxing our tense paranoia, we find individualizing awareness of the person and concern about ourselves. Aware of the pain that the person's behavior is bringing us, we try to appreciate the suffering that he or she is experiencing too. With compassion, we then try to turn our concern to the person, with the wish that he or she be free of this suffering and the worry that is causing it.

(7) Lastly, we choose someone who asked or told us to do something that we did not wish to do. Insensitive to others, we exasperated everyone around us with our complaints. Regretting this now, we try to note the dualistic appearances that fuel this turmoil. Arrogant and outraged, we felt inherently too good to have to do this task or to be told what to do. The task seemed innately degrading, while the person asking us to do it seemed to be trying to rob us of our independence

and dignity. If the person later reminded us of the task, we became even more furious, thinking that he or she did not trust our intention or ability to do it.

We try to relax our belief in this paranoid vision. The more we relax, the more tension we release. Our accomplishing awareness has been focusing on what needs to be done, and our reality awareness has been dealing with the issues of our ability to do the task and of the appropriateness of our doing it. Calmer now, we imagine deciding what to do and, no matter what we choose, we try to feel compassion for the person who needs the task done.

Then, we turn our attention to someone who complained about something that we asked him or her to do. Deconstructing our overreaction of annoyance at a "you" defying a "me," we try to relax. Seeing what needs accomplishing, we try to imagine calmly evaluating whether the person can do it and whether doing it ourselves would be more appropriate or perhaps less of a bother. We try to feel compassion for the person who has become so upset in the face of this task.

Overcoming Loneliness and Resolving Conflicts

During the second phase of the exercise, we sit in a circle and focus on other members of our group. Since we may not feel any disturbing emotions toward these people, we can work with the feeling of loneliness. Even if we are not lonely now, almost everyone has sometime felt lonely.

We begin by remembering the feeling of loneliness and then looking at the people around the circle. When we are obsessed with feeling sorry for ourselves, we are caught in the dualistic appearance of ourselves as inherently alone and of these people as unattainably distant. We may naively close ourselves off from any contact. Trying to relax our tension allows us to reach our mirror-like awareness. With it, we try to take in information about the people. Moreover, with awareness of reality, we try to see that each of them, with appropriate effort on our part, could become a friend. This vision helps to dispel our fear.

Next, we try to notice how loneliness colors our experience of seeing these people. By making us feel either better or worse than they are, it creates a distance. Feeling perhaps that they are not good enough for us, we do not want to open ourselves and share our feelings or thoughts in friendship. Perhaps feeling the opposite—that we are not good enough for them—we fear rejection. Now, we try to relinquish our paranoid fantasies and to discover the equalizing awareness that lies behind them. We have been considering these people and ourselves in the same moment. Appreciating the connection that this automatically creates, we try to extend our natural warmth to them.

Until now, we might have hoped for someone special to come. Attached to the dream of an ideal friend, we might have longed for such a person to end our loneliness as we looked around the circle. Realizing that no one can meet such a high ideal helps us to drop our fantasy. This opens us to the experience of the moment, namely looking at each person in the circle with awareness of his or her individuality. Trying to do this now, we realize that everyone has both strong and weak points. When we accept that fact, we can begin to form realistic friendships.

We might have often envied others for having close friends. Further, before our session began, we might have noticed someone in our group who aroused our interest and hopes. We were jealous that he or she was joking with others. Trying to relax, we find ourselves left with accomplishing awareness. We now look at the people in the circle with this awareness that to form a friendship we also need to approach them and speak.

Some of our previous friendships may have failed. We might now be bitter and angrily blame others for having been cruel. Trying to relax the dualistic feeling of oppressor and victim leaves us with mirror-like awareness of what took place. Further, with awareness of reality, we see simply that our former friends acted unacceptably and not as we would have preferred. This does not mean that all friendships will inherently turn sour or that everyone will inevitably hurt us. Realizing this, we try to look at each person in the circle with openness and no preconceptions.

We may have worried that others will dislike us. Trying to relax our anxiety leaves us looking at each person as an individual, with concern about how he or she will react to us. Our wish is that the person be happy with us. Recognizing that this wish for someone to be happy is the wish of love, we try to strengthen that loving concern. Love opens the door to forming friendships.

We might have complained about loneliness or about having to join groups to meet people. Trying to relax our feeling sorry for ourselves, we find ourselves looking at each person in the circle merely with awareness of what we have done. To meet these people, we had to come here. Happy at the opportunity for friendship that we now have, we try to look at each person with appreciation and gratitude that he or she has also come.

Following a similar technique is helpful for conflict resolution, especially if both parties agree to try the same approach. We need to switch from closed-minded naivety about the other's position to mirror-like awareness of reality. Dropping our arrogance, we need to see each other as equal and each other's position as equally valid. Unattached to how we would like things ideally to be, we need to use individualizing awareness to evaluate the specifics of the situation. Not jealous if the other party were to get his or her way over certain points, we need to work out compromises with accomplishing awareness.

Most of all, we need to drop our anger. With mirror-like awareness of reality, we need to see our differences objectively. This enables us to resolve them nonjudgmentally. Instead of worrying about how the other party will react, we need to feel concern that he or she be happy with our proposals. Therefore, we need to make them reasonable. In addition, instead of complaining if the person objects to any points, we need to see what has to be done to accomplish our aim. If we have a conflict with someone in our group, we may sit privately with the person and use this technique to try to resolve it.

Dislodging Low Self-esteem

We may be clinging to the image of an ideal weight and hair color that is outdated and unrealistic. Relaxing our attachment to this ideal, we try to look with individualizing awareness at how we are at this stage of life. Further, we might envy the way that we looked and felt when we were younger. Letting go of our envy, we try to look at ourselves with accomplishing awareness. We gained our previous look and level of energy because of youth. Those times are gone. Now, we can only accomplish what is realistic for our age. We may be angry with ourselves for having gained so much weight. Realizing that this does not help, we try to relax our anger. With mirror-like awareness of reality, we see simply that we are old, not young, and fat, not thin. Seeing the facts enables us to deal with them more soberly and sensitively.

If we are overly worried about how we look, we try to relax and look at ourselves with the warm concern that underlies our tension. Accepting the situation specific to our age, we set ourselves a reasonable goal for losing weight. If we frequently complain about having to diet, we try soberly to see what we need to do to accomplish our goal. Then, we try simply to do it.

We repeat the exercise putting down the mirror and just working with our feelings about ourselves. Lastly, we work with our emotional responses to the series of photographs of ourselves from the past.

PART IV

Responding with Balanced Sensitivity

18   Adjusting Our Innate Mental Factors

Balanced sensitivity requires deconstructing the deceptive, dualistic appearances our mind creates and harnessing our underlying deep awareness and natural talents. We also need to work with other mental factors that structure our mental activity but do not form part of our Buddha-nature. The abhidharma literature provides a clear picture of the relevant factors.

Ten Mental Factors That Accompany Each Moment of Experience

All abhidharma systems accept five ever-functioning mental factors. These are urges, distinguishing, attention, contacting awareness, and feeling some level of happiness. Certain systems include five more factors by defining them in their broadest sense: interest, mindfulness, concentration, discrimination, and intention. We shall follow their lead.

(1) *Urges* cause our mind to go in the direction of a particular experience. In some systems, this factor corresponds to *karma*—the factor, based on previous behavior and habits, that brings us to experience what we do in life. Other systems correlate urges with motivation.

(2) *Distinguishing* is the mental factor that differentiates specific objects within a sense field from their background, and specific mental or emotional states from within an experience. This factor is usually

translated as "recognition." Recognition, however, is a misleading term. This mental factor neither compares what it differentiates with prior experience nor ascribes a name to it.

(3) *Attention* directs us to a specific object within a sense field or to a specific mental or emotional state within an experience. It causes us to focus on or to consider an object in a certain way. We may pay attention to something carefully or we may pay attention to it as valuable.

(4) *Contacting awareness* is the awareness that establishes pleasant, neutral, or unpleasant contact with specific objects or with specific mental or emotional states. These are the objects and states that we simultaneously distinguish and pay attention to as pleasant, neutral, or unpleasant.

(5) *Feeling* refers exclusively to feeling some level of happiness—in other words, happy, neutral, or unhappy. It is always in harmony with the tone of the contacting awareness that also accompanies the experience it characterizes.

(6) With *interest*, our mind does not wish to leave what it is holding. It is not the same as attachment, which inflates the good qualities of a mental object. Here, we differentiate interest from motivation. A motivation brings us only to the initial perception of an object or of a mental or emotional state. Once we perceive the object, it may hold our interest.

(7) *Mindfulness* is the mental activity of keeping hold of an object or of a mental or emotional state once attention focuses on it. The same term also means "to remember something" and "to be conscious of something." Here, remembering something does not refer to the mental act of storing an impression. Nor does it refer to the mental act that establishes the focus on an impression. It only implies maintaining attention on a mental object after establishing a focus.

(8) *Concentration* is the mental activity of remaining placed on an object or on a mental or emotional state. It is directly proportionate to our mindfulness of the object. Some texts describe mindfulness and concentration as the active and passive aspects of the same mental function.

(9) *Discrimination* adds certainty about what we distinguish. It also decides between alternatives. The frequent translation of this term as "wisdom" is misleading. We may be completely certain about something incorrect.

(10) *Intention* leads to doing something in response to what we discriminate.

To understand these ten, let us take an example from everyday life. Suppose we have a young daughter and we have put her to bed for the night. An urge causes us later to look in her room. When we do so, we distinguish a form on the bed from the shape and color of the bed itself. We then focus on the form with attention. Moreover, we pay attention to the form as the sight of our child and as a pleasant sight to behold. We contact this sight with pleasant awareness and, on that basis, experience seeing it with a feeling of happiness.

Because of interest, we do not wish to look away from the sight of our sleeping child. Therefore, mindfulness holds our attention on the sight and we remain fixed on it with concentration. Discrimination brings certainty that our daughter has thrown back her covers. We also discriminate between how they are and how they should be for her not to catch a chill. Our intention is to enter the room and tuck her in. All ten mental factors are intimately involved in the mechanism for being properly sensitive to our sleeping child.

The Spectrum These Innate Mental Factors Encompass

Each of these mental factors spans a complete spectrum. (1) Urges arise for constructive, neutral, or destructive actions, each of which may entail either doing something or avoiding doing it. We may have an urge to look in on our child during the night or an urge to ignore her. Depending on what we see, on the routines we have established, and on our psychological makeup, we may have the urge to scold her for still having the light on, the urge to tell her gently that it is time to go to sleep, or the urge not to say anything.

(2) We distinguish many things when we look into our daughter's room—for example, our daughter being uncovered or the toys strewn on the floor. Moreover, we distinguish in different degrees of fineness. Looking at the floor, we may distinguish just toys in general or a particular item among them.

(3) We pay varying degrees of attention to what we distinguish, from full attention to little or none. We may be very attentive of the covers, but pay little heed to the toys, although we see and distinguish them from the rug. Further, we pay attention to what we distinguish in a variety of ways, some accurate and some not. Attentive of the toys on the floor, we may consider them a permanent mess or just

temporary disorder. Also, we are attentive to various objects as pleasant, unpleasant, or neutral. We may pay attention to the sight of our sleeping daughter as something pleasant, the strewn toys as something unpleasant, and the rug as something neutral.

(4) Contacting awareness of a mental object spans the spectrum from pleasant through neutral to unpleasant and is in keeping with how we consider or pay attention to that object. We contact the sight of our sleeping daughter, which we consider pleasing, with pleasant awareness, the sight of the toys with unpleasant awareness, and the sight of the rug with neutral awareness.

(5) Our feelings toward an object also span a spectrum from happy through neutral to unhappy, and accord with the tone of our contacting awareness with it. We feel happy seeing the sight of our daughter, unhappy at the sight of the toys, and neutral when seeing the rug.

(6) Interest is from strong through weak to no interest at all. We may see our sleeping child with great interest, not wanting to look elsewhere. On the other hand, we may have no interest in continuing to look at the rug when we see it. Our eyes immediately shift to the bed.

(7) Mindfulness encompasses the entire spectrum of strength and quality of mental hold on an object, from overly tight and tense to strong and stable, through medium to weak and loose, and lastly to almost no hold at all. We may hold our attention tightly on the sight of our daughter so that our mind does not wander or become dull. On the other hand, we may hold it only loosely on the sight of the rug so that we quickly look away.

(8) Concentration ranges also from strong through weak to none at all. Our attention may remain fixed on our daughter and not on the rug.

(9) Discrimination is about a wide assortment of variables and spans the entire spectrum of certainty concerning what it discovers about its object. We may discriminate how the covers are arranged and that our daughter may catch a chill, although we may not be completely sure of this. We may also discriminate what needs to be done. Our discrimination may or may not be correct. Sometimes, we discriminate something completely incorrectly and are even certain of it, although it is wrong. We might swear that we see the cat sleeping on top of our daughter's covers, when in fact it is her crumpled sweater.

(10) Lastly, we have all sorts of intentions concerning what we perceive, some of which are helpful and others not. We may intend to pull the covers up snugly or to shoo away the imagined cat that is not there. Sometimes, we may intend to do nothing.

How These Factors Function During Moments of Insensitivity

To heighten our sensitivity if it is weak, we need to realize that these ten mental factors are always functioning, even when they appear not to be. Although they may be operating at the bottom end of their spectrum, none are ever missing unless we are in a deep meditation trance. To become more properly sensitive to others or to ourselves, we need merely to strengthen or to change the operating level of certain mental factors that are already present. Seeing this makes the task less daunting.

Consider the case of sitting across from a relative at the dinner table and being insensitive to the fact that he or she is upset. Let us analyze the situation in order to recognize the ten mental factors involved. During the meal, we look mostly at our plate, lost in thought about ourselves. Occasionally, however, the urge arises to look up. At such times, we see the sight of our relative's face with knitted brow and twisted mouth. We distinguish it from the wall behind. We pay minimal attention to it, however, so that we hardly notice the expression. In fact, we consider his or her expression to be unimportant and we find the sight of our relative's face a neutral experience. Our contacting awareness of the sight is similarly neutral and we feel neither happy nor sad.

The interest with which we see our relative's face is minimal. We are preoccupied with ourselves. Thus, we hold on to the sight of him or her with hardly any mindfulness. We are soon lost again in our own thoughts. Our concentration on seeing his or her face is extremely weak and so we quickly look back at our plate. We discriminate something about our relative—that nothing is wrong—but this is incorrect. Our intention is to ignore him or her and watch television as soon as we finish eating.

The major source of our insensitive behavior here is self-preoccupation. To overcome that, we need discrimination of voidness and compassion for our relative. Deconstruction techniques help us to develop the two. Equipped with this pair of indispensable factors, we find that our urges, attention, interest, mindfulness, concentration, further discriminations, and intentions automatically change. We naturally become a more sensitive person, both noticing and responding kindly to whatever we experience.

EXERCISE 20
Adjusting Our Innate Mental Factors

The first phase of this exercise entails recognizing the ten innate mental factors and realizing that we can adjust them. We need to be careful, however, not to conceive of this adjustment process as done by a boss in our head, turning the dials on a complex control panel. Any alterations that occur are the result of motivation, urge, and willpower—mental factors that also accompany our experience. Moreover, although we shall work with each of the ten factors individually, we need to remember that all ten function simultaneously and interweave inextricably with one another.

As an aid for this phase of the exercise, we may place a sweater or another item of clothing on the floor before us if we are practicing alone or in a small group. If the group is large, we may hang the sweater on something high enough in front of the room so that everyone has an unobstructed view of it.

(1) We begin by sitting quietly and trying to observe what we experience. An urge may arise to look at the sweater, or to the side, or to scratch our head. As a result, we may either act it out or restrain ourselves. Although most urges arise unconsciously, we can also purposely generate an urge to do something through a conscious motivation. To practice doing this, we imagine being cold. Because of our concern to get warm, we decide to look for something to put on. This causes an urge to arise to look around the room for a sweater and we now do so. We confirm that we can similarly generate an urge to look at how someone is doing when we are motivated by concern.

(2) Next, we examine the mental factor of distinguishing. Looking around the room in which we are sitting, we naturally distinguish many things about what we see. Without thinking to do so, we automatically distinguish, for example, a chair from the wall, the leg of the chair from its other parts, and a scratch on the leg from the rest of its surface.

We can also direct what we distinguish, including the expression on someone's face. This depends on our interest. To practice distinguishing, we look at the sweater and purposely try to distinguish the whole garment from the floor and the neck from the sleeves, with interest to determine whether or not it has a v-neck.

(3) Attention is also a variable affecting our experience. We look again around the room and try to notice that certain things automatically catch our attention, while others do not. When motivated, we can also choose to pay more attention to something when we see it, for instance the expression on someone's face. We practice increasing our attention by turning to the sweater and deciding to look closely for any cat hairs on it, because we are allergic. We then try to give our full, painstaking attention to the sweater as we look at it carefully.

Another aspect of attention is *how* we pay attention to what we sense—how we regard or consider it. This is intimately connected with the type of awareness we have of (4) mental contact with the object and (5) the level of happiness or unhappiness we feel at that contact. For example, when we pay attention to an item as something we like, such as an attractive garment on a rack, we have pleasant awareness of contact with it and experience happiness. On the other hand, when we pay attention to an object as something we do not care for, such as a fly buzzing loudly, we experience unpleasant contacting awareness of it and are unhappy. We look again around the room and try to notice that we naturally pay attention to what we like, for instance a certain picture, quite differently from what we dislike, such as the scratch on the leg of the chair.

We can also consciously pay attention to things in a certain way, when we have a reason to do so. For instance, if we are short of money, we can choose to pay more attention than usual to the prices on the menu in a restaurant. Contacting awareness of an inexpensive but delicious item is pleasant and delights us. The opposite occurs when we see something we like but cannot afford. Similarly, we can choose to look at the expression on someone's face as something important, when we are concerned. If we see that the person is happy, we have pleasant awareness of contact with the sight, and feel happy ourselves. If we see that he or she is upset, we have unpleasant contact and are sad. Suppose, however, that we do not consider the person's mood important. Even if we notice his or her expression, our awareness of the contact is neutral. We feel neither happy nor sad.

To see the relationship between these mental factors, we try consciously looking at the sweater as our favorite item of clothing that a loved one has knitted. In doing so, we have pleasant awareness of contact with its sight and experience a feeling of happiness. We then try paying attention to it as a nuisance that leaves fuzz on our shirt. Our contacting awareness is unpleasant and seeing the sweater makes us unhappy.

(6) The next mental factor is interest, which strongly affects (7) mindfulness and (8) concentration. Certain things naturally interest us when we see them, for example a sports event on the television. When we watch it, our attention effortlessly holds on to the contents with mindfulness and remains fixed with concentration. We now look around the room and try to note that some things we see naturally interest us more than others do.

We can also affect our interest in continuing to look at or to listen to something. One way is through remembering the necessity to do so, such as when seeing the help wanted section in the newspaper when we are out of work. Another way is to remind ourselves of the good points of something, for instance of an award-winning movie when the opening scene bores us. When we change the way in which we regard an object or person, we decide to take more interest.

We can do this with respect to increasing our interest, mindfulness, and concentration on someone's mood. When we reaffirm our loving concern for the person, we regard his or her mood as something important. Consciously deciding to take more interest in it, we naturally look at the person's expression with increased mindfulness and concentration. We practice now by trying to imagine that sweaters suddenly become the height of fashion. All our friends are wearing them. When we see the sweater, we now look at it with new interest. Our attention naturally holds on to the sight and remains fixed.

(9) The next mental factor is discrimination. We naturally discriminate between various possibilities concerning whatever we encounter. For example, when we look in the refrigerator, we discriminate and choose what we want to eat. Looking around the room once more, we try to note that we automatically discriminate between what is neatly arranged and what is haphazard. If we see certain items strewn around, we further discriminate between tidying them and leaving them alone.

When motivated, we can also consciously decide to discriminate something about an object or person. Before going to sleep, if we need to wake up early, we may decide to check the alarm clock to determine whether we have set it. We can similarly decide, when concerned, to look at someone's expression with discrimination to determine whether the person is happy or upset and whether we need to say comforting words. We practice discrimination by imagining that we want to buy a sweater and by deciding to check the one before us to see if it might fit and whether we can afford it. We then try to look at it from that point of view.

(10) Lastly, we examine the mental factor of intention. We naturally accompany our perception of things with various intentions. We discriminate that something is boiling over on the stove and, without having to think about it, we naturally intend to turn down the heat. We now look once more around the room and try to observe the intentions that automatically arise. Depending on what we discriminate and on necessity and interest, we may intend to open the window or to buy some flowers.

We can also consciously generate an intention to do something, such as to go shopping for food today when we see that the refrigerator is empty. Similarly, when we discriminate that someone is upset, we can generate an intention to be more sensitive toward the person and to give him or her emotional support. We now consciously try to generate an intention by discriminating that the sweater fits us and that we can afford it, and then by looking at it with the intention to buy it.

Focusing These Factors on Others and on Ourselves

During the second part of the first phase of this exercise, we practice adjusting the ten mental factors that accompany our perception of people. For this, we work with photos first of someone we like, then of a stranger, and lastly of someone we dislike. We go through the entire sequence of steps with each person before proceeding to the next. Since mental images are usually not very vivid, merely imagining someone is not conducive for this practice. As we shall be focusing on the person's facial expression and body language, we need to choose a candid snapshot, not a posed portrait with a fixed smile. Moreover, we need to imagine that the photo is a live scene that we are encountering now. Using a video is best.

First, we consciously generate a motivated urge to look at the person. For example, we feel concern about the one we like, or we need to speak to the stranger or to the person we dislike. Then, we try to distinguish various aspects of how the person looks and what he or she is doing. For example, the person may be tired or busy. Trying to pay attention to these points as meaningful for knowing how to approach the person, we experience pleasant contacting awareness and feel happy to see him or her.

Reaffirming our concern or the necessity to relate to the person, we try to generate the interest to understand what he or she is feeling. Naturally, our mindfulness and concentration increase. With discrimination, we try to decide what mood the person is in and whether or not this is a good time to talk. Then, we consciously set the intention to approach or to delay the meeting accordingly. To help us maintain the sequence, our group facilitator or we ourselves may repeat the ten key phrases: "motivated urge," "distinguishing," "attention," "contacting awareness," "feeling," "interest," "mindfulness," "concentration," "discrimination," and "intention."

During the second phase of the exercise, we sit in a circle with a group and repeat the procedure two or three times, by using the ten key phrases and focusing each time on a different person for the entire sequence. We try to adjust our ten mental factors so that we can approach and relate to the person appropriately, with balanced sensitivity.

During the third phase, we focus on ourselves. First we look in the mirror. Normally, we use these factors to shave or to put on lipstick. Now, we try to apply them to seeing whether we look sick or haggard, for example, and, if we do, to setting an intention to do something about it, such as to take a rest. We use the ten phrases as before. We must be careful, however, not to view what we see dualistically, as if the person we look at were alien from the one who is doing the looking.

Putting down the mirror, we try next to adjust our ten mental factors so that we regard ourselves with balanced sensitivity throughout the day. We begin by trying to generate the urge to examine ourselves. We do this by reminding ourselves that if we are not in touch with our feelings, we may unconsciously cause others and ourselves problems today. Trying to distinguish our emotional state and level of happiness, we then try to pay close attention to them as important. In doing this, we try to avoid inflating our feelings into something so earth-shattering that we feel compelled to announce them narcissistically to everyone—as if others were interested or cared what we felt. We also try to avoid exaggerating them into something so overwhelming that we compulsively complain. Since we have pleasant awareness of contact with our feelings, we naturally experience happiness at bringing them to conscious awareness.

We may uncover deeply rooted loneliness, sadness, or insecurity. Nevertheless, if we consider our feelings relevant to our quality of life and as something we can change, we are happy, not frightened, to discover them. With such an attitude, we naturally take keen interest and hold our attention mindfully on our feelings with firm concentration. We try to discriminate between one feeling and another, and between detrimental and constructive ones. We then set our intention on trying to do something to improve our mood.

As a final step, we look at a photo or think of first someone we like, then a stranger, and lastly someone we dislike. We try to apply the ten mental factors to our feelings about each. We then do the same regarding the series of self-portraits from different periods in our life, using the ten key phrases.

The point of this practice with our feelings and emotions is not to become more self-conscious, but more self-aware. Self-consciousness, with which we view ourselves with either low or excessively high self-esteem, disables us from acting naturally. We make ourselves and others feel uncomfortable. With self-awareness, however, or self-understanding, we avoid compulsively saying or doing foolish things that we later regret.

Gaining a Balanced View of Others and of Ourselves

The classical Mahayana techniques for gaining equanimity suggest an additional area in which adjusting the ten factors is helpful. Sometimes, because of hatred or anger, we lose sight of someone's positive qualities. When we are infatuated with the person, we do the same regarding his or her weak points. In each case, our naivety and insensitivity cause an unhealthy relationship. Adjusting our mental factors returns us to reality and brings emotional balance.

First, we imagine or look at a photo of someone toward whom we normally have only negative feelings. Reminding ourselves of the inner turmoil our hypersensitive attitude brings and the emotional blocks in other relationships that it causes, we try to motivate ourselves to overcome these feelings. With this motivation, we generate a conscious urge to focus on the person's good points. Following this urge, we try to distinguish these points and to pay close attention to them as valid and important. If our motivation is sincere, we naturally experience pleasant contact with this knowledge and feel happy discovering it.

Delight with this experience helps us to develop the interest to re-solve our problems with the person. This leads us to focus on him or her with mindfulness and concentration. We try to discriminate a more balanced way of interacting. Lastly, we set our intentions on carrying out this approach in our encounters. If the person we have chosen has passed away, we try to develop the intention to remind ourselves of his or her positive qualities whenever negative feelings arise.

We repeat the process, choosing someone with whom we are in-fatuated. We try to motivate ourselves to discover and acknowledge the person's negative points so that we may stop being insensitive to our needs and behaving self-destructively. For example, we may not take care of our other affairs because we want to spend as much time with the person as possible. Contacting awareness with the person's negative aspects is naturally unpleasant and may make us temporarily feel sad. We need not worry when that happens. Sobering the rela-tionship does not mean a loss in warmth, love, or concern. In fact, balance enhances these aspects. Adjusting the rest of our mental fac-tors, we then try to set our intentions on relating more realistically.

As a final step, we work with the ten mental factors to balance our feelings about ourselves. To deal with present feelings, we focus di-rectly on them, without using a mirror. To resolve our feelings about the past, we turn to the series of photos of ourselves. Looking at each of them in turn, we work with self-hatred by distinguishing our good points then. We consciously decide to bear them in mind when we feel negative toward ourselves as we were at those times. To sober our conceit, we do the same with our weaker aspects.

19 Unblocking Our Feelings

Differentiating Various Aspects of Feelings

Adjusting the ten mental factors is an effective means for increasing attentiveness to problems and for enhancing the intention to respond. Several factors, however, may still hamper this response. One of the more troublesome is not feeling anything. Here, we shall not limit the term "feeling" to its definition as one of the ten innate factors, but use it also to mean emotions.

Often we experience what seems to be a block in our feelings. We speak of being "out of touch" with our feelings—in other words, alienated from them. We say we feel nothing. Sometimes, we are so confused that we do not even know what we feel. This is because our feelings are so complex that they can be bewildering. We can dispel our confusion about the feelings we experience by seeing their component elements. Two of the most relevant components when trying to gain balanced sensitivity are feeling some level of happiness or sadness and feeling some level of sympathy. Let us examine each in turn and then the relation between the two.

Feeling Some Level of Happiness or Sadness

Though we may not have sympathy for someone, we always feel something on the spectrum between total happiness and complete sadness. This is because feeling some level of happiness or sadness is an integral part of how we experience each moment of life. Therefore, when we say we feel nothing when we encounter somebody, our impression is inaccurate. If we examine ourselves carefully, we discover that we are actually feeling a low level of either happiness or dissatisfaction. Rarely are our feelings exactly in the middle so that they are neither one nor the other. Moreover, feelings in the low intensity range on either side of neutral are not bland. Nor do they suggest that we care little about anything because nothing impassions us. Such feelings are simply another portion of the happiness/sadness spectrum, no more and no less.

We can appreciate this point by considering our feelings while looking at a wall. If we lack interest and want to look away, we are dissatisfied. This means that we are experiencing low-level unhappiness. If we keep our gaze on the wall, even out of laziness or boredom, we are content with what we see. Thus, we are experiencing low-level happiness. We consider the sight soothing or neutral.

We need to keep in mind the definitions of happiness and unhappiness and not confuse the mental factor of feeling with feeling as a physical sensation. Happiness is a pleasant feeling that we wish to continue experiencing and unhappiness is an unpleasant feeling that we wish to end. A physical feeling, on the other hand, is a sensation perceived through the faculty of touch. Under novocaine, for example, we do not experience a physical sensation when the dentist drills our tooth. Nevertheless, we may still feel unhappy at the experience.

Understanding this difference, we discover that when we see the expression on someone's face, we do feel something. This occurs whether or not we have sufficient interest and attention to notice if the person is upset. We know that we feel something because either we continue to look at the person or we avert our eyes. In other words, either we are comfortable at seeing him or her or we are ill at ease.

Ridding Ourselves of Upsetting Feelings That Block Sensitivity

Any feeling on the spectrum of happiness/sadness can be of two types—upsetting or not upsetting. The difference between the two depends on whether we mix the feeling with confusion. According to Gelug-style analysis, when we are confused about our feelings we inflate them into what seem like solid entities existing on their own. They seem as if they had a thick line around them like something in a coloring book. We then color them in with a seemingly concrete identity that our confusion projects. Believing our feelings to have these imaginary "true identities," we regard them with attachment or fear.

For example, being happy may give us a greater capacity to be helpful to people in pain. Yet, if confusion makes our own happiness appear as the most wonderful and important thing in the world, we become attached and possessive when experiencing it. We do not want to meet or deal with anyone having problems, because it will ruin our good mood. Happiness experienced in this inflated way is an upsetting experience, despite it being pleasurable and even exhilarating. Because we are worried about being robbed of our pleasure, this type of happiness renders us insensitive to others and to ourselves. We often notice this syndrome in people who are under the influence of recreational drugs. Furthermore, if we do not have this seemingly wonderful, yet elusive happiness, we become fixated on attaining it. This also causes us to act insensitively toward others, for instance by being obsessed with our orgasm when having sex.

When we inflate sadness, our mind makes it appear monstrous and frightening. It seems capable of swallowing us in a pit of quicksand. Because of this, we want to avoid unpleasant situations so as not to become depressed. Consequently, we do not want to hear about others' troubles or to visit them when they are sick.

When we inflate neutral or low-intensity feelings, our mind makes them appear to be an unfulfilling "nothing." If we are not impassioned about an issue or a person, it feels as though we are not real. Thus, if we are hyperemotional, we may find neutral feelings upsetting. Trying to avoid them, we go to extremes and overreact to what people say. For example, we feel outraged at any injustice they suffer or we break down and cry. Our self-indulgent display of emotion makes others feel threatened, embarrassed, or uncomfortable to speak to us about their problems. Instead of receiving comfort, they have to calm us down.

Balanced sensitivity requires happy, sad, and neutral feelings, but only those that are not upsetting. To have such feelings, we need to divest them of inflation. We can do this by seeing that our fantasies about how they exist do not refer to anything real. The happiness of sharing life with a partner never matches what someone in a fairy tale experiences who lives "happily ever after" with a prince or a princess. The sadness of losing a loved one may last many years, but it never signals the end of our life. Similarly, neutral or low-level feelings do not exist as an empty nothing, incapable of making us feel alive. We are alive no matter what level of happiness, sadness, or between that we feel.

When we burst the balloons of fantasy about our feelings, we do not deprive ourselves of feelings altogether. We do not become completely insensitive to others or to ourselves. Non-upsetting feelings are not equivalent to a total lack of feelings. We still feel pleasure when having sex. Enjoying it for what it is, while it lasts, we do not whine over its loss once it is over. Similarly, when we hear of someone's misfortune, we still feel sad. Our sadness, however, does not upset us to the core. We also do not feel bored when experiencing neutral feelings. We are comfortable with them or with any level of happiness or sadness that we feel.

Overcoming Alienation from Feelings

Sometimes, we may find feelings so difficult to handle that we block them. Occasionally, doing this may be helpful. For example, when we have a serious accident or a loved one suddenly dies, we automatically go into shock as a survival mechanism. Our feelings are too intense and may overload us. At other times, we block our feelings for neurotic reasons. Our confusion makes feelings seem dangerous and so we consider them inherently upsetting for us. This causes us to be stiff and inwardly frightened.

The Kagyü approach to overcoming this problem is to see that our mind normally tears in half our experiences of levels of happiness. It makes them deceptively appear as two opposing elements, "me" and "them," that is, the feelings appear as "other." Conceiving of feelings as existing like that alienates us from them. It blocks us from responding to others and to ourselves with sensitive spontaneity. We may think, for example, that we will not allow ourselves to feel happy because we do not deserve it. In addition, we may not allow ourselves to feel sad because we are afraid we might lose control. Further, we may not allow ourselves to feel neutral because then we are not really responding to someone. Consequently, we force ourselves and fake feeling happy or sad at someone's news, which does not fool anyone.

We act as if feelings of happiness or sadness were somewhere menacingly or alluringly "out there." It then seems as if we were sitting safely at home with the choice of whether to go out and feel them. This is absurd. We need to experience whatever feelings naturally arise, without making something monumental of them or of ourselves experiencing them.

Serenity and Equanimity as the Container for Balanced Feelings

According to the Sarvastivada and Mahayana traditions of abhidharma, a mental factor of serenity (*upeksha*) accompanies all constructive states of mind. The Teravada tradition similarly presents equanimity (*upekka*). Balanced sensitivity requires both factors. Neither of them suggests an insensitive lack of feelings or response.

Serenity is a mental state free from flightiness or dullness. With flightiness of mind, our attention flies off to appealing objects or to compelling thoughts. For example, although someone may be speaking to us, our focus strays to the television or to self-centered thoughts. With dullness, our mind is unclear. We listen, but do not really hear what the person is saying.

To be properly sensitive, we need to rid ourselves of these two major hindrances, flightiness and dullness. Being serene is not equivalent to being spaced-out and not feeling anything. With serenity, we are focused, alert, and do not fall to an extreme. We are not so intense and nervous that we make the other person uneasy. Nor are we so calm and relaxed that we give the impression that we do not care about anything.

Furthermore, a serene state of mind is a happy mind. Neutral feelings that are neither happy nor sad accompany only the serenity experienced as part of a deep meditation trance. The happiness felt in non-trance serenity, however, has a special quality. It resembles a feeling of freshness. If our mind is restless or sluggish, we are not using its potentials. We feel unfulfilled. When we are free of these disabilities, our mind is fresh and uplifted like after a summer shower. We naturally wish to maintain such a feeling and thus, by definition, we are happy. Equanimity is a state of mind free from attraction, repulsion, and indifference. Suppose we are sitting next to someone on an airplane and the person starts to tell us his or her life history. If we feel sexually attracted, we are so preoccupied that we do not even hear what the person says. If we find our fellow passenger repulsive, we may interrupt and say something rude. On the other hand, if we are indifferent, we ignore the person and do not look up from our magazine. In all three cases, we are insensitive to this man or woman as a person. We feel uncomfortable in his or her presence and are unhappy.

Having equanimity is not equivalent to feeling nothing. Nor is it the same as polite resignation. We do not simply tolerate the person's words while considering them rubbish and inwardly wishing for the plane to land. If we have time, we pay attention with openness and interest. Our fellow passenger is a human being, like us, and could become a close friend. As we wish the encounter to continue, we experience it with happiness. If we are truly busy, equanimity allows us to tell that to the person, without losing our calm. We would love to listen, but unfortunately we have something important to finish before we land.

The happiness that comes with equanimity is a relaxed and mellow feeling of relief. We feel relief because we neither crave nor are frightened of anything. We are not pushing ourselves on anyone, nor are we so rushed that we have no time. This state of mind provides a protected space in which we are comfortable about responding warmly to others and to ourselves. Tantra practice acknowledges the need for a protected space by including the visualization of one before the practitioner attempts self-transformation. Here, a feeling of emotional ease acts as a safe container for transforming ourselves into someone with balanced feelings.

Components of Sympathy

Balanced sensitivity not only requires serenity, equanimity, and feeling a level of happiness or sadness that is not upsetting, but also requires sympathy. Sympathy is a complex of several emotions and attitudes, each of which spans a spectrum. The three major ones are empathy, compassion, and willingness to become involved. As with the happiness/sadness spectrum, some element of each factor accompanies our encounter with anyone.

The first component of sympathy is a degree of empathy. It ranges from empathizing fully with someone's situation to not empathizing at all. The variables that affect this component are the willingness and the ability to understand someone's situation by imagining ourselves in the same predicament. Suppose a friend suffers from cancer. We may be willing to try to appreciate his or her pain and be either able or unable to imagine it. Alternatively, for various reasons, such as lack of interest or fear, we may be unwilling to imagine the pain. This may happen whether or not we can conceive of it.

The second component of sympathy is some point on the spectrum between compassion, indifference, and malevolence. We might wish that someone be free of torment, not care whether he or she suffers, or wish that the person experience more pain. For example, even if we cannot imagine the physical and mental torture of terminal cancer, we may still wish our friend to be cured. On the other hand, we may know very well how much cancer hurts, but either not care about a malevolent dictator suffering from it or feel that such a person deserves the pain.

The third component is some element from the spectrum that runs from wishing to become involved to feeling antipathy toward any involvement. The variable that determines this factor is willingness to do something about someone's predicament. We may empathize with our friend, be concerned about his or her comfort, and wish him or her not to suffer pain. Yet, we may be unwilling to visit because of fear of the feelings that might arise. Clearly, this is different from being unable to visit because of having to go out of town on business.

Feeling No Sympathy

When we say we do not feel anything, meaning we feel no sympathy for someone, we must analyze carefully which components of sympathy are deficient. From this, we can know which steps to take for remedying the situation. For example, if our lack of sympathy for our friend with cancer is due to being unwilling to empathize, we need to heighten the factor of interest that accompanies our meeting. We can do this by thinking how everyone is interrelated in our complex world. As Shantideva pointed out, how would it do for our hand to refuse to take interest in the welfare of our foot? Similarly, how would it do for us to refuse to take interest in others who are part of our circle of friends or community?

On the other hand, if we feel nothing because our interest in our friend's problem is purely intellectual, we need to think how he or she is a human being like ourselves. Just as when we are in pain, it hurts, the same is true with our friend. As Shantideva also once said, pain needs to be removed not because it is my pain or yours, but simply because it hurts. Thinking like this helps us to take his or her situation seriously.

Suppose we take sincere interest in our friend's problem but cannot empathize because we are unable to relate to what he or she is feeling. We may recall something similar that we have experienced, like a severe stomachache. Although the pain of a stomachache does not approach that of cancer, still it can serve as an example to help us understand our friend's situation.

Perhaps we do take interest and do appreciate our friend's torment. In other words, we can fully empathize. Yet, because we are presently angry with him or her, we feel no compassion. We do not care whether our friend suffers from cancer or we think that he or she deserves the pain. To overcome our insensitivity, we can imagine ourselves in the same predicament. No matter how many cruel things we might have said or done in our life, we would intensely wish our agony to end. Our friend feels the same. Unless we were a masochist, we would not ignore our misery or refuse ourselves a reasonable amount of painkillers because we felt that we deserved to suffer. Similarly, why should we be indifferent to our friend's situation or think that he or she should be tortured with pain? We are all human beings with the same wish for happiness and aversion for suffering.

We may understand our friend's intense discomfort and feel the compassionate wish that it may quickly end. Yet, we might lack sufficient sympathy to visit in the hospital. If our reason for staying away is that we are too busy, we can think about how we would not appreciate someone making the same excuse to us. We must reevaluate the priorities for our time in human rather than financial terms. Moreover, if we do visit, we need to remind ourselves of these priorities so that we avoid looking constantly at our watch.

If we shun the hospital because of fear of emotion overwhelming us, we can apply deconstruction techniques to overcome the self-preoccupation causing our fear. We may try to see through the dualistic appearance our mind creates of a frightened, oversensitive "me" meeting an emotionally unbearable "you." We may also try to focus on the absence of any real referent to our fantasy when we inflate the visit into an ordeal that we will be unable to handle or endure. Nothing exists in this impossible manner.

Overcoming Fear of Unhappiness When Feeling Sympathy

When someone is suffering, we need to feel both sympathy and a level of sadness that is not upsetting. Fear of becoming unhappy, however, may block one or more of the components of sympathy: empathy, compassion, or willingness to become involved. Overcoming this fear is essential for a balanced and sensitive response.

Tibetan masters explain the etymology of *karuna*, the Sanskrit word for compassion, as connoting that which destroys happiness. When we see someone suffering and feel compassion, we naturally also feel sad. When we mix our compassion with confusion about reality, however, we experience a sadness that upsets us completely. For example, thinking that life cannot continue after a loved one with terminal cancer passes away, we may become totally depressed when we think of the person. It seems safer to feel nothing. Being afraid of an upsetting feeling of unhappiness is understandable. On the other hand, an uninflated feeling of sadness that rests on a stable foundation of serene equanimity is not upsetting. It offers nothing to fear.

When we rid ourselves of flightiness, dullness, attraction, repulsion, indifference, and confusion about reality, we achieve a stable peace of mind. Its hallmark is a deep, mature, and quiet feeling of joy. Ironically, we find that if we previously had emotional blocks that prevented us from crying, we now cry more easily. Yet, even when we feel sad about our own or others' suffering and are spontaneously moved to tears, we remain internally composed on an emotional level. We are not crying because of feeling hopeless, lost, or overwhelmed at the injustices of the world. We have no feelings of self-pity or outrage. Our basic happiness remains unchallenged and quickly returns. Although the sadness of compassionate sympathy briefly overrides our happiness, we are not afraid to experience it. Sadness is merely a wave that naturally arises on the ocean of the mind.

The Relation between Love and Happiness

Love is the wish for someone to be happy. Such a wish naturally follows from compassionate sympathy. Though we feel sad at someone's pain and sorrow, feeling morose is difficult while actively wishing the person to be happy. When we stop thinking about ourselves and focus instead on someone's happiness, our heart naturally warms. This automatically brings us a quiet feeling of joy. Thus, when love is selfless and sincere, a gentle happiness accompanies it that is not upsetting. Just as a parent suffering from a headache forgets the pain while comforting his or her sick child, similarly the sadness we feel at someone's misfortune disappears while we radiate thoughts of love.

Training to Respond to Problems with Non-upsetting Feelings

Having balanced sensitivity to someone's problems requires listening with sympathy and sadness and then responding warmly by trying to comfort and cheer the person. The traditional Mahayana technique for training to do this with non-upsetting feelings is *tonglen* (taking and giving). As an advanced practice, it requires emotional stability, strength, and courage, gained, for example, through training with the previous twenty exercises. We take on others' suffering and give them our happiness. With a feeling of compassion, we imagine others' pain, sorrow, sickness, or injury as a black light that leaves them, freeing them from it. This light then enters us as we breathe in; we experience the suffering that it represents; and the light subsequently dissolves at our heart. We then generate a loving wish for them to be happy. As we exhale, we imagine this happiness leaving our heart as white light. This light fills them completely with health, well-being, and soothing joy.

Several points are crucial when attempting this practice. First, we need not only compassion, but also the other two components of sympathy: empathy and willingness to become involved. Second, we need to feel appropriate levels of sadness and happiness. Doing this requires not having fear of these feelings. We lose any fear we might have when we experience sadness and happiness nondualistically, based on serenity and equanimity. Feelings experienced in this way are not upsetting.

Furthermore, we must be careful not to mix our practice with the dualistic feeling that we are a saint or a martyr taking on the sufferings of some pitiful wretch. We must also be cautious not to inflate the others' suffering into a solid monster that we now hold inside so that it overwhelms us. Although feeling the person's pain is important, otherwise we may not take it seriously, nevertheless we must let it go. One technique is to imagine the pain passing through us and ending. Another is to see it as a wave that does not disturb the depths of the mind. Understanding and wisdom must always accompany the practice of loving compassion.

Even in the saddest moments, such as at a funeral, this practice enables us to smile warmly, with sympathetic and understanding eyes, and to comfort other mourners with love. We feel sad at the loss and may even cry. Yet, our main concern is wishing happiness and wellbeing to both the deceased and those left behind. Our smile is not flippant, distasteful, nor disrespectful. Nor is it false. We do not force it before we have sufficiently mourned, nor do we scold ourselves for being silly and crying. Nevertheless, our tears quickly pass. We understand death, impermanence, and cause and effect. Anyone born must some day depart. With the wish that the other mourners might also understand this, we accept and imagine relieving their suffering and bringing them comfort.

EXERCISE 21

Accepting Suffering and Giving Happiness

During the first phase of this exercise, we look at a photo of a loved one or mentally picture the person. First, we try to settle into a state of serenity, free of flightiness and dullness. To quiet our mind of tension, worry, or speediness, we may use the technique of letting go or the image of writing on water. To uplift our energy if we are depressed or dull, we may imagine that we have just emerged from a refreshing shower. We then turn our attention to the person, without probing or intruding with insistent intensity, but also without feeling removed or distant. The more relaxed and fresher we are, the looser our intensity and the more sincere our concern.

Next, we try to compose ourselves further, with equanimity. We think how our loved one is a human being and, like us, does not like to be clung to, rejected, or ignored. The more relaxed and alert we are, the easier it becomes not to want anything from the person and not to feel repulsed or indifferent. Furthermore, when in need, the person does not appreciate someone who is overprotective, frightened, or too busy to spare any time. Releasing those attitudes as well—with the breath or the image of writing on water—we try simply to be open and attentive.

We now recall a problem our loved one may be facing and the pain and sorrow he or she might be experiencing. To develop full sympathy, we need to generate empathy, compassion, and the willingness to become involved. First, we think how the person and we are interrelated, like our hand and our foot. Ignoring his or her pain would be shortsighted. Then, we consider that this pain needs to be removed, not because it is our loved one's pain, but simply because it hurts. With these two thoughts, we develop the interest to try to empathize. Next, if we cannot imagine what his or her pain might be like, we recall something similar that we have experienced. The person's suffering is not so alien.

Once we can empathize with the physical or emotional pain, we reflect that if we were in the same predicament, we would want it to end. So does our loved one. With this line of thinking, we develop compassion: the wish for him or her to be free of the pain and its causes. To gain the willingness to become involved, we think that just as we would not appreciate someone's excuses, our loved one also would not welcome our hesitation.

If we are frightened of feeling his or her sorrow, we try to deflate our dualistic projections. To do this, we alternate tickling our palm, pinching it, and holding one hand in the other. We try to experience each as a wave of the mind without a dualistic impression of a seemingly concrete "me" and a seemingly concrete physical sensation. When we are successful, we naturally have no fear of these experiences. Just as feelings of physical pleasure or pain are not upsetting or frightening when experienced nondualistically, the same is true of feelings of mental happiness or sadness.

Now, without tension or fear, we try to imagine the suffering and its causes leaving our loved one as black light, freeing the person from his or her pain. As we breathe in, we picture this light entering our heart. We accept and try to feel his or her anguish. Then, viewing the experience of pain from the perspective of the ocean of our clear light mind, we try to see it nondualistically like a wave. What our loved one and now we are experiencing is unpleasant and naturally evokes a feeling of sadness. We do not trivialize it in any way. This feeling, however, does not upset the calm, composed depths of the ocean. We try to let it naturally subside and pass.

From our clear light heart, a warm and loving concern for the person's welfare now naturally arises. With the wish for him or her to be happy, we try to picture our concern as this happiness and its causes, but in the form of white light. Reinforced by the natural joy of the mind, we try to feel deep happiness ourselves as we imagine the light entering the person and filling him or her with joy.

Next, we imagine supplementing our gift of happiness with an additional present of understanding and possible solutions for his or her problems. To do this, we try to tap the abilities of the five types of deep awareness that also endow our clear light mind. We picture our understanding and solutions leaving us also as white light and filling the person. Sometimes, experiencing frustration and displeasure is healthy, as it may help our loved one to grow, as in the situation of a child learning social skills. In such cases, we may imagine taking away simply the rough edges of the experience and giving him or her valuable insight.

We may also give other factors related to clear light mind. For example, if a loved one needs self-confidence, we may recall Buddha-nature and transform the self-confidence we feel in our natural abilities into belief in our loved one's innate talents. Radiating confidence to the person, we try to imagine our loved one filled with the white light of both self-confidence and our faith in him or her. When we repeat this process during actual encounters with the person, our confidence reinforces his or her self-esteem.

Since mind's natural qualities automatically translate into physical and verbal expression, we also try to imagine our loved one acting and speaking self-assuredly. Moreover, we try to imagine ourselves interacting with the person with faith in him or her. In real life encounters, similar words and actions will stimulate our loved one to speak and act self-confidently.

We may follow a similar procedure if a loved one feels his or her self-dignity threatened, for instance by the ravages of disease or old age. Tapping the self-pride we feel in view of our innate good qualities, we try to imagine self-dignity filling the person with white light. We reinforce it by also sending the person our respect for him or her. Then, we try to picture our loved one acting with strengthened self-esteem and ourselves interacting with sincere deep respect.

Repeating the procedures of giving and taking with a stranger or with someone we dislike is not recommended for initial practice. Our feelings may not be sincere. We may attempt it only when we have gained some experience with the technique and are well advanced in our sensitivity training.

Helping Others and Ourselves to Overcome Insecurity

During the second phase of the exercise, we practice giving and taking while sitting in a circle with a group, by repeating the procedure two or three times and focusing each time on a different person. Doing this practice while facing a partner is too intense and, in real life encounters, may seem pretentious. The classical texts advise us always to keep the practice of giving and taking private so that no one knows that we are doing it, not even the person who is the object of our focus.

Here, in the circle, we may not know the specific troubles that anyone is currently facing. Nevertheless, we may work with the general problems that afflict most people. Let us take the example of insecurity.

First, while focusing on someone, we need to settle our mind into a state of serene equanimity and sympathy as before. To help the process, we may use the key phrases: "no tension, worry, speediness, or dullness," "relaxed and fresh," "no clinging, aversion, or indifference," "not overprotective, frightened, or too busy," "open and concerned," "interest," "empathy," "compassion," "willingness to become involved," and "no fear of feeling sad." Then, we imagine relieving the person of the suffering of being insecure. We do this by picturing that suffering entering us as black light. Not frightened to feel the person's pain, we try to view it from the perspective of the ocean of the mind and let it settle. Remaining in an oceanic clear light state free from the worries and tensions that feed insecurity, we try to experience the natural joy of our mind. With feelings of love, we then radiate this joy as white light, which we imagine fills the person.

Further, we try to understand that the person's insecurity stems from not viewing his or her experiences from the perspective of life's changes, parts and causes, and waves on the ocean. We also emanate as white light our understanding of these points and the consequent security and sense of well-being that it gives us. Feeling secure in ourselves, we try to reinforce the person's own feeling of security. If we know the person, we may also practice giving and taking with his or her specific problems.

During the third phase, we focus on ourselves, first in a mirror and then after putting the mirror aside. We begin by trying to identify any personal problems we may be currently facing. To settle ourselves into a state of serene equanimity and sympathy, we may use the seven key phrases as before. Next, with compassion for ourselves, we imagine taking on our difficulties as black light either drawn from the mirror image or extracted from our entire body and brought to our heart. In other words, we accept working on our problems and try to feel free of worry about them. Without tension, fear, or feelings of dualism, we try to experience the pain they cause, from the point of view of the ocean, and let the experience pass. Trying to find possible solutions with the understanding of our deep awareness, we radiate these remedies lovingly and joyfully as white light. The light fills our image in the mirror or fills our body from within if we are practicing without a prop.

Using the same procedure as when working in a circle, we may also try to take on any manifest or residual feelings of insecurity we may have. We then send out to ourselves a sense of security.

Lastly, we practice giving and taking while viewing the series of photos of ourselves from particularly difficult times in our life. If we have any unresolved problems, blocked feelings, or emotional turmoil left from or still concerning those times, we try to bring them to the surface. Taking them on compassionately, we try to experience the pain they produce, and deal with them now. We try to send loving wishes of joy to ourselves at those times and possible solutions we can presently use to resolve these problems. If we do not have pictures of ourselves from those periods, we may think of those times and practice as we did without a mirror. We try to draw the pain from our entire body as black light. Then, we try to emanate the white light of joy from the center of our heart so that it permeates our body. Finally, we try to feel this light beaming from all the pores of our skin.

20   Making Sensitive Decisions

Feelings, Wishes, and Necessity

Even when we are attentive to a situation and we feel some level of happiness, interest, and compassion about it, and some level of willingness to become involved, we need to respond sensitively and appropriately. Frequently, we need to decide between three choices: doing what we feel like doing, what we want to do, and what we need to do. Decisions involving someone else add the further choices between what the person wants and what he or she needs. Some or all these choices may coincide. Often, however, they differ. Choosing either what we want or feel like doing over what is needed, or what the other person wants over what he or she needs, is a form of insensitivity. When we make such a choice, we frequently feel guilty. This overreaction happens because we experience what we need to do dualistically as what we *should* do. On one side stands a defiant "me" and on the other the unsavory action that we should do, but are not doing. Usually, a moralistic judgment accompanies the dualistic appearance.

Deconstructing the decision-making process, by using images such as a balloon bursting, resolves any tension over the issue of "should." In place of what we should do, this process leaves what we need to do. Yet, we might not know what we need to do or what someone else needs. To find out, we may rely on the five types of deep awareness, knowledge, experience, intuition, discrimination, and trustworthy external sources of advice.

Even when we know what we need to do, we may neither want to do it nor feel like doing it. We may still feel tension, even if the issue of "should" does not complicate the matter. Do we need to be insensitive to our wishes or feelings? Is it an overreaction to feel frustration and disappointment at needing to ignore either one or both of them?

The issue is complex. Four combinations may occur between what we want and what we feel like doing. Suppose, for example, we are overweight and we know that we need to diet. (1) We may want to keep our diet, but not feel like doing so when our favorite cake is served for dessert. (2) We may feel like sticking to our diet, but not want to do so when we have paid much money for a hotel room and a breakfast buffet is included. (3) We may both feel like keeping to our diet and want to do so when people tell us how fat we have become. (4) We may neither want to keep nor feel like keeping our diet when we are aggravated about something and want to drown our annoyance by eating cake. In each case, we may choose either to eat some cake or to exercise restraint. How do we make a sensitive decision that we do not later regret?

Reasons for Feeling Like Doing Something and Wanting to Do It

Understanding the mechanism behind feelings and wishes helps to alleviate tensions between the two and between either of them and necessity. When we understand why we feel like doing something and why we might want to do something different, we can evaluate these factors. Weighing them against the reasons for what we need to do, we can then come to a reasonable decision.

The abhidharma presentation of mental factors and karma suggests the following analysis. The deeper we probe, the more sensitive and honest we are to the myriad psychological factors involved in making difficult decisions in life. For easier comprehension, we shall use the relatively trivial example of eating to illustrate the complexity of the issue. Appreciating the depth that any analysis must go in order to be accurate helps us to be thorough in considering the choices available in more serious decisions, such as concerning an unhealthy relationship.

An urge is the mental factor that leads in the direction of a certain course of action. There are two types of urges: those that bring on the thought to do something and those that lead directly to doing it. Feeling like doing something and wanting to do it are examples of the former type of urge. Deciding to do it is an example of the latter. Feeling like doing something arises when we are unaware of the reason. When we consciously feel motivated, we want to do it. Let us explore this distinction in depth.

Feeling like doing something may arise from a habit and preference, a physical reason, or the involuntary motivation of an emotion or attitude. For example, we may feel like eating something because of the habit and preference to eat at a certain time, because of hunger, or because of attachment to food. These three major causes may act either in combination with each other or independently. If we are in the habit of taking lunch at noon, we may feel like eating at that hour whether or not we are actually hungry and whether or not we are attached to food. On the other hand, when we are hungry, we feel like eating regardless of the time or our attachments. Further, when we are attached to food, we feel like eating at all times, no matter whether our stomach is empty.

When an urge to eat arises and we are unaware of the time or do not think about being hungry, we merely feel like eating. We do not necessarily want to eat. The same thing happens when the urge arises simply from attachment to food. Wanting to eat requires being conscious of a reason and feeling motivated by it.

We want to eat when we are mindful of what triggers our habit, of our preference, or of a physical reason for eating. For example, when we know it is noon or we think either about our preference for eating then or about being hungry, we want to eat. Similarly, we want to eat when we have a deliberated reason for doing so. For instance, we have no time later; if we are to eat at all, we must eat now. Awareness of feeling like doing something may also make us want to do it. Sometimes, we want to eat simply because we feel like eating. Although a psychological motivation for eating, such as attachment to food, is sufficient to make us feel like eating, it is insufficient to make us want to eat. We need another reason, such as it being lunchtime, and awareness of that reason. Attachment to food, however, may support our wish to eat.

Suppose an urge to eat arises from a habit, preference, or physical reason before we are mindful of that reason or it arises at the same time as we are mindful of a deliberated reason. In each case, we both feel and want to eat. For instance, we feel like eating because we are hungry. Subsequently, when we notice that it is noon or we realize that we have no time to eat later, we also want to eat. We may similarly experience both the feeling and the wish to eat when an involuntary psychological motivation supports a conscious, deliberated reason for eating. For example, we realize that we have no time to eat later and we are attached to food. We both want to eat and feel like eating despite it not being noon or our not being hungry.

On the other hand, if we are mindful of a reason for eating and an urge to eat does not arise either beforehand or from a psychological motivation, we want to eat but do not feel like doing so. For instance,

---

Feeling like doing something
> because of a habit and preference
> because of a physical reason
> because of an emotion or attitude
> may be supported by circumstances or the influence of others

Wanting to do something
> because of a habit and mindfulness of what has triggered that habit
> because of a preference and mindfulness of that preference
> because of a physical need that we realize
> because of a deliberated reason
> because of feeling like doing it
> may be supported by an emotion or attitude
> may be supported by circumstances or the influence of others

Merely feeling like doing something without necessarily wanting to do it
> when unaware of what is triggering the habit that causes the feeling
> when not thinking about the physical reason that causes the feeling
> when the feeling is motivated simply by an emotion or attitude

Both feeling like doing something and wanting to do it
> when an urge arises from a habit, preference, or physical reason
>> –before being mindful of that reason
>> –at the same time as being mindful of a deliberated reason
> when an emotion or attitude supports a conscious motivation

Wanting to do something but not feeling like doing it
> when mindful of a reason for doing something and
>> –an urge to do it does not arise beforehand
>> –an urge to do it does not arise from an emotion or attitude

---

Figure 4: Feeling like doing something and wanting to do it

although we realize that we have no time later, it is not our usual time to eat. We are not hungry and we are unattached to food. In this case, we want to eat, but do not feel like it.

Circumstances or the influence of others may support the arising of an urge to do something, whether we experience the urge as.a feeling or a wish to do it. Without other causes, however, neither supporting factor is a sufficient cause for the urge to occur. For example, when food is on the table or when our friends are ordering at the restaurant, we may also feel like eating something and want to eat. Yet, not everyone reacts in the same way. Without it being lunchtime, or without being either hungry or attached to food, or without having a deliberated reason, we will not feel like eating or want to eat even under these circumstances or in this company. What we decide to do is another matter.

Choosing between What We Want to Do and What We Feel Like Doing

Suppose we want to do one thing, but feel like doing the opposite. Let us leave aside for a moment the further complication of what we need to do. When we decide to do what we feel like doing rather than what we want to do, our habit, preference, physical need, emotions, attitude, or some combination of these factors, may be stronger than the deliberated motivation behind our wish or the emotional force behind that motivation. Our mindfulness of our reason for doing something may also be too weak or the circumstances or influence of others may be too overwhelming. For example, although we may want to lose weight, we may feel like eating a piece of cake. We choose to take a piece when our habit, hunger, greed, preference for a particular type of cake, our host's insistence, or some combination of these factors outweighs our vanity or mindfulness of how fat we are. When, in the same situation, we choose to do what we want rather than what we feel like doing, the strengths of the factors supporting each choice are reversed.

When we both want to do and feel like doing something, we choose not to do so when an extraneous motivation overrides all other considerations. For example, when we know that our host has specially baked the cake for us and would be hurt if we did not take a piece, we may decide to eat it despite wanting to keep to our diet and feeling like doing so.

Lastly, a deliberated motivation may cause us to do something though we neither want to nor feel like doing it. For instance, when we neither want to keep nor feel like keeping to our diet, we may refrain from eating anyway if we meditate on the disadvantages of being a slave to our greed. Here, our deliberated motivation of wanting to avoid these drawbacks outweighs any reason for wanting to break our diet, such as aggravation about work.

Doing What We Need to Do

We need to do something because it will benefit us, others, or both, or because of physical necessity or circumstances. For example, we may need to diet because losing weight will improve our self-esteem, will enable us to play sports with our children without losing our breath, or will improve our performance at work. We may also need to diet for health reasons or because we are traveling in an area where the food does not suit us. We do what we need to do when we are aware of the reasons for doing it, are convinced of their validity, feel motivated by them, and remain mindful of these three factors.

Someone may also force us to do what we need to do even if we do not see the need. For example, a strong-willed nurse or relative may bully us into eating when we are sick, even if we do not consciously wish to get well. This usually occurs because of physical or psychological weakness. We may be frightened of the person.

Unconscious motivations that derive from disturbing attitudes such as vanity may be behind our wanting to do something. They do not support, however, our needing to do it. They fuel, instead, our feeling that we *should* do it, such as vanity making us feel that we *should* go on a diet. On the other hand, certain attitudes, such as a sense of duty, family honor, or national pride, may make us feel either that we need to do something or that we should do it. This depends on whether we mix our outlook with confusion. Moreover, these attitudes are constructive, destructive, or neutral following from the ethical status of what we feel that we need or should do. Family honor may lead to helping the poor, vengeance killing, or living in a certain neighborhood.

At first, we may consciously have to motivate ourselves and exercise willpower to do what we need to do. Later, when we have built up new habits, we may spontaneously do what is needed and even feel like doing and want to do it.

Alienation from What We Want To Do or What We Feel Like Doing

Sometimes, we feel that we must suppress what we want to do or feel like doing and not "allow" ourselves to do it. We usually experience this as frustration. At other times, as a reward, we "allow" ourselves to do something that we both want to do and feel like doing, but in which we normally restrain ourselves from indulging. Then, when we actually do what we temporarily allow ourselves to do, we often feel irrational anxiety that someone will catch and punish us. We find it difficult to relax and enjoy what we are doing.

In addition, sometimes we feel that we have to force ourselves to do something that we know we *should* do, but that we neither want to do nor feel like doing. We often experience this with resentment. Moreover, often when we do what we feel like doing and not what we know we *should* do, we feel that we cannot control ourselves. Such experiences are often accompanied by feelings of guilt.

All such forms of alienation from our wishes, from our feelings, and from ourselves, stem from dualistic views. These are views of "me" and what I want to do, "me" and what I feel like doing, "me" and what I need to do, and "me" and what I actually do. Consequently, we experience these various "me"s in conflict, fighting to control each other, with each and what it wants, needs, does, or feels like doing bearing a concrete identity. When we identify with one of these "me"s that we imagine to be "bad," we feel guilty as the "bad" person who wants to do, feels like doing, or is doing something naughty. When we identify with one of these "me"s as the "good" person who must always be in control, we experience tension at having to be the police officer. We are never at ease with ourselves. To overcome these emotionally disturbing syndromes, we need the wisdom of nonduality.

Decision-making

Decisions occur as the result of a complex interaction of mental factors, without a concrete "me" in our head making the decision. This is true although the voice in our head worrying about which decision to take makes it appear as though a findable speaker is doing the worrying and making the choice. When a decision occurs, for instance to eat a piece of cake, all that happens is merely the seeing of the cake accompanied by the mental factors of discrimination and intention. These two mental factors arise from the interaction and comparative weights of (1) the habits, preferences, physical needs, emotions, and attitudes behind what we feel like doing, (2) the conscious, deliberated, and nondeliberate motivations for what we want to do, (3) the reasons behind what we need to do and our conscious motivation for doing it, and (4) any extraneous or deliberated motivations that might draw us to do something different from these three. We experience our intention to eat, accompanied by the decisiveness of discrimination, as our will. Willpower then brings on the urge that directly leads us to act. We experience this urge as a decision.

Neurobiology similarly describes a decision from the physical viewpoint as the outcome of millions of brain cells firing. It agrees with Buddhism that no findable agent sits in our head making the decision. If we remain mindful of this common conclusion of both Buddhism and science, we stop viewing our decision-making dualistically. In this way, we avoid feelings of frustration, alienation, or guilt.

If we ask who made the decision to eat the cake, there is no denying that it was "me," not someone else. This conventional person "me," however, is not some findable agent in our head manipulating events. This "me" is like an illusion, in that it seems concrete and findable, but in fact is not. Yet, it is not the same as an illusion. People make decisions; illusions do not.

Just because no concrete decision-maker sits in our head and our decisions arise dependently on causes and conditions, it does not follow that our choices are predetermined and inevitable. Predetermination implies that an all-powerful agent other than ourselves has independently decided for us. Neither we nor anyone else, however, can make choices independently of the affecting factors. Furthermore, when we decide between what we want to do, what we feel like doing, and what we need to do, we subjectively experience making a choice. This is conventionally and existentially true. We do not know beforehand which decision we shall take. Nevertheless, no matter which decision we choose, all decisions arise from causes and conditions. Nothing happens arbitrarily without any reason. Therefore, all decisions are understandable. Moreover, we are accountable for them.

To make a sensitive decision, then, we need to check (1) what we feel like doing and why, (2) what we want to do and why, and (3) what we need to do and why. We then weigh the strengths of each, without becoming either overemotional or devoid of all feelings, and decide what to do.

Decisions are not always clear cut. Often we need to compromise. The first fact of life or "noble truth" that Buddha taught, however, is that life is difficult. We may feel sad at having to compromise our feelings or wishes, but there is no need to feel frustrated, angry, or alienated. As in accepting any unfortunate situation, we need to view our experience of sadness like a wave on the ocean of the mind. In this way, we avoid being battered. Our sadness will pass, like everything else.

Not Identifying with What We Want to Do or Feel Like Doing

The realization that no concrete "me" exists as a basis upon which to project a fixed identity allows us balanced sensitivity not only toward decision-making, but also toward ourselves. If we do not identify with the feelings or wishes that arise to do this or that, we do not judge ourselves as "bad" and feel guilty when the feelings or wishes are to do something bizarre or destructive. We see that urges and wishes to do things arise as the result of habit, physical needs, various forms of motivation, and so forth. An intention to act them out does not need also to accompany them. This realization allows us more sympathy and tolerance toward ourselves as we work to eliminate the causes for destructive urges to arise at all.

Not Knowing What We Want to Do or Feel Like Doing

Sometimes, when faced with a decision, we do not know what we want to do or feel like doing. When we are uneasy about this, we experience the phenomenon as alienation. We imagine we are "out of touch with ourselves." On the other hand, when we make decisions based purely on necessity, without considering our wishes or feelings, we may experience life as cold and mechanical. To overcome these problems we need to examine the possible causes for not knowing our feelings or wishes.

Feeling like doing something derives from an urge, which comes from habits, preferences, physical needs, emotions, attitudes, and so forth. While we are not liberated from our compelling habits, involuntary urges to do things constantly arise. Not all these urges have the same strength of intensity. When we experience not knowing what we feel like doing, we may merely be inattentive to a low-energy urge that is arising in that particular moment. To overcome the uneasiness that often accompanies the experience of not knowing what we feel like doing, we need to increase our sensitivity. We accomplish this by quieting our mind and being more attentive to the low-intensity urges that arise. We can then consider these feelings when deciding our course of action. In so doing, we experience our decision-making as a kinder and fairer process.

Feelings and Intuition

Intuition takes three major forms, each of which can also help us to make a decision. We may have an intuition about someone, such as that a woman is pregnant. Based on that, we may decide to help her carry a bundle. We may also have an intuition that something will happen, such as the doorbell will ring. Consequently, we postpone taking a bath. These first two forms of intuition are stronger than a suspicion. They have a quality of certainty to them.

We may also have an intuition to do something, for instance to tell someone something about his or her behavior. Because of this, we may decide to speak to the person. A quality of certainty also accompanies this type of intuition. We intuitively *know* what to do; we do not merely have an opinion.

The English word *feeling* can be used in the context of all three types of intuition. We may intuitively feel that a woman is pregnant or intuitively feel that the doorbell will ring. We may also intuitively feel that we need to say something to someone. In each case, we do not merely feel these things; we feel them with certainty. In other words, intuitions are more compelling than feelings since they seem to derive from "inner wisdom." Moreover, intuitions often arise without an accompanying emotional tone. They may be intense or low-level, depending on our attention and mindfulness.

In deciding what to do, we also need to evaluate our intuitions. An intuition arises for unconscious reasons. Its source may be knowledge, innate deep awareness, or understanding built up from experience. However, what we take to be an intuitive feeling may also come from confusion or disturbing emotions. When we are paranoid, for example, our feeling that a journey will be dangerous may seem to us like an intuition of impending disaster. Intuition, then, may be a valid source of information or it may be incorrect. Although we need to consult intuition in coming to a decision, we also need to take care not to follow it blindly or impulsively.

Sometimes, we may feel like doing something, but intuition tells us something different. Here, too, we need to be careful. One or the other may be correct, both may be partially correct, or both may be wrong. Intuition may be either an asset or a liability.

Compromising Our Preferences for Those of Others

When we are properly sensitive, we see what is troubling others and what they need. Their needs always take precedence over what they might say that they want. Sometimes, however, what they might want and need—for example, a show of physical affection or the space and time to be alone—is something that we find difficult to give. We may also not like giving it, not feel like giving it, or not want to give it. Moreover, because we do not like to receive the same ourselves, we may think that anyone who likes to receive it is immature or foolish.

Such a need or request from someone is different from asking for our time or money when we have none to spare. Although we may have certain psychological blocks, everyone is capable of giving someone a hug or of not bothering a person. To decide what to do, we need to evaluate our own and the other person's motivations and the possible outcome of any decision we might take. Although giving in to someone's needs or refusing them may make the person or us temporarily feel better, we need to do what is of long-term benefit for each of us.

Saying No

In deciding what to do, we need to be sensitive to our own needs as well as to those of others. Giving the person what he or she wants or needs—for instance, more of our time than we have available—may be damaging to our physical or emotional health. It may also restrict the time and energy we have for others. We need to say no sensitively, however, so that the person does not feel that a restriction is equivalent to a personal rejection. We also need to say no without guilt or fear of rejection.

One way to handle the situation is to give someone, particularly a friend or a relative, a set time each week exclusively devoted to him or her, for example breakfast each Saturday. We also make it clear that we have a weekly appointment afterwards, so that our time together is not open-ended. Setting limitations is the only realistic and practical way of leading our life. We cannot give everyone who wants to be with us equal time.

Prioritizing is difficult, especially when people are involved. Although family responsibilities, loyalty, and duty cannot be neglected, the main criteria are the other person's receptivity to our help and our effectiveness in benefiting him or her in some significant way. We also need to consider how much we gain or are drained by the encounter. This affects our general sense of well-being and our ability to interact more effectively with others. The teachings on karma suggest that, although everyone is ultimately equal, prioritizing also requires considering the benefit the other person and we can realistically give to others, now or later in life. This guideline applies to deciding not only how much time to spend with each person, but also how much energy to devote to ourselves.

Again, we need to be aware of how our mind produces deceptive appearances of a seemingly concrete "me" who is overwhelmed with unfair demands and a seemingly concrete "you" inconsiderately making those demands. When we believe in this dualistic appearance and label ourselves and others in this confused fashion, we become tense and defensive. We have to ward others off with cunning excuses and, unless we are completely shameless, we naturally feel guilty. Deconstructing this dualistic appearance and trying to relate unselfconsciously allow us to prioritize our time without feeling guilty. Changing our mental labels to "someone trying to help" and "people in need" is also helpful when we do not concretize the two.

On another level, our mind may produce a dualistic appearance of a seemingly concrete "me" who needs to be useful to justify our existence and a seemingly concrete "you" who can provide that elusive security by allowing us to serve. Fooled by this appearance, we may feel that if we say no to our friends, we will be rejected ourselves and thus lose any hope of gaining concrete existence from always catering to their demands.

Even if a friend does reject us, we need to focus on how life goes on. We are sad to lose contact with this person, but his or her disappointment, annoyance, or departure does not render us a worthless person. If Buddha himself was unable to please everyone, what do we expect of ourselves? Keeping these points in mind allows us to say no in a relaxed, sincere manner, without guilt or fear. It also allows us to understand and accept someone saying no to us, without feeling hurt.

EXERCISE 22
Making Sensitive Decisions

As a preliminary to making sensitive decisions, we need to divest decision-making from feelings of dualism. A convenient way to train is to work with an itch. We try to sit quietly without moving. When the inevitable itch arises, we try to notice how we both feel like scratching it and want to do so. Deciding not to scratch it, we try to observe how our mind automatically creates a dualistic appearance of a tormented "me" and an unbearable itch. Our mind tears the experience further apart by also creating the impression of a controller "me" who will not give in to this annoying itch and of a weak "me" who wants to surrender and needs to be controlled. If we identify with the strong "me" and yet scratch the itch, we feel defeated by the weak "me." When this happens, we may experience the defeat with self-recrimination and thoughts that we should have been stronger. If we succeed in controlling the weak "me," we may gloat with overbearing pride at how strong we are. In each case, the experience is disturbing.

We may deconstruct our experience by focusing now on the itch that we have decided not to scratch. It is merely a physical sensation that our tactile consciousness is producing and perceiving. Paying attention to it in this way, we try to notice that an intention accompanies our perception of the itch – namely, to endure the sensation and to resist ending it by scratching. This intention becomes more decisive when we pay attention to the itch as something impermanent that will eventually go away by itself. Analyzing in this way, we discover that no controller is directing the incident and restraining our hand from scratching. Refraining from scratching the itch, we try to focus on our experience as devoid of a solid "me."

Next, we consciously change our mind and decide to scratch the itch. Examining what occurs as we slowly scratch, we try to notice that the only change is the intention that accompanies our awareness of the itch. The intention is now to scratch it. This intention, fueled by the consciously motivated wish to stop experiencing this physical sensation, gives rise to an urge that immediately translates into the motion of our hand as we scratch. Again, no concrete boss stands behind the act, taking in information from the sensors in our skin and sending out orders to our hand. We try to focus for a minute on the fact that we are capable of making decisions without dualistic feelings.

An additional factor enabling us to make sensitive decisions is being comfortable with ourselves. Nervousness and insecurity make us indecisive. Therefore, as a further preliminary we may repeat the third phase of Exercise Seventeen. Dismissing any feeling of two "me"s, we smooth our hair, tell ourselves we need to reach a decision, and hold our hand reassuringly. Stretching our legs and sitting comfortably, we try to feel our energy with total acceptance. We then relax and sit quietly for a minute or two, trying to feel the calm joy of being with ourselves.

Now we are ready to begin the main part of the exercise. We begin the first phase by focusing on a photo or on a thought of someone about whom we might have to make a difficult decision. Choosing, for example, someone with whom we are in an unhealthy or unsatisfactory relationship, we need to draw upon the various skills we have learned in the previous exercises.

First, we must decide whether something needs to be done. For this, we have to evaluate our impression of the situation. We begin by deconstructing any dualistic feelings we may be projecting. In other words, we try to stop seeing the relationship as a confrontation between a concrete "me" and a concrete "you." Imagining the balloon of that fantasy popping, we objectively check the facts, taking into account the other person's perspective and comments. Both sides undoubtedly have valid points. Placing the blame solely on one side is absurd. We may wish to consult an unbiased outside opinion. However, we need take care not lose our critical faculties and let bad counsel sway us.

Once we are certain of the facts, we need to determine with introspection (1) what we feel like doing, (2) what our intuition says, (3) what we want to do, and (4) what we need to do. For example, we may feel like doing nothing. Yet, our intuitive feeling is that this will only make things worse. Moreover, we want to say something and we know that we need to do that.

We then evaluate the reasons behind each of the four. Making a list is helpful. Doing so may seem removed and analytical. Nevertheless, without some structure, we may simply take the easiest course of action—which is to do nothing—or torture ourselves with indecision.

(1) Feeling like doing something arises from habits, preferences, physical factors, and unconscious motivations. Circumstances and the influence of others may also contribute. Here, we may feel like doing nothing because of our habit of keeping quiet and our preference for avoiding confrontation. Examining ourselves more deeply, we uncover fear of incurring the person's anger and also anxiety at the prospect of loneliness if he or she rejects us. Overwork and tiredness may also be contributing to our feeling of reticence.

(2) Intuition of what to do arises from knowledge, innate deep awareness, or understanding gained from experience. We intuitively know that keeping quiet will worsen the situation because we have

seen this happen with others. Since what we take to be intuition may also come from a hidden attitude, we need to examine if this is the case. An unconscious drive to be in control may be reinforcing our intuition.

(3) A wish to do something arises from both conscious and unconscious motivations. Circumstances and the influence of others may also contribute. We want to say something because we can no longer tolerate the pain that the unhealthy relationship is causing us. Although we usually never acknowledge it, we may also feel oppressed. Moreover, several friends have been encouraging us to say something and the circumstances are right: we are spending the weekend together.

(4) Lastly, the need to do something comes from the benefits that both parties will derive. Even if the decision brings short-term pain, we need to aim for long-term benefits. Moreover, physical necessity and circumstances may also contribute to the need for action. Here, we know that we need to do something because the present situation is negatively affecting our work, our health, and our other relationships. Further, the relationship as it stands is unhealthy for the person too and for his or her relations with others. We love the person and wish him or her to be happy. Neither of us is happy now. Thus, our love and concern confirm the need. The person may feel hurt if we say something and we may feel sad afterwards. In the end, however, doing something now will benefit us both.

The first decision we need to take is whether or not to do anything at all. Having brought to the surface all the factors involved, we need to evaluate the positive and negative reasons for each choice. The main constructive reasons for action are the long-term benefits both of us will gain, our love for the person, and our honest concern for the welfare of both of us. Although our feeling of oppression may be a hypersensitive reaction, our intolerance of our present emotional pain is reasonable. Experience tells us that unless we do something it will only get worse. Our other friends' counsel corroborates this choice. The only negative factor behind doing something is our unconscious drive to be in control. To keep that in check, we need to listen carefully to what the other person has to say.

The advantage of saying nothing is that we avoid a potentially explosive confrontation, the other person's anger, and our possible future loneliness. The negative reasons for keeping quiet are our fears and insecurity. Since long-term benefits always outweigh short-term disadvantages, our anxiety is clearly a hypersensitive reaction. It is not a valid reason for inaction. The fact that we are overworked and tired suggests that perhaps we need to wait a short while, but we must do something soon. Weighing all factors, we see that the reasons for changing the relationship are more valid than the ones for doing nothing. We resolve to act.

Once we make up our mind like this and our motivation of love is clear, we are ready to decide what to do. The choices are either to try to restructure the relationship or to leave the person. To reach a conclusion, we need to adjust our ten mental factors and apply the five types of deep awareness. With a motivated urge, we focus on the person. With mirror-like awareness, we distinguish and pay attention to various aspects of his or her behavior. Using awareness of equalities and individualities, we further distinguish the patterns and yet respect the individuality of each instance. Pleasant contacting awareness and a feeling of happiness at the prospect of resolving the problem enhance our interest, mindfulness, and concentration. These, in turn, lead us to discriminate a course of action. We do this with accomplishing awareness. We then evaluate the wisdom and effectiveness of this choice with awareness of reality. Lastly, if the choice seems to be the most reasonable one, we set our intention to suggest it to the other person as we begin our discussion.

The decision-making process requires gentleness, warmth, and understanding, not the zeal of planning a battle. We must make sure that whatever we choose to propose is ethically pure—neither dishonest nor destructive to the feelings of the people involved.

To avoid insensitivity toward ourselves, we need to be clear about our limits. Yet, within those limits, we need to be prepared to say either yes or no about specific points as the discussion develops. We also need to choose an appropriate moment to broach the matter, when both of us will be receptive. Acting rashly may bring disastrous results. Most important, we need to approach the encounter without preconceptions. Maintaining awareness of reality allows us to give the person the room to change his or her ways, while realizing that no one changes instantly. It also allows us to remain open to his or her viewpoint and suggestions. If we find it helpful, we may rehearse possible things we will say and the steps we are willing to take ourselves. Nevertheless, like in settling any dispute, we need the flexibility not to follow a fixed agenda.

We try to imagine doing all this calmly and gently. Even if the other person becomes angry, hurt, or upset, we must resolve the problem. This requires courage and strength. Ridding ourselves of self-consciousness gives us that courage. When we speak and act nondualistically, we are no longer frightened or insecure. The abhidharma literature lists indecisiveness among the six most disturbing states of mind. When we waver or hesitate in making a decision about an unhealthy relationship, we lose time and energy in immature, painful psychological games. This prevents us from making progress in life.

If we later realize that we made the wrong decision, we need to accept our limited ability to know what is best. After all, we are not omniscient. Moreover, our decision was not the sole factor that affected what happened to the person or to us. Learning from experience, we can only try to use compassion and wisdom to go on from there.

During the second phase of the exercise, we sit in a circle with a group and focus on one of the members with whom we need to decide something. If we know any of them and have a dispute, we may work with that. If we have no quarrels or do not know anyone, we may deal with such issues as improving our relationship or establishing one. Approaching the challenge nondualistically and with warm concern, we try to assess the situation objectively and to evaluate what we feel, intuit, want, and need to do. We then try to use our ten mental factors and five types of deep awareness to decide a course of action and to resolve to do it.

We practice the third phase by directing our focus at ourselves, first in a mirror and then without one. Choosing a difficult decision we need to make about ourselves, we apply the same techniques. Useful topics include what are we going to do with our life, what work shall we do, where shall we live, whom shall we live with, shall we change jobs, when shall we retire and then what shall we do, and so forth. We need to apply the sensitivity skills we have gained through this program to help resolve the most difficult issues in life. Doing so benefits both ourselves and others.

Bibliography

Major Tibetan, Sanskrit and Pali Sources Consulted

Akya Yongdzin (A-kya Yongs-'dzin dByangs-can dga'-ba'i blo-gros). *Blo-rigs-kyi sdom-tshig blang-dor gsal-ba'i me-long* (A Compendium of Ways of Knowing: A Mirror to Clarify What Is to Be Adopted and What Is to Be Discarded).

Anuruddha. *Abhidhammattha Sangaha* (An All-inclusive Text of Points of Special Topics of Knowledge).

Asanga. *Abhidharmasamuccaya* (Chos mngon-pa kun-las btus-pa; An Anthology of Special Topics of Knowledge).

Buddhaghosa. *Visuddhimagga* (The Path of Purification).

Chandrakirti (Candrakīrti). *Madhyamakavatāra* (dBu-ma-la 'jug-pa; A Supplement to [Nagarjuna's "Root Stanzas on] the Middle Way").

Chekawa (mChad-kha-ba Ye-shes rdo-rje). *Blo-sbyong don-bdun-ma* (A Cleansing of Attitudes in Seven Points).

Jetsünpa (rJe-btsun Chos-kyi rgyal-mtshan). *Rigs-kyi spyi-don* (The General Meaning of Family-traits) from *bsTan-bcos mngon-par rtogs-pa'i rgyan 'grel-ba-dang bcas-pa'i rnam-bshad rnam-pa gnyis-kyi dka'-ba'i gnad gsal-bar byed-pa'i legs-bshad skal-bzang klu-dbang-gi rol-mtsho* (An Ocean of Play of the Fortunate Naga King: An Explanation Clarifying the Difficult Points of the Second Topic of [Maitreya's] "The Treatise: A Filigree of Realizations" [*Abhisamayālaṃkāra śāstra*] and Its Commentary [by Haribhadra]).

Third Karmapa (Kar-ma-pa Rang-byung rdo-rje). *De-bzhin gshegs-pa'i snying-po bstan-pa'i bstan-bcos* (A Treatise Indicating the Essential Factors Allowing for Authentic Progress).

Eighth Karmapa (Kar-ma-pa Mi-bskyod rdo-rje). *dBu-ma gzhan-stong smra-ba'i srol legs-par phye-ba'i sgron-me* (A Lamp for Opening up the Tradition of Other Voidness Madhyamaka).

Ninth Karmapa (Kar-ma-pa dBang-phyug rdo-rje). *Phyag-chen ma-rig mun-sel* (Mahamudra Eliminating the Darkness of Ignorance).

Kaydrub Norzang-gyatso (mKhas-grub Nor-bzang rgya-mtsho). *Phyi-nang-gzhan-gsum gsal-bar byed-pa dri-med 'od-kyi rgyan* (An Adornment for the *Stainless Light*, Clarifying the External, Internal and Alternative [Kalachakras]).

Kongtrül ('Jam-mgon Kong-sprul Blo-gros mtha'-yas). *De-bzhin gshegs-pa'i snying-po bstan-pa'i bstan-bcos-kyi rnam-'grel rang-byung dgongs-gsal* (Clarifying the Intentions of [the Third Karmapa] Rangchung [dorjey]: A Commentary on "A Treatise Indicating the Essential Factors Allowing for Authentic Progress").

Longchenpa (Klong-chen Rab-'byams-pa Dri-med 'od-zer). *Chos-bzhi rin-chen 'phreng-ba* (The Four-themed Precious Garland).

Maitreya (Maitreya, Byams-pa). *Mahāyānottaratantraśāstra* (Theg-pa chen-po rgyud bla-ma bstan-bcos; The Furthest Everlasting Stream: A Mahayana Treatise).

Mipam ('Ju Mi-pham 'Jam-dbyangs rnam-rgyal rgya-mtsho). *bDe-gshegs snying-po'i stong-thun chen-mo seng-ge'i nga-ro* (The Lion's Roar: A Great [Collection of] Thousands of Points Concerning the Essential Factors Allowing for Blissful Progress).

Pabongka (Pha-bong-kha Byams-pa bstan-'dzin 'phrin-las rgya-mtsho). *rNam-grol lag-bcangs* (A Personal Gift for Being Utterly Freed).

First Panchen Lama (Paṇ-chen Blo-bzang chos-kyi rgyal-mtshan). *dGe-ldan bka'-brgyud rin-po-che'i phyag-chen rtsa-ba rgyal-ba'i gzhung-lam* (A Root Text for the Precious Gelug/Kagyü Tradition of Mahamudra: The Main Road of the Triumphant Ones).

Shakya Chogden (gSer-mdog Paṇ-chen Shakya mchog-ldan). *Shing-rta'i srol-chen gnyis-las 'byung-ba'i dbu-ma chen-po'i lugs-gnyis rnam-par dbye-ba* (Differentiating the Two Traditions of the Great Maha-madhyamaka Derived from the Two Great Forerunners).

Shantideva (Śāntideva). *Bodhisattvacaryāvatāra* (Byang-chub sems-pa'i spyod-pa-la 'jug-pa; Engaging in a Bodhisattva's Deeds).

Tsongkapa (Tsong-kha-pa Blo-bzang grags-pa). *Lam-rim chen-mo* (A Grand Presentation of the Graded Stages of the Path).

Vasubandhu. *Abhidharmakosa* (Chos mngon-pa'i mdzod; A Treasure House of Special Topics of Knowledge).

_____. *Abhidharmakosabhāsya* (Chos-mngon-pa'i mdzod-kyi rang-'grel; An Auto-commentary on "A Treasure House of Special Topics of Knowledge").

Recommended Reading

Akya Yongdzin. *A Compendium of Ways of Knowing*, with commentary by Geshe Ngawang Dhargyey (Alexander Berzin and Sharpa Tulku, trans. and eds.). Dharamsala: Library of Tibetan Works & Archives, 1977.

Berzin, Alexander. *Fünf Weisheiten: im Aryatara Institut e. V., München (1993)*. Munich: Aryatara Institut, 1994.

_____. *Taking the Kalachakra Initiation*. Ithaca: Snow Lion, 1997.

Buddhaghosa. *The Path of Purification*, 2 vols. (Bhikkhu Nyanamoli, trans.). Berkeley: Shambhala, 1976.

Chodron, Thubten. *Open Heart, Clear Mind*. Ithaca: Snow Lion, 1990.

The Dalai Lama. *Kindness, Clarity, and Insight* (Jeffrey Hopkins and Elizabeth Napper, trans. and eds.). Ithaca: Snow Lion, 1984.

_____. *The World of Tibetan Buddhism: An Overview of Its Philosophy and Practice* (Geshe Thupten Jinpa, trans. and ed.). Boston: Wisdom, 1995.

The Dalai Lama and Alexander Berzin. *The Gelug/Kagyü Tradition of Mahamudra* (Alexander Berzin, trans. and ed.). Ithaca: Snow Lion, 1997.

Deshung Rinpoche. *The Three Levels of Spiritual Perception* (Jared Rhoton, trans.). Boston: Wisdom, 1995.

Dhargyey, Geshe Ngawang. *An Anthology of Well-spoken Advice*, vol. 1 (Alexander Berzin and Sharpa Tulku, trans. and eds.). Dharamsala: Library of Tibetan Works & Archives, 1984.

Jamgon Kongtrul. *The Great Path of Awakening: A Commentary on the Mahayana Teaching "Seven Points for Training the Mind"* (Ken McLeod, trans.). Boston: Shambhala, 1987.

Karmapa IX. *Mahamudra Eliminating the Darkness of Ignorance*, with commentary by Beru Khyentse Rinpoche (Alexander Berzin, trans. and ed.). Dharamsala: Library of Tibetan Works & Archives, 1978.

Lati Rinpochay. *Mind in Tibetan Buddhism* (Elizabeth Napper, trans. and ed.). Ithaca: Snow Lion, 1980.

La Vallée Poussin, Louis de (trans.). *L'Abhidharmakoṣa de Vasubandhu*, 6 vols. Brussels: Institut Belge des Hautes Études Chinoises, 1971.

Loden, Geshe Acharya Thubten. *The Fundamental Potential for Enlightenment in Tibetan Buddhism*. Melbourne: Tushita, 1996.

Longchenpa. *Dzog-chen: The Four-themed Precious Garland*, with commentary by Dudjom Rinpoche and Beru Khyentse Rinpoche (Alexander Berzin and Matthew Kapstein, trans.). Dharamsala: Library of Tibetan Works & Archives, 1979.

McDonald, Kathleen. *How to Meditate: A Practical Guide*. London: Wisdom, 1984.

Newland, Guy. *Compassion: A Tibetan Analysis*. London: Wisdom, 1984.

Pabongka Rinpoche. *Liberation in the Palm of Your Hand* (Michael Richards, trans.). Boston: Wisdom, 1991.

Rabten, Geshe. *Mind and Its Functions* (Stephen Batchelor, trans.). Mt. Pèlerin: Tharpa Choeling, 1978.

Rahula, Walpola (trans.). *Le Compendium de la super-doctrine (philosophie) (Abhidharmasamuccaya) d'Asanga*. Paris: École française d'extrême-orient, 1971.

Śāntideva. *A Guide to the Bodhisattva Way of Life*. (Vesna A. Wallace and B. Alan Wallace, trans.). Ithaca: Snow Lion, 1997.

Thrangu Rinpoche. *The Uttara Tantra: A Treatise on Buddha Nature, A Commentary on the Uttara Tantra Śāstra of Asanga* (Ken and Katia Holmes, trans.). Delhi: Sri Satguru, 1994.